The London Bible

A guide to living and working in the capital

By Katherine Harlow and Katya Holloway

Interlink Books
An imprint of Interlink Publishing Group, Inc.
New York • Northampton

First American edition published 2004 by

INTERLINK BOOKS
An imprint of Interlink Publishing Group, Inc.
46 Crosby Street, Northampton, Massachusetts 01060

Originally published in Great Britain by Summersdale
Publishers Ltd

Library of Congress Cataloging-in-Publication Data

Harlow, Katherine.
The London bible / by Katherine Harlow and Katya Holloway.
p. cm.
ISBN 1-56656-524-3 (pbk.)
1. London (England)--Guidebooks. 2. Life
skills--England--London--Handbooks, manuals, etc. I. Holloway,
Katya. II. Title.
DA684.25.H366 2003
914.2104'86--dc21

2003014798

Cover design by Blue Lemon Design Consultancy.

Photos by:
Jamie Cooper (pgs 108, 127)
Stewart Ferris (pgs 13, 28, 59, 73, 139, 153, 182, 208, 215, 235, 243,
251, 265, 271, 277, 283, 295, 312)
Iain Findlay (pgs 44, 82, 114, 147, 159, 174, 190, 198, 220, 302)
Katherine Harlow (p 92)
Katya Holloway (pgs 169, 229, 260)

Printed and bound in Canada by Webcom

About the Authors

Katherine Harlow moved to London in 1998 at the age of 20, and has been working in television as an artwork executive. She is now writing her first novel.

Katya Holloway moved from Canada at the age of 20 to work in the British publishing industry. Trained as a journalist, she is now the deputy editor of a travel magazine in London.

Acknowledgements

Katya: I would like to thank Mom and Dad, Daniel and Grandma for their steadfast support over the years. Big hug to Fin and Louise for sticking by me during all my frazzled moments – things are about to get exciting.

Katherine: I would like to thank Mom, Dad, Siobhan and Caroline for all the years of encouragement and for their understanding when I needed to try my luck on the other side of the world. Also to Albert Thackway, who I never had the fortune to meet, may our books one day sit on the shelves side by side.

We would like to offer enthusiastic thanks to everyone who helped us to plug up the holes that we were unsure about. Our thanks go to Phil Buxton for his help with the sports section, and to Mark Mayne for his uncanny awareness of the underground nightlife scene and his help with the Camberwell/Brixton area guide. Sincere gratitude goes to Dave Hoyland and Graham Hudson for sharing their in-depth knowledge of the London art scene. Also, we are hugely grateful to Iain Findlay, Jamie Cooper and Cathy Thornhill for their brilliant photographs.

Please note: the information contained in this book was accurate at the time of going to press. However, things change so please don't phone us up in tears if you arrange to meet a hot date at a club and find that it's recently closed down and that your date has gone off with someone else. That's not our fault – particularly the bit about the club being closed (it's the fault of the club owner defaulting on his overdraft and doing a runner to the Costa Brava with all his clients' cash). But we would like to be able to update future editions of this book, so if you happen to come across any information that is out of date or want to recommend additional entries, please e-mail the publishers: info@interlinkbooks.com and we'll check it out and consider including it in the next printing of the book. London's a big place and it's better to be selective by just including the best of everything, so we can't promise to include any entries sent to us willy-nilly, but we're happy to consider them. *Cheers!*

Words & Terms

bloke	guy
CV	resume
chemist	pharmacist
chips	fries
dodgy	seedy
flat	apartment
flatmate	roommate
flog(ging)	sell(ing)
football	soccer
high street	main street
hire	rent
holiday	vacation
let(ting)	rent(ing)
lift	elevator
loo	bathroom
mains	entrées
Marmite	a dark brown-colored salty spread
mate	friend
mobile phone	cell phone
motoring	driving
naft	tacky, tasteless
petrol	gas
pie-eyed	wasted
post	mail
postcode	zipcode
punters	customers
queue	line
quid	pound
snog(ging)	kiss(ing)
tat	trinkets
telly	TV
trainers	sneakers

Contents

Introduction

There are many reasons to move to London, whether it is to work, study, or just try your luck in the big city. But the reason that you'll stay in London, the reason that you'll put up with delayed Tube trains and constant drizzle, is that you love it here. Embrace the past, present, and future of London with open arms, a wide smile, and an umbrella. I wouldn't dream of living anywhere else, hell, I'm even thankful for the crap weather, because if it was sunny all the time the place would be swarming.

The streets of London aren't paved with gold; they are cobbled with a priceless history. Every winding street you walk down holds a secret. The haunting cries of starving medieval peasants, Victorian highwaymen pickpocketing and pillaging, 1950s bohemian artists drinking themselves into the gutters of Soho, 60s mods driving scooters and following the latest fashions on Carnaby Street, and punks thrashing their piercings about in the sweating crowds in dodgy clubs. Every time you step out onto the pavement in London, it is on the ash and dust of hundreds of forgotten footsteps.

Last year I lived in Whitechapel near the street where Jack the Ripper disembowelled one of his unfortunate victims. A few years ago, while living in south London, every evening I walked along Waterloo Bridge to get to work, and could picture The Kinks standing on the bridge composing "Waterloo Sunset" at dusk. Wandering the Kings Road it's easy to forget that before the boutiques and high street chains opened, girls in miniskirts and false eyelashes shopped alongside suited and booted cravat-clad gents. These things seem like they are part of a filmmaker's ideal, ideas conjured up in the mind of an executive sitting at a boardroom table. But they aren't whimsical thoughts. They are facts. In decades to come people will think about the dawning of this century and will fondly evoke images of people like you sitting in your jeans and trainers sipping pints of lager and listening to the DJ spin tunes on his decks. You are a part of history in London like you would never be anywhere else.

But although there are many reasons to move to London and to embrace it wholeheartedly, I won't deny that acclimatising yourself to the big city can be hard. Relocating may be one of the most difficult things you've ever faced, but it shouldn't have to be. During those dismal first few weeks, we had a million questions to ask, but nobody to answer them properly. Forget about your anxieties – this book will answer all your questions before you even have a chance to ask them. As soon as you get a flat, a job, and a social life, London will become more than just your home: it will become part of you.

"We are all in the gutter but some of us are looking at the stars"
Oscar Wilde

PART ONE:
THE BASICS

Chapter One:
Accommodation

Time to move

If you've recently arrived in London and are horrified to find the conditions of your new life don't measure up to the comforts of mom's home, then it's time to get your accommodation sorted. Perhaps you've found yourself camped out in your distant cousin's sitting room, watching her take detailed notes on episodes of Oprah, and have to endure her lecherous boyfriend leaving the soap furry. Desperate times call for quick action. You need to find a flat, and fast. So where do you start?

Before you begin flicking through newspapers and calling up estate agents, you're going to have to get your head around just what sort of property you will be looking to rent, and how much you are willing to pay out for it. Pick up *Loot* newspaper from any newsagent and scan the extensive property listings, which will give you an idea of how much you will be required to pay for the luxury of living in certain areas. This paper lists properties all over London, and breaks it down by accommodation, price, and postcode. Other good sources for accommodation ads include the *Evening Standard* newspaper, *Time Out* magazine and the *Guardian*'s Saturday supplement, *The Guide*, all available from local newsagents. Also try *TNT* and *SX*, free weekly antipodean magazines available from bins outside most Tube stations.

To check out London hotels on the web try:

www.hotel-london.co.uk

www.londonnights.com

www.lastminute.com

www.hotels.in-london.co.uk

www.hotelsoflondon.co.uk

www.london-hotels.co.uk

Where to look

Properties in London are either rented individually by their private owners, who advertise in the mainstream press or local shop fronts, or through letting agencies, which have been hired to do the dirty work.

It is up to you to decide whether you choose to approach letting agents, or real estate agents, to find a property or whether you decide to scan the newspapers and magazines for ads on your own. By dealing with a real estate agent, you will save yourself the time and hassle involved in calling around and arranging times to view properties, but you will also pay an administration fee for the service. This can be anything from £100 upwards. Make sure you check about all fees (inventory, checking in, checking out and general administration) before you place down a deposit.

Real estate agents often advertise their properties in the windows with descriptions and pictures of those available to buy or let. However, the best places tend to go quickly, so make sure you keep in constant contact with the agencies if you are serious about finding a new home. Once you register with an agent, they will contact you with suggestions as properties come to them suiting your requests.

If you opt to do your own legwork, regularly check the publications listed above for their accommodation advertisements. Also look for private postings in shop windows in the areas that appeal to you. But you are going to have to move fast – properties in London don't stick around very long. Especially the good ones, as you will soon find out.

Pick up a *London A to Z* streetmap guide from a bookshop or newsagent to help find your way around the capital. This costs about £7 and offers detailed maps to all streets and landmarks, including tube stations. It is invaluable, regardless of how long you've been in London.

Types of properties to let

Those who are new to London or on a tight budget often check themselves into a bedsit temporarily, which is a single room in a house where tenants share a common kitchen and a bathroom. The obvious downside to this sort of accommodation is that you will not have a lounge area for socialising with others in the house, and the shared bathroom is guaranteed to always be busy and unkept. Consequently, bedsits are most often the accommodation for the young, the poor, and singles.

One step up is to move into a flat, which come in all shapes and sizes. Flats in tall buildings are called tower blocks, unless they are purpose-built council blocks. A flat in a house split into multiple dwellings is called a conversion, and if it's a luxurious building, it will be called a mansion block. Whatever the case, all flats have a kitchen, a bathroom, and a living room.

A flat advertised as ex-council means that it was formerly owned by a borough council, bought from the government by its tenant. Council flats are government-owned housing estates normally in tower blocks, which are rented to residents for a cheap price. To qualify for this type of housing, you must contact your local council and provide evidence that you have lived in the borough for at least three years and have evidence of financial need. Even so, there are long waiting lists for this type of accommodation.

Houses in London generally fall into three categories. The first is a terraced house, which shares walls with identical houses on either side of it. Semi-detached houses are two identical houses side by side, and a detached house is free standing.

Unless you are minted, or plan on scoring a six-figured salary in your new job, it is unlikely that you will be financially able to rent an entire house – or even a flat –on your salary alone. Most 20-somethings in London live in shared flats or houses with at least two others. Take time to shop around for your new home, and be sure to move in with people you know you will get on with, because they will soon become a central part of your social life. You don't want to get stuck with a twitching anti-social sloth who only comes out of his room to forage for Marmite. I once shared a house with two budding DJs. They were absolutely terrible, but that didn't stop them from scratching and pulsating all through the night. It might sound like an ideal house for all you little ravers, but seven nights a week is a bit tiring. A normal Sunday morning would find me in the kitchen trying to make a cup of tea with out-of-sync hard house blaring and a wasted Aussie dancing on the kitchen table in a mini skirt and smeared make-up. Shudder.

> The streets of London were lit by gaslights for the first time in 1807. Before that, torches were used.

Letting a room or property

Starting fresh in a new city can be a costly experience, especially if it means purchasing a whole new set of dishes, sitting room furniture, a vacuum cleaner, and all those essentially household items you will need to get by. Luckily for you, the majority of properties let in London are fully furnished. This means that your basic pieces of furniture – including your bed, couch and television – will be included in the cost of your rent. But the quality of the furnishings can certainly vary. I'm sure you can live with mismatched dishes and glasses that all appear to have been nicked from The Old Queen's Head down the road, but take a look at the main bits of furniture. If you're stuck with a bed that will turn you into the Hunchback of Holland Park you may want to check on the possibility of a new one before slapping down your deposit and writing the guest list for your housewarming party.

Here is a list of some of the acronyms you will encounter while flipping through the pages of *Loot*:

gch	Gas central heating
gfch	Gas fired central heating
osp	On site parking

wfb	Wooden floorboards
w/m	Washing machine
WC	Water closet
N/S	No smokers
No DSS	No welfare/Social Security (dole) receivers
c/h	Central heating
p/g	Private garden
s/c	Self contained
ff	Fully furnished
pw	Per week
pcm	Per calendar month
pppw	Per person per week
inc	Inclusive of bills
excl	Exclusive of bills
d/g	Double glazing windows
BR	Close to British Rail station
dep	Security deposit required
tube	Close to a Tube station

Whether you are planning on renting an entire apartment, or simply moving into a room in a shared house, there are a few questions you will want to ask before traipsing all the way across London to take a look at the property.

Things to ask before viewing or letting a property:

1) What is the monthly rent?
2) Is the room fully furnished? Does it have a double/single bed?
3) Does this price include utilities (electricity, gas and water)?
4) Who pays the council tax?
5) How much is the bond/deposit?
6) How long is the walk to the tube station?
7) What is the length of the tenancy?
8) Is there a lounge? Is the kitchen separate from the lounge?
9) How many people live in the house?
10) How old are they? What do they do?
11) Is there a washer/dryer?

Searching by postcode

I will never forget the first day I flipped open the accommodation listings pages of *Loot*. Not only are the properties divided by price, but they also have a foreign numbering system (the London zipcodes called "postcodes"), which can be incredibly frustrating to make head or tail of.

London postcodes consists of two parts (i.e. SW11 1HT). The first part tells the general area of your address, while the second part tells where your property is positioned on the street. For example, the address starting with SW indicates the property is in South-west London. An address starting with E means the property is in East London. The lower the postcode number, the more central it is to that area (SE1 is the most central of the south-east zones). Be aware that some areas fall under more than one postcode.

Using this list (opposite) of the main postcodes in central London, you should be able to get an idea of where the property is located.

The basics

Once you have found a flat that suits you without having unlivable rat, ant and moisture ratios, it's time to sort out the basics. The easiest way to set up your electricity account is by taking over whatever service arrangement the previous occupiers used. If the landlord doesn't know which electricity company was used, then just call around the suppliers and check which one has an account with your address and register your new details.

Thames Water (0845 920 0888) supplies water to most of London. In most cases, water is not metered on your household, but if one is installed, you will need to take over the account from the previous tenant.

You may also want to consider getting either building or contents insurance to protect the goods in your house. Owners will need both kinds but renters will only need contents insurance to protect their valuables.

Finally, you will need a residential phone line in the flat. If there isn't already a line installed, you will need to contact your chosen telephone provider to arrange an appointment to have one set up. See the communication chapter in this book for further information about London telephone companies.

If you have a gas, electricity, or water meter at your house or flat, then be sure to take a reading on the day you move in so that you don't pay for any utilities that you don't use.

Council tax

Council tax payments go towards financing local government expenses including education, police, roads, waste disposal,

EC postcodes:
EC1 - Aldersgate, Finsbury, Holborn
EC2 - Bishopsgate, Cheapside
EC3 - Aldgate
EC4 - St Paul's

E postcodes:
E1, E2 - Bethnal Green, Whitechapel
E3 - Bow
E5 - Clapton, Homerton
E6 - East Ham
E7 - Forest Gate
E8 - Dalston
E9 - Homerton
E12 - Manor Park
E13 - Plaistow
E14 - Poplar (Isle of Dogs)
E15 - Stratford, West Ham
E16 - Victoria Docks, N Woolwich

NW postcodes:
NW1 - Regent's Park, St Pancras
NW3 - Hampstead
NW5 - Kentish Town
NW8 - St John's Wood

SE postcodes:
SE1 - The Borough, Waterloo
SE3 - Blackheath
SE4 - Brockley
SE5 - Camberwell
SE6 - Catford
SE8 - Deptford
SE11 - Kennington
SE12 - Lee
SE13 - Lewisham Central
SE14 - New Cross
SE15 - Peckham
SE16 - Bermondsey, Rotherhithe
SE17 - Walworth
SE21, 22 - Dulwich
SE23 - Forest Hill

WC postcodes:
WC1 - Bloomsbury, High Holborn
WC2 - Strand, Holborn

W postcodes:
W1 - West End
W2 - Bayswater, Paddington
W6 - Hammersmith
W8 - Holland Park
W9 - Maida Vale, Paddington
W10 - North Kensington
W11 - Notting Hill
W12, 14 - Shepherd's Bush, Hammersmith

N postcodes:
N1 - Angel
N5 - Highbury
N4 - Crouch End
N7 - Holloway
N16 - Stoke Newington
N19 - Upper Holloway

SW postcodes:
SW1 - Westminster, Victoria
SW2 - Brixton Hill
SW3 - Chelsea
SW4 - Clapham
SW5 - Brompton, Earl's Court
SW6 - Fulham
SW7 - Knightsbridge, South Kensington
SW8 - South Lambeth
SW9 - Brixton
SW10 - West Brompton
SW11 - Battersea
SW12 - Balham
SW15 - Putney
SW16 - Streatham
SW17 - Tooting
SW18 - West Wandsworth
SW19 - Wimbledon

libraries and community services. Each council determines its own rate based on the number of residents and how much money they need to finance their services. The tax rate is adjusted yearly. The amount of council tax you will be required to pay varies depending on which borough you live in and the number of people in your household.

You should notify your local council as soon as you move into your new home. If you don't do this straight away, they will catch up to you later down the road – and force you to pay up in arrears. Speaking from experience, having got stung with a £300 bill in one lump sum, you do not want to make this mistake.

Council tax can be paid by direct debit, at the bank, by post with a personal cheque, in person at your local council offices, by credit card, or at a post office. Payments can be made all at once, or in ten installments spread throughout the year. Average rates can vary from £500 per year all the way up to £1500.

If all residents in the property are full-time students, you may be exempt from paying Council Tax. Check with your borough.

For contents insurance, try one of the following:

www.insurance.co.uk

www.ms-home-insurance.co.uk

www.alliance-leicester.co.uk

www.insurance4homes.net

www.directline.com

Short-term accommodation

London has a huge range of short-term accommodation. Whether you're a backpacker with only a few pounds left in your pocket after a round-the-world extravaganza, you'd rather gouge your eyes out than stay in a hostel yet don't have a massive budget, or you want to experience the height of London's upmarket hotels, you'll find what you're after.

Youth hostels

Earls Court has traditionally been one of the best locations to head for if you are looking for short-term accommodation in London at a reasonable price. The area is a bit of a mecca for travellers so just follow the sticky trail of hunched over backpackers struggling down the streets under the weight of their packs to find the hostels. The area is fairly central so you won't be forced to pay extortionate amounts to catch the Tube into the center, and it has a very backpacker-friendly, social atmosphere. Everyone heads out to the local pubs in the evenings for a pint so you'll never be short of drinking buddies. Dorm beds cost as little as £15 per night, but be sure to book in advance during the high season, or you'll have to lug your belongings all over the area after being turned away from inn after inn.

Oxford Street YHA

14 Noel Street, London, W1
Tel: 020 7734 1618
Tube: Oxford Circus
www.yha.org.uk

Bordering the bustling shopping epicenter of Oxford Street and the trendy bars of Soho, locations don't come much better than this. The rooms are impeccably clean, quiet, and can be securely locked. This hostel comes with all the facilities a backpacker desires, including the rare privilege of on-site washing machines. But be prepared to pay dearly for such luxuries. The YHA membership costs £12.50 per year and a bed in a dorm room for four people costs £21.50 per night. Advanced booking in peak seasons is essential.

Barmy Badger Backpackers

17 Longridge Road, Earls Court, London, SW5
Tel: 020 7370 5213
Tube: Earls Court
www.barmybadger.com

The best thing about this hostel is its spacious kitchen, which is dominated by a huge dining table that serves as a social focal point every evening. The dorm rooms feel a bit cramped, but the bunk beds are wooden and sturdy, meaning that your upper bunkmate won't shake you awake after too many pints at the local pub. The toilets have fairly new fixtures, but because of the high levels of traffic using them, the standards are understandably low – especially after a Saturday night. A dorm bed in a room with five others will set you back £13 per night or £78 a week.

Ayers Rock Hostel

16 Longridge Road, Earls Court, London, SW5
Tel: 020 7373 2944
Tube: Earls Court

The crowd of weary nomads hovering outside the steps on Longridge Road marks the entrance to this popular youth hostel. The lounge area is also always packed with travellers watching television, reading books, or having social drinks. This is the place to come if you want to make friends and party hard while sorting out your next destination. The rooms are pretty dirty – which is what you'll expect everywhere – so make sure you own a pair of flip flops when it comes to taking that shower. A bed in a dorm room for six costs £12 per night or £65 a week.

Other hostels

Hampstead Heath, 4 Wellgarth Road, NW11. Tel: 020 8458 9054 or e-mail hampstead@yha.org.uk. Tube: Golders Green. This 199-bed hostel is in a three-story house situated in the leafy Hampstead area. A real gem during summer. Beds cost £19.90 including breakfast.

Hyde Park Hostel, 2–6 Inverness Terrace, W2. Tel: 020 7229 5101 or see www.astorhostels.com. Tube: Bayswater. Hardly the cleanest place available, but it's in a good location and has all the basic facilities. A bed will set you back £12–17.50.

St Christopher's Inn Camden, 48–50 Camden High Street, NW1. Tel: 020 7388 1012 or see www.st-christophers.co.uk. Tube: Camden Town. Perched above Belushi's, a lively late bar, this is a good place if you're looking to party – rather than sleep. Beds cost £17–23 per night in high season.

For those of you in blissful coupledom who couldn't possibly face bunking up with six new-found mates spreading gaseous rectum fumes and shedding hairs all over the floor, there's no need to lose sleep. Double rooms are available in many hostels and some may even have their own sink – so go ahead and play house together before actually unloading your backpacks into that new studio flat in Clapham. Here is a selection of hostels in London offering double rooms:

London City YMCA, 8 Errol Street, EC1. Tel: 020 7628 8832. Tube: Barbican or Old Street. Located in the City, the price of a double room may be slightly costly at £45, but at least you can count on this YMCA to be clean. Book ahead.

Oxford Street, 14 Noel Street, W1. Tel: 020 7734 1618. www.oxfordst@yha.org.uk Tube: Oxford Circus. This West End hostel has 75 beds with rooms for singles, couples, and even threesomes. You must have YHA membership to stay here. One night costs £24 per person.

Leinster Inn, 7-12 Leinster Square, W2. Tel: 020 7229 9641. www.astorhostels.com Tube: Queensway or Notting Hill Gate. This lively hostel in Notting Hill has a great atmosphere and double rooms are available for £22 per person, or £27 with your own shower. Under 30s only.

Budget hotels

If you don't want to slum it with the backpackers discussing the cheapest place to find hash in Koh Samui, but you don't have the budget for the mini-bar and a fluffy bathrobe, then the inexpensive hotels listed below are your best bet.

Regent Palace Hotel

Glasshouse Street, London, W1
Tel: 0870 400 8703
Tube: Piccadilly Circus
Rates from £40
This large impressive Victorian building set in the heart of London is just a five minute walk from Trafalgar Square and the National Gallery, and only a 10-minute walk to Covent Garden. While the standard rooms only have a wash basin, the newly refurbished rooms have both a shower and toilet facilities. Great for budget travellers.

Enrico Hotel

77–79 Warwick Way, Victoria, SW1
Tel: 020 7834 9538
Tube: Victoria
Rates from £40
This clean and comfortable bed and breakfast hotel is centrally located in Victoria. Of its 26 rooms, most have showers, but none have lavatories. All toilets are located outside the rooms, off the corridors.

The Abbey Lodge Hotel

51 Grange Park, London, W5
Tel: 020 8567 7914
Tube: Ealing Broadway
Rates from £45
Based in Ealing, which is slightly out of the way, this intimate hotel offers good value for money. Recently refurbished, each of its 17 rooms has an en suite bathroom with color TV, radio and alarm clock.

Chelsea Lodge Hotel

268 Fulham Road, London SW10
Tel: 020 7823 3494
Tube: Earls Court
Rates from £55
Nestled above the Fulham Tup pub, this little hotel promises good value for money, is fairly centrally located, and its rooms are well equipped with private baths or showers plus all the usual amenities. Having just 14 bedrooms, it is advisable to book ahead.

Mid-range hotels

If you want a nice place to stay, but can't part with the cash for a five-star room, then try one of these mid-range hotels.

Best Western Burns Kensington Hotel

18–26 Barkston Gardens, London, SW5
Tel: 020 7373 3151
Tube: Earls Court
Rates from £69

A full English breakfast is included and the rooms have phones, tea-making facilities, and 24-hour room service. The hotel is located close to the museums and shops of Kensington and is near to the West End.

The Abbey Court Hotel

20 Pembridge Gardens, London, W2
Tel: 020 7221 7518
Tube: Notting Hill Gate
Rates from £99

This elegant five-story Victorian town house hotel has been restored to exacting standards offering 22 bedrooms with antique furnishings. The beds range from brass to four-poster, and the Italian marble bathrooms are equipped with jacuzzi-jet baths.

Grange Adelphi Hotel

127–129 Cromwell Road, Kensington, SW7
Tel: 020 7373 7177
Tube: Gloucester Road
Rates from £60–148

Located in the luxurious borough of Kensington and Chelsea, The Adelphi is a 70-room establishment just a short ride by Tube to central London. There is a sophisticated and quiet restaurant for likewise clientele.

The Sydney Hotel Chelsea

9–11 Sydney Street, Chelsea, London, SW3
Tel: 020 7376 7711
Tube: South Kensington
Rates from £50

This distinctly original nineteenth-century town house has rooms themed around other places and other times. This four-star hotel is located close to the shopping at Knightsbridge and South Kensington.

The Commodore Hotel

50 Lancaster Gate, Hyde Park, W2
Tel: 020 7402 5291 or e-mail: reservations@commodore-hotel.com
Tube: Lancaster Gate
Rates from £110
This three-star hotel near Hyde Park offers lavishly refurbished rooms ideal for families and business travellers. Superb location for taking in the sights, eating at fine restaurants, and doing some shopping.

Windermere Hotel

142–144 Warwick Way, Victoria, London, SW1
Tel: 020 7834 5163
Tube: Victoria
Rates from £58
This award-winning, cozy little hotel is full of charm and character. Most rooms have en-suite, satellite television and tea-making facilities. The hotel is close to Victoria Station and is easily reachable from the West End.

Posh hotels

London has some of the top hotels in the world. The service is impeccable, the rooms are lavish, and restaurants and bars at the hotels are highly rated. Go on, book a room at one of these hotels for a dirty weekend away without ever setting your eyes on a sheep or placing your feet in a cow pie. Lock the doors, order room service and get down to some serious copulating.

The Ritz

150 Piccadilly, W1
Tel: 020 7300 2308
Tube: Piccadilly Circus
www.theritzlondon.com
Rates from £255
The Ritz. What more can we say? Opened in 1906, this hotel offers unparalleled style and true British sophistication. It has been totally refurbished to restore even the fabrics to their original Louis XVI style.

The Dorchester Hotel

Park Lane, London, W1
Tel: 020 7629 8888
Tube: Hyde Park Corner
www.dorchesterhotel.com
Rates from £340
Built in 1931, this grand hotel is now a favorite amongst film stars and the elite, offering exceptional services and keeping to high

standards. Overlooking Hyde Park, The Dorchester is well placed for taking in the shops, galleries and nightlife of Knightsbridge and Mayfair. This hotel boasts 195 king, twin and queen bedrooms with satellite television, plus 53 suites.

Sanderson Hotel

50 Berners Street, London, W1
Tel: 020 7300 1400
Tube: Oxford Circus
Rates from £205
This hotel in lively Soho has a distinctly modern feel. From the giant red lip sofa that greets you when you enter, to the art installations and sculptures – this is no ordinary hotel. Rooms are all state of the art and the hotel has been called 'the hippest hotel in the world' by *GQ* magazine.

The Metropolitan Hotel

Old Park Lane, Park Lane, London, W1
Tel: 020 7447 1000
Tube: Hyde Park Corner
Rates from £205
This hotel embodies all that is stylish and trendy. It is probably most famous for The Met Bar downstairs, which is a major celebrity hangout. The members-only door policy is strict, but guests are allowed in with no hassles. Rooms are contemporary and chic.

The Westbourne Hotel

163–165 Westbourne Grove, London, W11
Tel: 020 7243 6008
Tube: Notting Hill Gate
Rates from £120
This classy hotel in the heart of Notting Hill is a favorite for fashionistas, media darlings, and celebrities. It was styled by top designers and some of the rooms were designed by top British artists. Trendy, modern and refined.

The Great Eastern Hotel

40 Liverpool Street, London, EC2
Tel: 020 7618 5000
Tube: Liverpool Street
Rates from £185
This trendy five-star hotel is located near lively Shoreditch. The area is crammed full of the hippest bars in London and Hoxton Square is just moments away, as is the bustling Spitalfields Market. Whatever you want you will find at this hotel, from contemporary to Victorian styled rooms, all full of every amenity you could ask for.

The Radisson Edwardian Berkshire Hotel

350 Oxford Street, W1
Tel: 020 7629 7474 or e-mail: resberk@radisson.com
Tube: Oxford Street
Rates from £159
Handily located next to Oxford Street's department stores, this is the ideal hotel for doing plenty of shopping in as little time as possible. The hotel attracts an international business clientele, offering 135 elegant bedrooms.

Making reservations

To save yourself the hassle of calling around to make a reservation, you may want to contact the **London Tourist Board**, who will do the work for you for just a £5 fee.

Phone 020 7932 2020, e-mail book@londontouristboard.co.uk or see www.londontouristboard.com. It may also be worthwhile to pick up its annual publication *Where to Stay and What to Do in London*, which lists approved hotels, bed and breakfasts and apartments throughout the capital. The tourist board also produces a free pamphlet called *Where to Stay on a Budget*.

If you would like to stay in a bed and breakfast or private home, reservations can be made through London Homestead Services on 020 8949 4455 or see www.lhslondon.com. The British Hotel Reservations Centre also makes reservations. Call 0800 282 888 or see www.bhronline.com.

Buying a property

If your grandfather has left you a mattress stuffed with money you might want to consider buying property in London. It will cost you dearly but since prices are constantly rising, it makes sense to get on the property ladder as soon as possible – if it's within your budget.

The first thing you'll need to do is visit a bank or building society to find out about getting a mortgage. Foreign nationals should not have too much trouble finding a suitable lender. You will also need to hire a solicitor to make sure that all contracts are above-board. Both the seller and the buyer normally hire solicitors to oversee the conveyance (or the transferring of property), and this should cost you in the region of £400. To find properties you can try an independent real estate agent in the area that you hope to live in, a larger estate agent chain such as Foxtons, Chestertons, or Stirling Ackroyd, or look in *Hot Properties* – the free supplement with the *Evening Standard* on Wednesdays. For a detailed listing of London estate agents, look on www.numberone4property.co.uk

Chapter Two:
Recruitment and Money

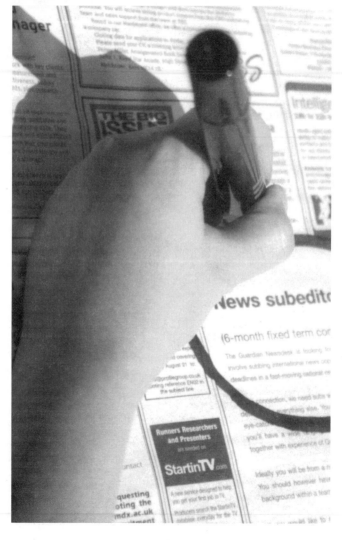

Get a job

Until you marry into aristocracy, sign that lucrative record deal, or succeed in starting a self-sufficient commune to live off the land in Crystal Palace Park, you'll probably need to get a job to survive. Donning a pressed shirt, shined shoes and a freshly coiffed hairstyle, you'll be ready to hit the pavement. London awaits and you'll have to give it all you've got. But where do you start? Understandably, trying to make a mark in a new place can be a terrifying experience, especially when you may be competing against thousands of equally valuable candidates.

Writing an impact CV

You should think of your CV (curriculum vitae, or resumé) as an advertisement for your life. It should grab the attention of the potential employer in less than 15 seconds by offering a succinct overview of your main achievements. If your CV rambles on for three or more pages, it is likely that the recruiter will not give your application the time and attention it deserves.

This is where rule number one comes in. Keep it short. One or two pages will be sufficient. Whether you are applying for a job with a telecommunications company, an art gallery, or a restaurant, no potential employer will want to scroll through page after page of autobiographical content on your life.

So what are the basic rules for making your CV stand out from the crowd? Firstly, make sure it covers the four necessary ingredients – key skills, career history, education and training, and a personal profile.

When stating your job experience, make sure you include your job title, the name of the company, and the dates that you worked there. This should be followed by a succinct two sentence description of the role plus a couple of bullet points stating key responsibilities, tasks and achievements. List each job in chronological order on the page starting with the most recent position.

Try to avoid using over-used phrases such as "was a good team player". Rather, use direct statements such as "restructured picture department" or "increased company turnover by 25 per cent".

It is also a good idea to cut the word "I" out of your CV. Rather, when describing your skills and duties, start your sentences with affirmative phrases, such as: Dealt with, Responsible for, Performed, etc.

Another secret of the trade is always to use positive language. If you find the words couldn't, wouldn't, or haven't, try to reconstruct the sentence – or cut it out completely. By sounding confident of your skills, you are selling yourself as being a potential benefit to the employer.

Lastly, to make your CV stand out from a stack of papers, take some time to lay out the page dynamically. Experiment with bold and plain text, as well as unusual fonts. As a general rule, however, try to avoid using more than two fonts on one page.

Your CV will also look more effective if you print it up on a good quality paper: either one that is of a heavier weight, unusual texture, or perhaps a slight off-white shade. That said, stay clear of bright colors, as this will likely portray the opposite effect.

You may need to tailor your CV for individual applications to ensure it is relevant for the job you are applying for. For example, if you are a nurse who is trying to get some freelance work as a journalist, make sure to include your relevant writing experience, associated awards and educational background.

At the end of your CV, you may want to include a personal profile detailing any non-work attributes or activities that will help in your application.

And finally, don't forget to get a neutral person to do a final proofread for grammar, spelling and presentation.

Attention-grabbing cover letter

Stun your potential employer with your fantastic wit and intelligence with an attention-grabbing cover letter that provides a brief insight into your employment history. Here is your chance to make a good first impression and influence the recruiter to read on.

The cover letter must be formal and concise – taking up no more than three paragraphs – and must be addressed to the named individual who is in charge of the hiring. Be sure to spell this person's name correctly.

In the first paragraph, introduce yourself and your job title and state the position you are applying for. This is followed by a paragraph outlining why you are suitable for the job, what skills you can offer the employee, and key attributes that make you the best candidate for the position. Briefly state your relevant experience and show how and why you are the best person for the job.

The closing paragraph should be punchy and confident. Rather than typing a bland "Yours sincerely", try a proactive phrase such as: "I look forward to hearing from you again soon. Please contact me at any time if you would like to arrange an interview."

Make sure the final paragraph also contains your contact details.

The cover letter must be typed using the same fonts and paper as your CV.

Sending out your application

In terms of presentation, it is always best to send your CV and cover letter by post in an A4 envelope, so that it doesn't have to be folded. E-mail is another good option, although be sure to send everything as a Word document attachment to avoid formatting problems. Fax is the least efficient method of sending your CV because the output may appear blurred, the pages may get lost, and if the employer doesn't have a plain paper fax, it will come out as an annoying curly roll of paper which will not be read properly.

> **Jobsites listing London jobs:**
>
> www.jobserve.com
>
> www.jobsite.co.uk
>
> www.monster.co.uk
>
> www.newmonday.com
>
> www.workthing.com

London salaries

Rather than hop directly into a permanent job, many newcomers to London decide to work as a temporary employee, giving them the option of hopping between one or more organisations. This way, you will gain experience working for numerous employers and will also get a better feel for the industry. Another option is to work on a contract basis, which means that you will not be owed the same dental and healthcare benefits as the permanent employers, but you have the option of leaving the job when the contract has run out. Temping and contract work is also a good way to earn quick money if you arrive in London and are in quick need of some cash. This chart should give you an idea of the salaries you can expect to earn per hour on a temping basis in London.

Accounting

	Rate per hour
Accounts assistant	£10–15
Credit controller	£9-14
Part-qualified accountant	£10–18
Newly qualified	£18–22
Qualified	from £21

Banking and Finance

	Rate per hour
Clerical accounts	£8–10
Part-time qualified	£13-23
Newly qualified	£17–23
Qualified with experience	from £25

Legal

	Rate per hour
Lawyers	from £13
Legal receptionist (untrained)	£9-10

Legal receptionist (trained)	£9–11
Legal secretary	£12–£15

Secretarial — Rate per hour

Office junior	£6–£8
General administration and receptionist	£7–£10
Trained secretaries	£9–£11
Personal Assistants (PAs)	£11–£14
Switchboard operator	£8-10
Data entry operator	£7-10

Technology — Rate per hour

IT specialist	£12–£16
Website or media designer	£12–£20

Engineering — Rate per hour

Engineer	£10–£20

Other popular professions — Rate per hour

Nannying (£150–£350 per week – some live-in)	£3–£7
Nursing	£8–£12
Teaching (from £115-120 per day)	£10-13
Supply teaching (£105–£115 per day)	£10–£13
Waitressing and bar staff (£140-170/week live-in)	£5-6.50 live-out
Chef	£5–£11
Head chefs	up to £20
Call center advisor	£6–£8
Telesales	£8–£10 plus commission
Permanent call center	£6–£10
Waitressing and bar work	£3–£6 (some live-in)
Construction	£10–15
Production and industrial labour	£5

Recruitment agencies

When approaching a recruitment agency for the first time, write a brief description of your work history followed by one line describing the type of job you are seeking. Enclose a cover letter with your CV; the latter must be listed in chronological order starting with your most recent position. Don't worry about making your cover letter too precise because your initial enquiry will be followed up by an informal interview with a recruitment consultant, who will want to discuss your job prospects further.

However, if you are approaching the agency with regard to a specific job advertised in a magazine or newspaper, take the time to type up a cover letter explaining why you think you are best suited to the job. In this case, the agency will only give up time to meet with you if they think you are suitable for the job.

It will be in your best interests to fire off your CV to every recruitment agency specialising in your field. By registering with as many agencies as possible, you will have jobs coming from all directions, meaning you will be in the position of being able to choose the best positions at the best rates. Initially, send your CV either by post or e-mail to the department responsible and wait a couple of days for a recruiter to get back to you. If you don't hear a response, make a polite telephone call to introduce yourself.

Accountancy and finance

London is Europe's financial hub and there is no shortage of jobs within the accountancy and banking fields. Staff within the commercial, public and industrial sectors are in hottest demand, and there are also regular vacancies for those with internal audit experience.

The best way to search for jobs is by sending your details to a specialist recruitment agency (such as the ones listed below) or checking the local newspapers for appointments, such as the *Evening Standard* on Mondays and Tuesdays, the *Metro* on Tuesdays and the *Guardian* on Saturdays. Make sure your CV highlights your academic qualifications, previous experiences and computer literacy.

Agencies to try:

Accountancy Additions
Tel: 020 7247 6414 or www.accountancyadditions.com
Andersen Leigh Associates
Tel: 020 7307 6565 or www.andersenleigh.com
David Chorley International
Tel: 020 7242 0509 or email holborn@davidchorley.co.uk
FSS Financial Tel: 020 7209 1000 or www.fss.co.uk
Joslin Rowe Tel: 020 7786 8085 or www.joslinrowe.com
Martin Ward Anderson
Tel: 020 7240 2233 or www.martinwardanderson.com
Michael Page International
Tel: 020 7831 2000 or www.michaelpage.co.uk
Robert Half International Tel: 020 7389 6900 or www.rhi.net
Robert Walters Tel: 020 7379 3333 or www.robertwalters.com

Administration/secretarial

If you are computer literate, have good conversation and telephone skills, and a typing speed of at least 50 words per minute, you shouldn't have a problem finding a secretarial job in the capital. Additional skills such as shorthand ability, audio skills, and the knowledge of other languages will also boost your chances and pay packages.

Unfortunately, the industry took a dive late last year due to a slowdown in the economy, meaning that temping secretarial jobs are not as abundant as they were a couple years ago. Saying that, demand in London for secretaries, PAs, and general administrators will never die out. If you look the part and boast all the relevant skills, good paying jobs are plentiful, although you may want to veer towards a permanent or contract position rather than a temporary one.

Agencies to try:

City People Tel: 020 7557 7222 or e-mail: secretarial@citipeople.com
Joslin Rowe Tel: 020 7786 8060 or www.joslinrowe.com
Judy Fisher Associates
Tel: 020 7437 2277 or e-mail: info@judyfisher.co.uk
Office Angels Tel: 020 7626 3550 or www.office-angels.com
OfficeTeam (temping)
Tel: 020 7389 6900 or e-mail: westend@officeteamuk.com
Robert Walters Tel: 020 7379 3333 or www.robertwalters.com
TMP Worldwide Tel: 020 7406 3869 or see www.monster.co.uk

Education

There is certainly no shortage of work for either supply or permanent teachers in London. In fact, a drastic shortage means that the pay is relatively high and the options of where – and when – you want to work will be available to you.

Look in the *Guardian* newspaper on Tuesdays, the *Evening Standard* on Mondays and the *Independent* on Thursdays for job ads. Also, be sure to pick up *The Times Education Supplement*, which can be purchased at your local newsagent. Other good sources for ads are *TNT* and *SX* magazines, available outside most Tube stations.

Agencies to try:

1st Contact Education Tel: 0800 039 3075 or
www.1stcontact.co.uk or e-mail: education@1stcontact.co.uk
Abacus Education Tel: 020 8646 1001 or
www.abacuseducation.co.uk
Ambition Tel: 020 8288 9071
Blue Education Tel: 020 7861 8955 or e-mail: info@bluecare.co.uk
Capita Education Resourcing Tel: 0800 731 6871 for primary, 0800 731 6872 secondary, or see www.capitaers.co.uk
Dream Education Tel: 08701 605958 or email: teachers@dream-education.co.uk

Hays Education Personnel Tel: 020 7931 9040 or
www.haysworks.com
Match Education Tel: 020 7927 8344 or www.matcheducation.com
Protocol Teachers Tel: 020 7440 8441 or www.protocol-teachers.com or email: info@protocol-teachers.com
Select Education Tel: 020 7638 1849 www.selecteducation.com
Verity Education Tel: 020 7629 8786 or www.verityeducation.com
or e-mail: info@verityeducation.com

Trades/industrial

There is plenty of work available in a whole variety of trades ranging from construction and light industrial labour to plumbing or hairdressing. However, because some of these jobs tend to be seasonal, skilled tradesmen may find themselves hopping from construction in the summer to maintenance work in the winter to keep the money flowing in.

Another booming industry in Britain at the moment is the call center market, which has huge demand for round-the-clock call center operators. The demand for workers is said to be growing by 40 per cent each year, and hourly pay rates can range from £6–10 per hour.

Agencies to try:

BBL Recruitment Tel: 020 8514 8866
or e-mail: garyw@bblrecruitment.co.uk
Blue Arrow Tel: 020 8681 8333 or www.bluearrow.co.uk
Euro Personnel Services
Tel: 020 7623 0101 or www.optionsemployment.com
Keyman Personnel Tel: 020 8771 8363 or www.keyman.co.uk
Manpower Tel: 01727 854393 or www.manpower.co.uk
Reed Tel: 020 8944 3000 or www.reed.co.uk
Robert Walters (for call-center work)
Tel: 020 7379 3333 or www.robertwalters.com
Securicor Tel: 020 7407 0313 or www.securicor.co.uk

Retail

The best way to land a job in retail is to approach the individual shop you are interested in working for and personally deliver your CV to the manager. Dig out your most stylish outfit and act confidently to make a good impression. However, if you would rather a recruitment agency did the work for you, there are a few specialising in the retail industry.

Agencies to try:

Reinforcements Tel: 020 7494 0050 or www.rossgroup.co.uk
Talisman Retail Tel: 020 8228 1734
or e-mail: alison.macleod@talismanretail.co.uk

Technical and engineering

Architects, engineers and surveyors should not have a problem finding work in London. Be sure to register with specialist agencies (such as the ones listed below) and check out permanent job postings in the *Evening Standard* on Wednesdays and the *Guardian* on Thursdays.

Agencies to try:

Anders Elite Tel: 020 7256 5555 or www.anderselite.com
Bluetec Tel: 020 7861 8960 or e-mail: bluetecinfo@bluetec.co.uk
Carmichael Site Services Tel: 01844 212 058 or email: cv@carmichaelsiteservices.com
KeyMan Personnel Tel: 020 8771 8363 or www.keymanpersonnel.com

Information technology (IT)

Despite the recent downturn within the global technology industry, staff with good qualifications and experience are still in demand in London. Check out the permanent IT job ads in the *Guardian* on Thursdays and the *Evening Standard* on Monday and Wednesdays. Also pick up trade publications such as *Computer Weekly* and *Computing* from the local newsagent for a selection of jobs for computer analysts, programmers, project managers and sales staff. The systems most sought after in London are Oracle 7, C++, SAP/R3, Visual Basic and Netware 3.x/4.1.

Agencies to try:

Computer People Tel: 020 7440 2000 or www.computerpeople.co.uk
Haymarket Consulting Group Tel: 0871 871 1000 or www.haymarket.com
Lester Associates Tel: 020 7413 3900 or www.lester-assoc.com
Michael Page International Tel: 020 7269 2285 or www.michaelpage.co.uk
Reed Technology Group Tel: 020 7636 2722 or www.reed.co.uk/it
Robert Walters Tel: 020 7379 3333 or www.robertwalters.com

Legal

Whether you are a legal secretary or a top lawyer, you have come to the right city to get a high-paying job. London is home to some of the biggest legal firms in the world, including some of the major US corporations that work on a highly beneficial pay scale, meaning more money for you.

Agencies to try:

David James Associates Tel: 020 7628 5535 or
www.djameslegal.com
Hays ZMB (lawyers and paralegals)
Tel: 020 7523 3838 or www.zureka.com
Lawson Clark Tel: 020 7256 6666 or www.lawson-clark.co.uk
LPA Legal Recruitment
Tel: 020 7430 1199 or www.legalrecruitment.co.uk
Verity Legal (legal secretaries)
Tel: 020 7493 0437 or www.verityappointments.com

Media, sales and marketing

The best source of jobs within these sectors is by checking the *Guardian's* media insert on Mondays or logging on to www.jobsunlimited.co.uk and www.workthing.com. Also, pick up *Broadcast*, *The Press Gazette* or *Marketing Week* magazines from your local newsagent.

Agencies to try:

Career Moves Tel: 020 7292 2900 or www.cmoves.co.uk
Formula Won Tel: 020 7987 1422 or www.formula-won.co.uk
Judy Fisher Associates Tel: 020 7437 2277
Michael Page Marketing
Tel: 020 7269 2556 or see www.michaelpage.co.uk
Recruit Media Tel: 020 7704 1227 or www.recruitmedia.co.uk
Searchlight Tel: 020 7383 3850 or www.search-light.com
Simpson Lang Associates
Tel: 020 7379 8388 or e-mail: simpsonlang@staffwise.co.uk
The Media Network Tel: 020 7637 9227 or www.tmn.co.uk

Hospitality

If you are looking for a pub job, the best way is simply to walk into the establishment and ask to speak to the manager. No previous experience is usually necessary, although you must be able to portray that you are a trustworthy, sociable and hardworking person. Another great source of job ads is *TNT* magazine and *SX* magazine, both distributed free on Mondays and Wednesdays from bunkers outside most Tube stations. Additionally, the *Evening Standard* and *Metro* newspapers run job sections for the hotel and catering industries on Thursdays.

Agencies to try:

Reed Tel: 0207 623 2014 or see www.reed.co.uk
Hot Recruit www.hotrecruit.co.uk
Dee Cooper Tel: 01764 670 001 or www.livein-jobs.co.uk
Golden Keys Recruitment
Tel: 020 7581 5739 or www.goldenkeys.co.uk or e-mail CV to: goldenkeys@goldenkeys.co.uk

Health

Due to a serious shortage in health staff within the UK, medics should have no problem securing a good job in London. In fact, hospitals have been known to travel internationally in the hopes of luring staff from abroad by promising good wages and working conditions. In addition to contacting recruitment agencies, you may want to consult specialist journals such as the *British Medical Journal* and *Nursing Times* for vacancies. Also, try the *Guardian* on Wednesdays, *TNT* magazine on Mondays, and the *Evening Standard* on Mondays. To register with an agency, you will need to provide proof of academic certificates, passport photos, a work permit, and professional references.

Agencies to try:

Bluecare Tel: 0800 376 4922 or www.bluecare.co.uk
Mediplacements Tel: 020 8491 8899 or www.mediplacements.com
Elite Recruitment Specialists
Tel: 020 7235 1900 or www.elitemedical.co.uk or e-mail CV to: recruit@elitemedical.co.uk
EM Nursing Recruitment
Tel: 020 8709 6570 or e-mail: nursing@emrecruitment.co.uk
Nursing UK Tel: 020 7499 9070 or www.nursing-uk.com
Pulse Nursing Recruitment Tel: 0800 772 299
Strand Nurses Bureau Tel: 020 7836 6396 or
www.strandnursing.co.uk

Additional health information

* **Doctors** must register with the General Medical Council (Tel: 020 7580 7642).
* **Speech therapists** must register with the Royal College of Speech and Language Therapists (Tel: 020 7378 1200).

* **Occupational therapists** must become a member of the Council of Professional Supplementary Medicine (Tel: 020 8735 0632).
* **Physiotherapists** need to register with the Chartered Society of Physiotherapy (Tel: 020 7306 6666).
* **Radiographers** from abroad must check if their qualifications are transferable in the UK. Contact the Society of Radiographers on 020 7391 4500.
* **Nurses** must register to join the UK nursing workforce by calling 020 7637 7181. If approved, you may want to join the UK Central Council for Nursing Midwifery and Health Visiting (Tel: 020 7637 7181). This is not essential but will improve your chances of finding work.

Nannies and carers

The majority of jobs in the UK within the nannying and carer industries are live-in, ranging from caring for the elderly to nannying a household of children in the suburbs. For those who are considering becoming a carer, be prepared to dispense medicine, give baths, make beds, prepare meals and spend hours entertaining your patient. You can expect to get two hours off each day and one day free a week.

Many live-in jobs are in the countryside, while live-out jobs tend to be in London and will be slightly better paid to cover your travel and rental costs. Most recruitment agencies will require that you provide personal and work references to apply for any job, plus some require you to have a full driving licence and previous experience in the field.

Agencies to try:

Consultus Tel: 01732 355 231 or www.carersagency.co.uk or e-mail: info@consultuscarers.co.uk
Colvin Nursing Tel: 020 7794 9323 or www.colvin-nursing.co.uk
Ena Live-In Carers Tel: 01727 825 000 or www.ena.co.uk or email: jobs@ena.co.uk
Kids Unlimited Tel: 01625 587 324 or email: info@kidsunlimited.co.uk
Premier Global Au Pairs and Nanny Services Tel: 01932 855 327 or email: contact@globalaupairs.com
Trinity Homecare Tel: 020 8307 7662 or www.trinity-homecare.com or e-mail: trinityhomecare@cs.com
Walleroo Nannies Tel: 020 7736 2331 or www.walleroonannies.com

If you're a hardcore antismoker, London will be a bit of a shock. But this isn't California sweetheart, and life isn't all yoga and macrobiotic green tea. So unfortunately, there aren't many pubs that are entirely smoke-free. Nevertheless, there are a few places where you can drink in a non-smoking section.

The Albion
10 Thornhill Road, Barnesbury, N1. Tel: 020 7607 7450.
Tube: Angel or Highbury & Islington.

Duke of Cambridge
30 St Peter's Street, N1. Tel: 020 7359 3066.
Tube: Angel

Marquess of Angelessay
39 Bow Street, WC2. Tel: 020 7240 3216.
Tube: Covent Garden

The Shakespeare
99 Buckingham Palace Road, SW1. Tel: 020 7828 4913.
Tube: Victoria

The William Morris Pub
2–4 King Street, W6. Tel: 020 8741 7175.
Tube: Hammersmith

The Windmill Pub
Clapham Common South Side, SW4. Tel: 020 8673 4578.
Tube: Clapham Common

The basics

Starting a new job is always stressful, but if you have concerns over and above the usual daily gripes, speak to your HR (Human Resources) manager to see if anything can be done. If you have concerns about pay entitlement, public holidays, employment rights, or unfair redundancy, go to the Department of Trade and Industry's website at www.dti.gov.uk/er/ to read about UK policies and regulations. Other good sources of employment news, information and inspiration include recruitment websites: www.newmonday.com and www.workthing.com

Holiday pay

It is up to your full-time employer to decide how many weeks of paid vacation you will be allocated each year. In the UK, the average is anywhere from 20 to 25 days, although some finance and technology companies offer generous packages in excess of the norm.

If you are working as a temporary worker, or on a part-time basis, you are also by law due to receive paid vacation time. For further information about what you are allotted, check out the BECTU (Broadcasting Entertainment Cinematography and Theatre Union) website at www.bectu.org.uk.

Tax

Once you begin earning a salary, your employer has to make National Insurance contributions on your behalf. These contributions, which translate to roughly 10 per cent of your total earnings, go towards paying a state pension, unemployment and social security benefits and funding the National Health Service (NHS) which runs all the state hospitals and medical facilities.

Inland Revenue is the government department responsible for collecting income tax. Your employer's payroll department should apply for your NI number for you, although if you are working on a temporary basis, you will have to do this on your own.

Contact your local Department of Health and Social Security (DHSS) and provide a passport and proof of employment. To make an appointment with your nearest DHSS, phone 020 7210 5983. There is often a wait to see an officer, so if you don't have an appointment, try to get there as early in the morning as possible.

When you visit the local office, you will have a one-to-one confidential interview, and your permanent NI number will be posted to you approximately 12–16 weeks later. For further information, call National Insurance on 0191 2204 222.

Banking

Unless you intend to sing showtunes to tourists for spare change, live off daddy's trust fund, or travel with a shopping trolley and stash your cash in a Tesco's bag under your mattress, you will probably need to open a bank account. It's not too much of a palaver, and at least you'll have a shiny new debit card to nestle in your wallet next to your wad of cash and those unflattering photo booth snaps of your ex.

Most Londoners bank with one of the high street banks, including Barclays, NatWest, Royal Bank of Scotland, Abbey National, HSBC and Lloyds TSB. However, another option is banking with a building society such as the Woolwich. While building societies have historically operated as mutual, non-profit institutions mainly offering mortgages and savings accounts, most today offer the same services provided by banks, including current and savings accounts, cheque guarantee cards, debit and credit cards, personal loans and insurance.

Opening an account

If you are planning on working in Britain, it will be necessary to open a current bank account, as your employer will probably transfer your salary directly into it. Your day-to-day dealings will be made through a current account and you may also decide to open an additional savings account for stashing away funds for next year's full moon party in Thailand.

When choosing a bank, select one that is conveniently located either next to your workplace or your home. Also, check what the queues are like at that particular branch – you don't want to be wasting your entire lunch hour waiting to cash a cheque.

Before opening an account, compare bank charges, interest rates on credit cards and fees for other services that you may take up in the future. These may include overdraft charges, loan and mortgage rates.

Finally, when you have made your selection, simply walk into your bank or building society of choice and speak to a personal banker. You will be asked to show a passport or a UK drivers licence showing that you are over age 18 plus proof of your new address in the form of a gas, electricity, phone or council tax bill. Many banks will also request to see a letter from your employer.

In return, you will be handed a crisp new cheque book, a debit card, the option to request either monthly or weekly statements, an automatic authorised overdraft facility, the option to apply for a credit card, plus free telephone and Internet banking.

Your choices

For the most current information on branch locations, opening hours, fees or rates, check out the individual websites or walk into your local branch.

Natwest	www.natwest.co.uk
Bank of Scotland	www.bankofscotland.co.uk
Barclays	www.barclays.co.uk
Lloyds TSB	www.lloydstsb.com
Halifax	www.halifax.co.uk
Abbey National	www.abbeynational.co.uk
HSBC	www.hsbc.com
Woolwich	www.woolwich.co.uk

Opening hours

Normal banking hours are from 9 a.m. to 4 p.m. on weekdays, with some branches staying open until 5 p.m. However, if you can't make it to the bank within working hours, most have cash points outside the branches available for 24-hour cash withdrawals.

Credit cards and loans

To apply for a credit card or loan, the easiest way is to walk into your branch and speak to a personal banker. It may be in your best interest to put on a nice outfit to impress the bank, although these days, most of the decision making process is actually done by computers which run an instant credit check on your accounts.

Also, take the time to shop around competing banks for the best rates. Fill out the application forms for the ones you wish to do business with, and post them off. Again, the bank will run a credit check on your previous financial history before making a decision on whether to issue you a credit card or loan.

Internet banking

Internet banks often offer lower rates, if you don't mind placing your money in the precarious world of the web. However, if you would like to check on your finances from the comfort of your desk without placing your trust in a less established bank, most major banks also offer Internet banking. Go to www.egg.co.uk, www.firstdirect.com, or www.smile.co.uk for details.

Chapter Three:
Transportation

The Tube (Underground)

Deep in the darkest bowels of hustling, bustling London lies a network of more than 500 trains zipping passengers all over the city. If you believe the grumblings of locals, you may think that the Tube more closely resembles a horse-drawn carriage with a bent wheel that's stuck in the mud than a twenty-first-century transportation system. But while it's true that delays do often occur, without it the streets of London would be rammed with triple-decker buses and bottle-necked traffic jams at every roundabout.

The London Underground is the oldest in the world, made up of 287 stations, some of which date back to the 1860s. Attracting 2.5 million passengers a day, you'll have to expect some overcrowding, but that is hardly what you'll be thinking the first time you are rammed into a carriage on the Central line during rush hour like chickens in a cage on the way to slaughter. Occasionally you'll have to wait a few minutes for the next train, and every now and again a station will be shut for a suspect package, overcrowding, or an "incident". You can't do anything to change it, so don't bother sighing: just grab a newspaper, keep your mind busy, and don't bore everyone with your complaining. For official information see www.thetube.com

Navigating the Tube

The Tube map is a network of colored lines, and is quite simple to navigate once you get used to it. Each of the 12 lines are named and color-coded on maps. Small, folded Tube maps are available free at all stations and you'll probably find it necessary to carry one until you get more used to the system. Once you get down the escalators or lift, simply follow the signs to the line you wish to travel on and then check that you are on the correct platform for the direction you want to travel. Services run from 5.30 a.m. until just after midnight, although fewer trains run on Sundays and public holidays.

Tube etiquette

Be prepared to give up your seat for a pregnant or elderly person.

Stand on the right on the escalators so that people in a hurry can pass by on the left.

Stand clear of the closing doors. Obstructing the doors causes delays and annoys passengers.

Let passengers get off the train before you get on.

Fares

Tickets can be purchased from machines and ticket windows in the station and the price varies depending on where you plan to travel. The network is divided into six zones that form rings around the innermost Zone 1, which includes the City, Westminster, and small parts of inner London boroughs. Zone 2 forms a concentric circle around Zone 1, and so on. If you are one of the lucky ones to live and work in central London, the cheapest way to get around is by purchasing Carnet cards for Zone 1. These are single tickets, can be bought in books of ten for the discounted bulk price of £11.50, and are used the same as normal Zone 1 single tickets.

A single journey ticket within Zone 1 will cost £1.60, a ticket from any station in Zone 1 to any station in Zone 2 will cost £2, and a single fare from Zone 1 to 6 will set you back £3.70. As a return ticket is simply double the price, buy a Travelcard to save money if you plan to make more than one journey a day. Daily, weekend, one week, one month, or one year Travelcards can be purchased for unlimited travel on all forms of transportation – including the Tube, bus, and trains.

To avoid the hassle of standing in Monday morning ticket queues, you may want to consider buying your monthly or annual tickets over the telephone, on 0870 849 999, or online at www.ticket-on-line.co.uk. For additional information about prices, see www.londontransport.co.uk or call the 24-hour London Travel Information line on 020 7222 1234.

One-day Travelcard

There are two types of One-day Travelcard, depending on the times you want to travel. The cheapest is the off-peak pass, which can only be purchased and used after 9.30 a.m. Mondays to Fridays, restricting early morning commuters from buying this pass. However, this Travelcard can be used any time on Saturdays and Sundays.

One-day Travelcard (Off-peak)

Zones Cost

Zones	Cost
1-2	£4.10
1-4	£4.50
1-6	£5.10
2-6	£3.60

If you must travel before 9.30 a.m., you're going to have to bite the bullet and fork out dearly, unless you get organized and buy a weekly, monthly or yearly Travelcard. This is a scheme set up by London Transportation to try and disperse traffic between its peak morning commuting hours.

One-day Travelcard (Peak)
Zones Cost

Zones	Cost
1-2	£5.10
1-3	£6.20
1-4	£7.00
1-5	£8.80
1-6	£10.70

Another option is to purchase a Weekend Travelcard for travelling between Zones 1 and 2 all day on Saturday and Sunday.

Tube facts

In 1987, an improperly extinguished cigarette in a pile of garbage beneath the escalators at King's Cross Station caused a fire that killed 31 people. All stations are now non-smoking.

Angel has the longest escalator in Western Europe. It is 60 meters long.

Victoria and King's Cross record the highest number of Tube suicides each year, with Tooting Bec and Mile End coming third and forth. The new Jubilee line extension is equipped with a glass barrier to prevent such grisly occurences.

The air in the Underground is on average 10 °C hotter than the air on the surface.

The Tube is home to an estimated half a million mice, and a species of rat that has become resistant to most poisons.

The Piccadilly Line was formerly known as the Great Northern, Piccadilly, and Brompton Railway.

The old Aldwych Station (closed in 1994) was used as a bomb shelter for Egyptian mummies and other artefacts from the British Museum during the Second World War. It is now used as a set whenever a film company wants footage filmed on the Tube (like *Superman 4*, and Prodigy's *Firestarter* music video).

There are 48 disused, or ghost, stations.

The world's first electric underground, the City and South London Railway, opened in Stockwell in 1890.

Weekend Travelcard

Zones	Cost
1-2	£6.10
1-4	£6.70
1-6	£7.60
2-6	£5.40

If you plan on doing a lot of travelling during peak hours, it will be in your best interests to purchase a Seven-day Travelcard, which may be used at any time of day for seven consecutive days. You will need to get your photo taken at one of the sit-down booths, found at most Tube stations, and you must fill in a form to get a designated Photocard to accompany your pass.

Seven-day Travelcard

Zones	Cost
1 or 2	£16.50
1-2	£19.60
1-3	£23.10
1-4	£28.40
1-5	£34.10
1-6	£37.20

Once you have landed a full-time job and have charted out your easiest travel routes, the cheapest and most convenient method for purchasing your Travelcards is by purchasing a monthly or annual pass. Although it may be a big lump sum all at once, this will save you time and money in the long run. These can also be used at any time of day and on night buses.

Monthly and Annual Travelcard

Zones	Monthly	Annual
1	£63.40	£660
1-2	£75.30	£784
1-3	£88.80	£924
1-4	£109.10	£1136
1-5	£131.00	£1364
1-6	£142.90	£1488

Docklands light railway

The DLR railway, which was opened in 1987, is a network of routes serving the east and south east of London including the City, Canary Wharf, Greenwich and Lewisham. Hop on this lightrail service from either Bank or Tower Hill on the London Underground. All Travelcards are valid for use on this railway, although you also have the option of purchasing a one-day DLR Rail and River Rover Ticket for £7.80, which provides unlimited travel on the City Cruises riverboat and DLR between Westminster and Greenwich. See the section below on riverboat services for further details or call London Transport on **020 7222 1234**. Tickets can be purchased at ticket machines and all DLR stations.

> Keep in mind that the tube map is not to scale. Some stations may look far away on the map but are really only a few minutes walk. A few very close stations are Leicester Square and Covent Garden, Charing Cross and Embankment, and King's Cross and Euston.

Bussing it

Although it may be a slower form of transportation than The Underground, hitching a lift on a double-decker bus can be a much more pleasant experience than travelling in a stuffy, crowded carriage during rush hour – and it will also help you gather understanding of your bearings above ground.

All buses are identified on the front and back by a route number. The front also has a screen showing its major destinations and the direction it is travelling, which may include the names of major Tube stations or landmarks.

When you see your bus approaching, be sure to put out your arm to indicate to the driver that you want it to pull over. Buses do not automatically pull over just because people are standing at the stop.

Also, be forewarned that there are two types of buses and these must be boarded in different ways. The old Routemaster double-decker buses require that you climb on at the back through an open platform. Take a seat and wait for the conductor to come around and collect fares or check your Travelcard. To indicate your stop, pull the wire that runs along the left-hand side downstairs, or press the red button on the pole upstairs.

To board one of the newer buses, however, board from the front doors, pay your fare to the driver – or flash your Travelcard – and later alight from the rear doors. You must have coins to pay for your fare, although it doesn't have to be the exact change. If you know the fare, simply state the price and give the driver your money. If you don't know, give your destination and the driver will determine the price.

Your one day, weekend, weekly or monthly Tube pass can be used on London Transport buses. If you don't have a pass, you will have to buy a single ticket on the bus. This will cost £1 to travel anywhere within Zone 1, or 70 pence outside Zone 1. One-day Zone 1 to 4 bus passes are available for £2.

Also, if you plan to use buses frequently and don't have a Travelcard, it is advisable to buy a bus pass from your local newsagents. You can also buy Bus Saver tickets, a book of 6 tickets to be used for single journeys, which costs £3.90.

Bus passes

Zones	Seven-day	Monthly	Annual
2, 3, or 4	£7.50	£28.80	£300
1-4	£8.50	£32.70	£340

Daytime buses run until just after midnight, at which time night buses take over. These start with the letter "N" and run hourly along more than 50 routes until dawn. Most pass through Trafalgar Square before heading outwards, so this is a good place to head to if you are in central London and looking for an inexpensive way to get home. The fare for a night bus is £1.

You may also want to pick up the Central London Bus Guide, which includes a night bus map, to find out the latest routes. Alternatively, program the London Transport hotline number into your mobile phone (020 7222 1234) so that you are only a telephone call away for up-to-the minute information on routes, prices and schedule times.

Go by coach

One of the great things about living in London is that you can be in a totally different city in less time than it takes you to track your friend down in the Topshop on Oxford Street on a Saturday afternoon. Escape the madness to go shopping in Manchester, land of the Happy Mondays and Oasis; pop down to the seaside resort of Brighton for a weekend clubbing session; or see a band play at the Cavern Club in Liverpool. They are all cheaply and easily reachable by coach.

Although travelling by coach may take considerably longer than hopping on the train, it is nearly twice as cheap as travelling by rail, and just as convenient.

National Express coachlines, which has a nationwide network of over 1,000 destinations, departs from Victoria Coach Station in central London. It's only a five-minute walk from Victoria Tube station. Full-time students and under 25s can purchase a Coach Card pass for £9, which is valid for one year and gives you a 20–30 per cent discount on all fares. To book tickets or check times, call National Express at 0990 808080, log on to www.gobycoach.com, or go directly to Victoria Coach Station at 164 Buckingham Palace Road, SW1.

Riding the rails

Travelling by train is by far the fastest way to get around Great Britain. There are a number of mainline stations throughout London which provide direct lines to thousands of destinations outside the city. Trains to the north leave from Euston, Kings Cross and St Pancras terminals. To travel to Essex or other eastern places, head to Liverpool Street; and for southern destinations, trains leave from either London Bridge, Waterloo or Victoria.

Be aware that if you plan to travel during peak travel periods such as bank holidays or on weekends, it is advisable to phone ahead and reserve your seat. Simply buying a ticket for a longer journey does not guarantee a seat, and the last thing you'll want to do is stand for an entire three-hour ride.

If you plan on doing a lot of rail travel out of London, you may want to apply for a Young Person's Railcard, which is available for those aged 16–25 or full-time students. This costs £18 for one year and gives a 34 per cent discount on most train tickets. To purchase this card, head to any rail station with a passport-sized photo and proof of age or status, plus the annual fee.

Regular train commuters can buy weekly, monthly or annual season tickets, although these are pricey. You will need to show a passport-sized photo for the Photocard.

A number of companies offer train services across the UK – including Virgin, Southwest Trains and Silverlink Trains – and each offer competitive rates. To find out time, route and price information, contact National Rail Enquiries at 08457 48 49 50 or log on to www.railtrack.co.uk or www.thetrainline.com.

International travel

If you plan on heading to France, Holland or Belgium, a quick and efficient means of travel is by taking the Eurostar train, which leaves from Waterloo station. Standard fares to Brussels and Paris start as low as £70 for a weekend day return. It takes 2 hours, 40 minutes to travel from London to Brussels, or three hours to Paris. Check out its website at www.eurostar.com or call 08705 186 186 for booking and information.

Taxis

The Tubes stop just after midnight, but that doesn't mean that you have to turn into a pumpkin. Night buses can be a bit grim, as the lurching and stopping doesn't usually bode well with nauseous drunks, and don't think that someone will wake you up if you pass out: you'll simply wake up in a bus depot in Watford. A much better option is to take a cab.

There are two types of taxi services operating in the city. The traditional black cabs are registered taxis and its drivers have undergone extensive training, dubbed "The Knowledge", which includes learning all the major routes before getting a licence. Black Cabs are fully insured in the case of an accident, but are more expensive to take than the privately owned taxis.

To hail a black cab, wait for one with the light on top to be lit up and wave your arm to flag it over. These have meters that start ticking as soon as you step inside. Beware that surcharges will be more expensive at night and for luggage and extra passengers. Also, most cabbies will expect a tip of 10–15 per cent.

As a cheaper option, taxis or minicabs are privately owned cars with a two-way radio or mobile phone connecting the driver to a central operator. Essentially anyone driving a car can be a (licensed or unlicensed) minicab driver. These are generally found loitering outside of nightclubs and bars, and punters can bargain with the drivers on the spot to drive down the cost of your journey.

However, because many minicabs don't follow the same legal guidelines as black cabs, they come with a risk. Newspaper reports throughout London warn about rising incidents of minicab sexual assaults, and horror stories about people being ripped off by unscrupulous drivers are also not uncommon. Single, or even two women travelling together, should be suspicious about taking minicabs.

To ensure you don't get stung with a pricey cab fare, make sure you determine the rate up front, and just hope he doesn't change his mind at the end of the journey.

It is highly recommended to program telephone numbers of taxi firms that you trust in your area – or the areas that you frequent often – into your mobile phone, so that you can easily contact them should you need a ride home. You can also call London Transport on 020 7222 1234 to check whether your local taxi firm is licensed.

Some other useful numbers include the 24-hour Radio Taxis line (for black cabs) at 020 7272 0272, or Lady Cabs at 020 7254 3501, which has a guaranteed female driver to drive female passengers.

In 1851, following numerous complaints by visitors to the Great Exhibition that cab drivers didn't know where they were going, 'The Knowledge', an intense geographical exam of London, was introduced. This exam is so difficult that eight out of ten people that attempt the test drop out before the end.

Get motoring (Driving)

If you have been enjoying the luxury of cruising around on four wheels up until now, times are about to change. The fact is: very few Londoners own a car, simply because of the high costs of petrol, parking, taxes and insurance. Not to mention the traffic.

Also, because very few employers provide workplace parking, and parking meters are for temporary stays of up to two hours only, the possibility of commuting to work by car is out of the question. Most Londoners rely on the Tube, trains and bus networks as their main means of transportation and hire a vehicle on special weekends should they get the urge to explore the countryside. So you should probably banish all thoughts of that new Renault from your mind.

However, if you are planning to purchase a vehicle, it is advisable to hire a car for a few weeks to gain experience of driving in the capital to decide if the costs and hassle are worth it.

It may be that you simply cannot face the reality of being stuck in London every weekend while the rest of the country waits to be explored. So if your salary can allow it, it may be worth keeping a vehicle should you need to get away from the havoc of the city.

Some good places to look for a new or used vehicle include *Loot*, *Auto Trader*, or online merchant www.jamjar.com. Also take a look in your Yellow Pages for a listings of car dealers near you.

Hitting the road

Driving on the left-hand side of London's narrow roads can be a tricky experience for those who are used to being in the opposite lane. But whether you are from the U.S., Canada, Sweden or Birmingham, there are a number of pointers you should be aware of before hitting the streets in London. If you want to avoid being bombarded with traffic tickets, take special note of the speed limits of and parking restrictions imposed throughout the city.

The speed limits are 30 mph in built-up areas, 70 mph on the highways, and 60 mph on most other roads outside the central area.

> If you've got a bit of extra cash to spend you can purchase a black cab for your own personal use. Look on www.taxicab.co.uk, but just be prepared to see lots of waving hands when you drive down the road.

Parking

Unless you want to be hunted down by overzealous traffic wardens busily spreading their evil pollen to illegally parked cars, make sure you pay attention to where you pull over. Otherwise, I guarantee you will return to find the dreaded plastic envelope with a ticket attached to your windscreen, or perhaps even be clamped or towed away and impounded. If the latter happens to you, call 020 7747 4747 to retrieve your vehicle.

If you are new to the UK, pick up a Highway Code manual from bookstores and driving schools, or take a look at the parking information available online at www.driving.co.uk.

Below is a listing of the main parking restrictions you will encounter while driving in London:

Double yellow lines: No parking at most or all times; signs nearby will indicate if and when you can park there. OK to stop if you are dropping off or picking up a passenger without leaving the wheel of the car.

Single yellow lines: Restricts parking for at least eight hours between 7 a.m. and 7 p.m. on four or more days a week.

Broken yellow line: Check nearby signs for restrictions.

Double red lines: Absolutely no stopping for any reason whatsoever.

No line: Parking permitted but keep an eye out for "Residents Only" signs in neighborhoods.

Hire cars (Rental Cars)

To hire a car, you will need at least one year's driving experience and must be at least 21–25 years old, depending on the hire company. Expect to pay at least £150 per week for a small car and be sure to check whether you have any mileage limitations and how much full insurance costs.

Below is a list of the larger car rental companies located in London. However, you may find that smaller local hire companies have cheaper rates than the multi-nationals.

Avis	0870 6060 100
Budget	0800 181 181
Europcar	0345 222 525
Hertz	0990 996 699
National Car Rental	020 7278 2273
Thrifty	0990 168 238

Easyrentacar book online at www.easyrentacar.com

Travelling in style

Abfab Limos	01753 663 660
Capital Limousines	020 7624 1800
All Stretched Out	0800 068 5632
LA Stretch Limos	020 8554 9292

Getting a driver's licence

For those of you who have international driving licences, it may be a good idea to transfer your licence to a British one if you plan on living in the country for more than a year. This will be required if you plan on owning a vehicle in the UK and to purchase insurance.

Some countries have a reciprocal deal with Britain, whereby a valid licence in one country can simply be exchanged for a British one. You will have to check with the DVLA (the Driver and Vehicle Licensing Agency; see www.dvla.gov.uk for the restrictions); and in some cases, you may have to retake both the theory and practical driving tests.

To find out your nearest testing station, look up 'Transport, Department of' in the business telephone directory. Pick up your application forms from any post office and send these to the station where you want to take your test.

Once you get your British driving licence it will be valid until you are 65, provided that you live in the country and do not get your licence revoked. You will be disqualified from driving if your points total 12 or more during a period of three years.

Insurance

When looking to buy vehicle insurance, the best way to find a reputable company is by asking fellow Londoners for names they recommend. Otherwise, check the press and billboards for companies that cater to your demands and tastes. One company definitely worth contacting is Direct Line at 0845 246 8701 or see www.directline.com.

Driving without valid car insurance has a £5,000 maximum fine and between six and eight points penalty.

Some driving organizations that offer 24-hour breakdown assistance include the Automobile Association (AA) on 0800 444 999 or www.theaa.co.uk, and the Royal Automobile Club (RAC) at 0800 550 0550 or www.rac.co.uk. A one-year membership for each will cost about £40.

Air miles

If your introduction to the city wasn't made at one of London's five airports, the chances are that it won't be long before you will be paying a visit to one of these busy circuses. Thanks to a recent boom in budget airlines, including services from EasyJet and Ryanair, air travel has been made much cheaper and accessible to Londoners, with return flights into continental Europe costing as little as £30.

Keep your eye out for cheap deals advertised in the newspapers, as well as the websites of the budget airlines, including www.ryanair.com, www.go-fly.com and www.easyjet.com.

Wherever it is you plan to travel, one of the capital's major airports will have a flight waiting to serve you.

London Gatwick Airport (LGW) – The fastest way to get to the airport is by catching the non-stop Gatwick Express from Victoria Station, which costs £10.50 one-way or £20 to return anytime within a month. This runs every 15 minutes and the journey takes 30 minutes (www.gatwickexpress.co.uk). A cheaper option is to hop on a Connex South Central train from Victoria Station, which stops at Clapham Junction and East Croydon station before arriving in Gatwick, adding about 15 minutes to the time (www.connex.co.uk). This will only set you back £8.20 for a single of £16.40 for a period return. Also, Thameslink rail services run from King's Cross, Farringdon, Blackfriars and London Bridge stations costing £9.80 one-way (www.thameslink.co.uk). For train times and ticket info, call National Rail Enquiries at 08457 484 950. If you prefer taking the scenic route, an Airbus A5 shuttle service is also available, leaving from Victoria Coach Station at 25 minutes past every hour. The first service departs at 6.35 a.m., the last at 11.25 p.m. and the journey time takes 90 minutes. This costs £8 single or £10 return.

Heathrow Airport (LHR) – London's largest airport has four terminals and mainly services major international destinations. Located on the Piccadilly Line, trains run to and from central London every five minutes, and the journey takes just under one hour from the city center. A faster option is by hopping on the Heathrow Express, which offers non-stop trains to and from Paddington Station in central London (www.heathrowexpress.co.uk). This journey takes 15 minutes and costs £12 for a single or £22 return. Tickets can be purchased at the time of travel, or see www.heathrowexpress.co.uk for further info. National Express also runs coaches from Victoria Coach station every 30 minutes, the journey takes approximately 45 minutes depending on the time of day. Ring 08705 80 80 80 or see www.gobycoach.com. To contact Heathrow Airport, call 0870 000 0123.

London City Airport (LCY) – This central location is easy to reach by the Jubilee Tube line or Docklands Light Railway, and the airport mainly services business routes. Hop off at Canning Town for a connecting shuttle service, which will cost £2. An Airbus shuttle service is also available from Liverpool Street, which runs every 10 minutes. For further info, call the airport on 020 7646 0000 or log on to www.londoncityairport.com.

London Luton Airport (LTN) – If you are flying by one of the main charter flights such as EasyJet, you will probably be leaving from this airport. The best way to get here is by taking a Thameslink train from London Bridge, Blackfriars, Farringdon or King's Cross station to Luton Airport Parkway station, which will take up to 40 minutes and costs £9.50 one-way. A free shuttle bus service will take you to the terminal from here. It is also possible to catch a coach from Victoria Coach Station, which will take approximately 1 hour 15 minutes depending on the time of day. Contact 08705 80 80 80 for details or see www.gobycoach.com.

Stansted Airport (STN) – You will need to catch the Stansted Express from Liverpool Street station, which takes 45 minutes. Tickets cost £13 one-way or £23 return. Call 08457 484950 for train times. You can also catch a bus from the Victoria Coach station, although these only run once an hour, and the journey takes an hour and a half. For coach details call 08705 80 80 80 or see www.gobycoach.com. Contact the airport at 08700 000 303.

Boat

Beneath the muddy Thames River's fluid soul lies a history lesson of London's turbulent past. Gold coins, sunken ships and Roman ruins remain buried under centuries of accumulated silt, discarded garbage and remnants of rotting dead fish. At one point in history, the Thames was the major routeway for conducting trade throughout the capital. During winter, the river would freeze over, and Londoners would open stalls and hold markets along its icy terrain.

Today, however, trains have taken over as the most efficient means of transportation, and you would be hard-pressed to find anyone who actually commutes to work by boat – although this isn't to say it isn't entirely possible.

Riverboats run along the Thames River to and from Greenwich to as far as Hampton Court in West London. There are over 20 piers along this stretch of the river and tickets can be bought at the pier.

However, this boat may not be a practical option for commuting, given the price, and the amount of time it takes to make the journey. A commuter route is available between Chelsea Harbour and Embankment, which costs £4 for a single ticket or £8 return. For further details on times and prices, call 020 7352 5888.

If you've got the time to spare, the 50-minute trip from Westminster to Greenwich offers a scenic view of the city but will set you back £7 one-way or £11 return.

To check out a route map online and for the latest information on times and prices of both leisure and commuter services, log on to www.transportforlondon.gov.uk or call London Transport river services at 020 7222 1234.

By foot and bicycle

Invest in a good pair of walking shoes and an umbrella, because if you plan on getting around the city like a true Londoner, you're going to have to do a lot of walking. Given that the city's central area is just one square kilometer, it is actually easier, faster, and cheaper to walk between central points rather than hopping on the Tube or a bus.

It will take a few years before you get a sense of orientation above ground. In the meantime, it is definitely worth investing in a pocket-sized A–Z streetmap, which can be purchased at newsagents and bookshops. These maps chart out the major tourist spots, Tube stations, and even the most obscure cobbled alleyways throughout the capital.

If you would like to hire a bicycle for a day, The London Bicycle Tour Company offers pushbikes to hire along with full insurance and helmets. Call 020 7928 6838 or see www.londonbicycle.com for further details.

Be forewarned that pedal cyclists who ride at night must have lights on the front and back of the cycle. It is also advised that you wear a helmet. Riding a bike in London can be like playing a Super Mario Brother's video game and you never know what obstacle will be popping up next.

> The Thames barrier, in south-east London, is the largest moveable flood barrier in the world. Since its completion in 1982, it has been raised more than 25 times to keep London from flooding.

Chapter Four:

Healthcare and Safety

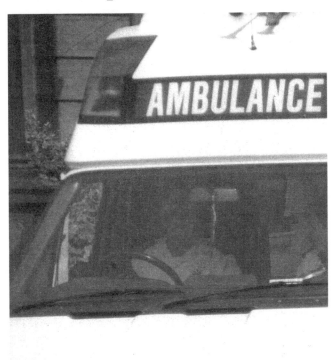

Healthcare

Unless you've spent most of your life living in an airtight anti-bacterial polythene boilersuit, you will probably need to see a doctor eventually. If you think you're immune to pesky illness and disease and haven't coughed up phlegm since 1987, then welcome to London: things are about to change. The Tube network in particular seems to be the capital's biggest source of illness. Urban legends race around London with nasty tales of human and bestial bodily fluids embedded deep in the cushions, but that certainly doesn't stop anyone from conducting intricate football (soccer) maneuvers in order to get a seat during rush hour. The culprit of disease spreading between the inhabitants of London is usually an infected individual coughing, dribbling and sneezing in your carriage, so you'll just have to start practicing breathing exercises in order to hold your breath between stations. Now that you are aware of what your poor immune system will have to battle on a daily basis, it's time to sort out a doctor.

> All the proceeds earned from James M. Barrie's book *Peter Pan* are bequeathed to the Great Ormond Street Hospital for Sick Children in London.

The NHS

The NHS is Britain's free healthcare system, which is available to anyone living in Britain. As with the Tube, the weather and the traffic, it has become somewhat of a popular pastime to moan about the NHS. However, despite shortages in funding, long waiting lists and older facilities, it's not too bad overall. Because the NHS is funded through government revenues, it won't cost you a penny to see a doctor, visit the hospital, or use the ambulance service for emergencies. Over a million people work for the NHS to provide care for the many millions who need it.

Private healthcare

The NHS provides free healthcare for all, but the waiting lists for surgery can be long and the quality of service is sometimes lacking. Private healthcare is very expensive, but if you can afford it, then you will get some of the world's best doctors. Many of these doctors are located on Harley Street and the best way to find the right one for you would be by word of mouth or from friends. Some employers provide a private healthcare scheme such as BUPA to their employees. If your office does, make sure you sign up for it right away, as you will not be eligible if you have already seen an NHS doctor about your complaint.

The average lifespan of London residents in the middle of the nineteenth century was 27 years. For members of the working class, that number dropped to 22 years.

Signing up with a doctor

If any of you out there think that you'll just wait until you are ill to locate a doctor (GP, General Practitioner) in your neighborhood, then let me warn you now that that would be a foolish, foolish idea. Signing up with a doctor takes time. As soon as you move into your new neighborhood, log on to www.nhsdirect.co.uk, and enter your home postcode for a list of doctors offices in your area who are accepting patients. Simple. Then just choose the one that you prefer and call them for an appointment to sign up. Be warned, however, that you will not be able to see a doctor on this visit; it is purely for registering. You'll be asked the usual questions as they open your file, such as whether or not you smoke, your health history and how much you drink – so be prepared for a look of shock on your doctor's face and a lecture on the evils of alcohol. Due to the strains on the NHS, you will often have to wait at least a week before the next available appointment. GPs can deal with most things in their offices, but if you need anything out of their area, you will be referred to a surgeon, clinic or local hospital.

Emergencies

Emergency ambulance transportation and treatment at a hospital's A&E (Accident and Emergency) departments are free to all. If you have an emergency, dial 999. Health authorities can charge a fee if you use 999 in a non-emergency. Police stations keep a list of doctors' and chemists' private telephone numbers in case of an emergency. Not all London hospitals have A&E departments, and not all of the ones that exist are open 24 hours.

London Hospitals with 24-hour emergency facilities:

Central

St Mary's Hospital, Praed Street, W2.
Tel: 020 7886 666. Tube: Paddington

University College Hospital, Grafton Way, WC1.
Tel: 020 7387 9300. Tube: Euston Square or Warren Street

North
Royal Free Hospital, Pond Street, NW3.
Tel: 020 7794 0500. Tube: Belsize Park

Whittington Hospital, St Mary's Wing, Highgate Hill, N19.
Tel: 020 7272 3070. Tube: Archway

South
St Thomas's Hospital, Lambeth Palace Road, SE1.
Tel: 020 7928 9292. Tube: Waterloo or Westminster

Guy's Hospital, St Thomas Street, SE1.
Tel: 020 7955 5000. Tube: London Bridge

St George's Hospital, Blackshaw Road, SW17.
Tel: 020 8672 1255. Tube: Tooting Broadway

West
Charing Cross Hospital, Fulham Palace Road, W6.
Tel: 020 8846 1234. Tube: Barons Court or Hammersmith

Chelsea and Westminster Hospital, 369 Fulham Road, SW10.
Tel: 020 8746 8000. Tube: Fulham Broadway or South Kensington

East
Hackney and Homerton Hospital, Homerton Row, E9.
Tel: 020 8510 5555. Rail: Homerton (Silverlink)

Royal London Hospital, Whitechapel Road, E1.
Tel: 020 7377 7000. Tube: Whitechapel

Prescriptions
Prescriptions are subsidized by the NHS, so you only have to pay a minimal dispensing fee for certain prescriptions. For a list of chemists in your area, check on the NHS website (address above), or simply take a wander down your nearest high street.

Dentists
Some dentists are available on the NHS, but because of recent changes by the government, it is now in the dentist's best interest to go private. A private dentist charges around £50 for a check-up and up to £80 for a cleaning.

If you need a dentist, you can search by postcode on www.nhsdirect.nhs.uk or you can call NHS Direct on 0845 46 47 (note that this number is shorter than normal 0845 numbers).

There are often long waiting lists, but it is worth it to register so that by the time the boiled sweets catch up with your nasty gnashers you won't have too much of a hassle. As a cheaper alternative to going with a private dentist, you can try the dentistry school at **Guy's Hospital**. Sounds scary, but most of London's dentists are accredited here, and they kindly sorted out a painful wisdom tooth for me a few years ago without any oral catastrophes.

United Medical and Dental Schools of Guys' and St Thomas' Hospitals, Lambeth Palace Road, SE1. Tel: 020 7922 8013. Tube: Waterloo

Opticians

If you're in need of new glasses or contacts in London there are plenty of opticians and optometrists to chose from in central shopping areas and on local high streets.

Many employers pay for sight tests as part of the basic benefit package. However, if you have to pay, the cost will normally be about £20. Sight tests can be done at most major opticians, though you may have to book in advance.

Clinics

Walk-in clinics

If you haven't taken my advice and you find yourself ill in London without a GP, then all is not lost. You'll be hard pressed to convince a GP to see you unless you are desperate – in which case they'll probably just send you to A&E. Below is a list of walk-in clinics around London. They are all NHS funded so you won't have to pay for a consultation and appointments are not necessary, though you may be in for a bit of a wait. For Birth Control Pill services please see Family Planning and Women's Health Clinics, as walk-in clinics do not dispense them.

Central

Soho NHS Walk-in Centre, Soho Centre for Health and Care, 1 Frith Street (off Soho Square), W1. Tel: 020 7534 6500. Tube: Tottenham Court Road

North

Edgware NHS Walk-in Centre, Edgware Community Hospital, Burnt Oak Broadway, Edgware, Middlesex, HA8 0AD. Tel: 020 8732 6459. Tube: Edgware (Northern line, not Edgware Road)

South
Tooting NHS Walk-in Centre, Clare House, St George's Hospital, Blackshaw Road, SW17. Tel: 020 8700 0505. Tube: Tooting Broadway

West
Charing Cross NHS Walk-in Centre, Charing Cross Hospital (next to A&E), Fulham Palace Road, W6. Tel: 020 8846 7490.
Tube: Barons Court or Hammersmith

Parsons Green NHS Walk-in Centre, 5–7 Parsons Green, Fulham, SW6. Tel: 020 8846 6758. Tube: Parsons Green

East
Whitechapel NHS Walk-in Centre (Next to the Royal London Hospital A&E department), 174 Whitechapel Road, E1. Tel: 020 7943 1333. Tube: Whitechapel

Newham NHS Walk-in Centre, Glen Road, E13. Tel: 020 7363 9200. Tube: Plaistow

Family planning and women's health clinics
All right ladies, you take the Pill nearly every morning like clockwork but you've run out of stock and you can't get an appointment with your doctor for another week. What's a girl to do? Luckily you don't have to, heaven forbid, go without. London has a number of clinics that deal solely in women's issues from dispensing the Pill, to pregnancy and smear tests. Make sure you call ahead to check which services they provide and set up an appointment. The Morning After Pill is now available in the UK over the counter from most pharmacies, so you just have to go in and ask for it. Pregnancy tests can be done by your GP, at Family Planning Clinics, or at most walk-in clinics.

For clinics in your area, check your local telephone book or see www.yell.co.uk The major central ones are listed below. Both are pro-choice.

The Margaret Pyke Family Planning Centre, 73 Charlotte Street, W1. Tel: 020 7530 3650. Tube: Goodge Street

Marie Stopes Pregnancy Advisory, 108 Whitfield Street, W1. Tel: 0845 300 8090. Tube: Warren Street

Sexual health clinics
The statistics about young people contracting STDs (sexually transmitted diseases, known as sexually transmitted infections in the UK) show that the numbers are constantly rising. From drunken fumbles in the loos of a club, to an unprotected romp at a

house party in Hackney, or even sex with a long-term partner who doesn't know they are infected, diseases can be caught and passed on with almost no symptoms. We all know that we should be tested at least every year or every time we change partners, but how many people do it? You may know how to go about being tested for HIV or STD's with discretion in your home town, but where do you turn in London? Below is a list of Sexual Health/GUM (Genito Urinary Medicine) clinics.

Some of these clinics have walk-in sessions, but call ahead as it may be necessary to make an appointment.

Central
The Lydia Clinic, St Thomas's Hospital, 1st Floor, Lambeth Wing, Lambeth Palace Road, SE1. Tel: 020 7955 2108. Tube: Waterloo

The Lloyd Clinic, Guy's Hospital, Thomas Guy House, SE1. Tel: 020 7955 2108. Tube: London Bridge

Victoria Clinic, South Westminster Centre for Sexual Health, 82 Vincent Square, SW1. Tel: 020 8746 8066/8700. Tube: Victoria or Pimlico

North
Patrick Clements Clinic, Central Middlesex Hospital, Acton Lane, NW10. Tel: 020 8453 2221. Tube: Harlesden or Park Royal

Archway Sexual Health Clinic, Clerkenwell Building, Whittingdon Hospital, Archway Road, N19. Tel: 020 7530 5800. Tube: Archway

Marlborough Clinic, The Royal Free Hospital, Pond Street, NW3. Tel: 020 7830 2047. Tube: Belsize Park

South
The Caldecot Centre, King's Healthcare,15–22 Caldecot Road, SE5. Tel: 020 7346 3453. Tube: Brixton or Oval

GUM Clinic, St George's Hospital, Blackshaw Road, SW17. Tel: 020 8725 3353. Tube: Tooting Broadway

West
John Hunter Clinic, Chelsea and Westminster Hospital, 369 Fulham Road, SW10 Tel: 020 8846 6154/6171. Tube: Fulham Broadway or South Kensington

West London Centre for Sexual Health – walk-in service, Charing Cross Hospital, Fulham Palace Road, W6. Tel: 020 8846 1576. Tube: Barons Court or Hammersmith

Jefferiss Wing, St Mary's Hospital, Praed Street, W2.
Tel: 020 7886 1225. Tube: Paddington

East

Ambrose King Centre, Royal London Hospital, Whitechapel Road, E1. Tel: 020 7377 7306/07. Tube: Whitechapel

Department of Sexual Health, Homerton Hospital, Homerton Row, E9. Tel: 020 8510 7989. Rail: Homerton (Silverlink)

Bart's Sexual Health Clinic, St Bartholemew's Hospital, West Smithfield, EC1. Tel: 020 7601 8090. Tube: St Paul's

HIV and AIDS

Getting tested for HIV is a terrifying experience, but the most off-putting part can be the long wait for the results. However, there is no need to wait days or weeks to get your results anymore. Below is a list of clinics that take your blood in the morning, test it and ask you to come back in the early evening for your results. They tell you the results face to face and normally have a counsellor on hand to give you advice.

This service is normally by appointment only.

Central

The Lydia Clinic, St Thomas's Hospital, Lambeth Palace Road, SE1. Tel: 020 7928 6651. Tube: Waterloo

The Lloyd Clinic, Guy's Hospital, St Thomas Street, SE1.
Tel: 020 7955 4510. Tube: London Bridge

Victoria Clinic, South Westminster Centre for Sexual Health, 82 Vincent Square, SW1. Tel: 020 8746 8066. Tube: Victoria or Pimlico

North

Marlborough Clinic, The Royal Free Hospital, Pond Street, NW3.
Tel: 020 7431 0970. Tube: Belsize Park

South

GUM Clinic, St George's Hospital, Blackshaw Road, SW17.
Tel: 020 8725 3353/3354. Tube: Tooting Broadway

West

Jefferiss Wing (Sexual Health Clinic), St Mary's Hospital (for registered clients. Prior visit to clinic needed), Praed Street, W2.
Tel: 020 7886 1225. Tube: Paddington

East
Sexual Health Clinic, Royal London Hospital, Whitechapel Road, E1. Tel: 020 7377 7312. Tube: Whitechapel

Wheelchair accessibility

Tube
Much of the tube network is very old and unfortunately is inaccessible for wheelchair users. The Underground is trying to rectify this, and there are some stations that you can use, but not many in central London. The easiest way would be to contact London Underground directly to plan your journey. London Transport publishes a booklet with information on access to buses and the Tube. The Wheelchair Access Guide, available at tube stations, is an easy to read and very informative listing of accessibility at stations. For information contact Access and Mobility on 020 7941 4600.

Tube Travel (www.thetube.com) will help you to find the best way to travel on the Underground.

Buses
Though the old fashioned Routemaster buses are inaccessible, newer low floor buses are being introduced. Call the Access and Mobility line below for detailed information.

Transport for London Access and Mobility: 020 7941 4600

Textphone: 020 7918 3015

24-hour London Travel Information: 020 7222 1234

Taxis
Almost all of London's Black Cabs are now wheelchair accessible. If they are, they have an illuminated chair symbol next to the for hire sign on the roof. If you order a taxi in advance, you must state that it is for a disabled person to ensure that you don't get an older inaccessible cab. Call 020 7272 0272 to book a taxi.

Accessible attractions
There has been new legislation implemented in the last couple of years to improve attractions and make London more accessible. Though many are impossible to visit with a wheelchair, there are still plenty of things to check out.

The London Eye

The 30-minute flight around the 135-meter wheel gives amazing views over London and is fully accessible. The wheel can be temporarily slowed or stopped to allow enough time to enter the pods safely. There is a disabled toilet in the County Hall nearby and plenty of disabled parking on Belvedere Road. Tel: 0870 5000 600. Admission: £7.65 (group)–£8.50. Carers go free.

The London Zoo

The zoo has 65 live animal exhibits that are all built to allow wheelchair users a good look. The new Web of Life exhibit has been designed for maximum disabled access, and most of the main site is accessible. Wheelchair-users' helpers are admitted free. Tel: 020 7722 3333. Admission: £9.30–£11.

The British Museum

This amazing museum has now opened the Queen Elizabeth II Great Court, which has coffee shops, incredible views, and accessible toilets. The information desk at the south end provides plans and accessibility advice. The museum has ramps at the front entrance. Tel: 020 7636 1555. Admission: free.

The National Portrait Gallery

The new wing is almost completely accessible, except for two landings, and the older parts can be accessed by a ramp at the Orange Street entrance. The gallery often holds events for their deaf and hearing-impaired guests. Tel: 020 7312 2463. Admission: free.

The Tate Modern

This stunning, newly converted power station on the south bank houses an incredible collection of modern art. Wheelchair access is very good at the gallery, and there are lifts to all floors. There are six wheelchairs available, pre-booking is essential, and chair access is available via the North Entrance, near the chimney. Tel: 020 7887 8000. Admission: free.

Wheelchair-accessible clubs and music venues

(part or fully accessible – call for further details)

Barbican, Silk St, EC2. Tel: 020 7638 8891
Brixton Academy, 211 Stockwell Rd, SW9. Tel: 020 7771 2000
The Bug Bar, Brixton Hill, SW2. Tel: 020 7738 3184
Cargo, 83 Rivington St, EC2. Tel: 020 7739 3440
Dingwalls, Camden Lock, Camden High St, NW1. Tel: 020 7267 1577
The Dogstar, 389 Coldharbour Lane, SW9. Tel: 020 7733 7515
The Elbow Rooms, 89–91 Chapel market, N1. Tel: 020 7278 3244

Fabric, 77a Charterhouse St, EC1. Tel: 020 7336 8898
The Garage, 22 Highbury Corner, N5. Tel: 020 7607 1818
Herbal, 12–14 Kingsland Rd, E2. Tel: 020 7613 4462
I.C.A., The Mall, SW1. Tel: 020 7930 3647
Jazz Café, 5 Parkway, NW1. Tel: 020 7916 6060
Ministry of Sound, 103 Gaunt St, SE1. Tel: 020 7378 6528
National Theatre, Upper Ground, South Bank, SE1. Tel: 020 7452 3000
Ocean, 270 Mare St, E8. Tel: 020 8533 0111
Old Vic Theatre, Waterloo Rd, SE1. Tel: 020 7928 7616
Royal Festival Hall, South Bank, SE1. Tel: 020 7960 4242
Spitz, Old Spitalfields Market, 109 Commercial St, E1. Tel: 020 7392 9032
Union Chapel, Compton Terrace, N1. Tel: 020 7226 1686

Theatre

For details of wheelchair accessible theatres, check out www.theatre-access.co.uk.

To ensure that you are always seated in the most appropriate area, order your tickets through the theatre box offices and not a ticketing agency.

Useful websites

London Disability Arts Forum: www.dail.dircon.co.uk

Holiday Care: www.holidaycare.org.uk

Artsline: www.artsline.co.uk

Deaf and hard of hearing

Things are slowly changing in London to make entertainment easier for people who are deaf or hard of hearing. As long as you know where to look, there are plenty of attractions to be found with sign language interpretation and subtitles.

Cinema and theatre

For a listing of cinemas that are showing blockbusters with subtitles, look at the RNID (Royal National Institute for Deaf People) website www.rnid.org.uk or else contact your local cinema or theatre directly.

For the most up-to-date listing of theatre venues with sign language interpreted, captioned, and audio-described performances for the blind, check out www.theatre-access.co.uk

Video rentals

Post Script is a video hire service, where members can borrow any subtitled film from the National Subtitling Library for Deaf

People through second-class post. Membership costs £5 and video rental is £3.50.

To join Post Script contact:

Victoria Mill, 3rd Floor, Compstall Mill Estate, Andrew Street, Compstall, Stockport, Cheshire, SK6 5HN. Tel: 0161 449 9650 (voice and Minicom 5)

Magazines

BDN – British Deaf News www.britishdeafassociation.org.uk/bdn/
One in Seven – RNID's membership magazine. www.rnid.org.uk

Sports

For an upcoming calendar of events check out
www.deafsports.org.uk

Television

The BBC runs *See Hear*, a weekly magazine show at 8.15 a.m. Saturdays on BBC2. www.bbc.co.uk/see_hear

For an up-to-date list of BBC's signed programmes, look on their website at www.bbc.co.uk

> One in seven people in the UK are deaf or hard of hearing, so why not learn British Sign Language? Courses are available all around London, and not only will it look good on your CV and improve your customer relations, but you could help to make someone's life a lot easier. Full-time, part-time and weekend courses are available all across London. www.hotcourses.co.uk has a good listing, and *Hotcourses* and *Floodlight* course catalogues are available in most major bookshops.

Personal safety

London is a major city and unfortunately there will always be some elements of crime. You just have to keep your wits about you, be careful, and trust your instincts. Don't talk on your mobile phone at night as it could be snatched, and always use well lit busy roads at night or else take a licensed mini cab. Keep the number of a reputable cab company stored in your mobile phone.

It is obviously best to avoid confrontation so keep in mind your wallet or mobile phone is not worth your life. However, if you are being attacked then follow your gut instincts and if possible try to talk to your attacker without provoking them. Draw as much attention to the situation as possible by shouting "call the police".

Police advise that if it is necessary for you to fight back to 'bash and dash'. Target the aggressor's eyes, nose, mouth, groin, shins, knees, or throat – whatever is easiest. And then run. If you are grabbed from behind and struggle forward, you will simply exhaust yourself. Instead, throw your bodyweight backwards to catch the attacker off guard, or else stamp on their foot or shin.

Use whatever you have with you as a weapon. An umbrella, keys, or anything you have to hand. Don't put up a major fight, just surprise your attacker and then run.

I hope that you will never find yourself in an undesirable situation, but, if, heaven forbid, anything does happen to you, immediately call the emergency services on 999. For all incidents, no matter how small, make a detailed report at the police station nearest to the incident. Keep in mind that not all police stations are open 24 hours.

Self-defense classes are available at community centers, gyms, and colleges throughout London. Check in your area or try one of the following, which all offer a variety of short and long self-defense classes for men and women:

City Lit, 16 Stuckley Street, WC2. Tel: 020 7831 7831. Tube: Holborn or Covent Garden. www.citylit.ac.uk
Lewisham College, Lewisham Way, SE4. Tel: 0800 834 545. Tube: New Cross. www.lewisham.ac.uk
Morely College, 61 Westminster Bridge Road, SE1. Tel: 020 7928 8501. Tube: Lambeth North. www.morelycollege.ac.uk
St Francis Xavier College, Malwood Road, SW12. Tel: 020 8772 6060. Tube: Clapham South. www.sfx.ac.uk

For further advice check out:

www.homeoffice.gov.uk

www.suzylamplugh.org

www.crimereduction.gov.uk

The Black Death

In 1348 the Black Death moved from Asia to Europe and passed into Dorset leaving bodies in its wake. When the disease hit London, it preyed upon the unsanitary conditions in the overcrowded medieval city and killed 30,000 people. The dead outnumbered the living and the only way to cope with the ever-mounting stacks of bodies was to build massive plague pits and chuck in the bodies. And then the plague mysteriously went away on its own …

The Bubonic Plague

In 1665, a ghastly disease causing black patches on the skin, swelling under the arms, and a quick death, swept London – The Bubonic Plague. The streets were still unhygienic and it wasn't yet known that the plague was caused by fleas on rats turning to human hosts for food when the rats perished. Over 68,000 people died, though this official figure is thought to be greatly underestimated. The bodies were chucked into large pits once the cemeteries were all full to bursting. Then came the Great Fire in 1666, blamed on a baker in Pudding Lane, which killed off the Plague, but devastated the city in its own right.

During the Bubonic Plague of London, the city was sealed off to avoid contamination, and therefore, no food was allowed in. The only people willing to trade with London were the Dutch, who left food on jetties and then would take the money left there. They used to steel their nerves with liquor before landing on the plague-infested shores, hence the saying "Dutch courage". To this day, the Dutch still have the freedom of the River Thames, which was granted as a reward for their courage and kindness.

Remember this children's nursery rhyme?

"Ring a round of roses
A pocketful of posies
A-tish-oo, a-tish-oo
We all fall down."

Though it seems like a harmless song taught to children in primary school, it actually has a more disturbing meaning. The ring of roses is the effect of the plague on the skin, the pocketful of posies represents the plants that people carried to ward off the plague, "a-tish-oo" is for the quick spread of the disease, and "all fall down" signifies death.

Chapter Five:
Education

Many people come to London specifically to study at universities, and others seize the chance to further their wealth of skills by attending a part-time or evening course. London has thousands of courses and you'd be foolish not to take the opportunity to learn a new skill. You'll probably be surprised by what's on offer; you could even take a circus workshop and learn how to throw knives and swing a lasso – a talent that is sure to come in handy one day. Don't smirk, I've done it.

Where to start?

London has two definitive catalogues of all part and full-time courses, which lead to qualifications or degrees:

Floodlight (www.floodlight.co.uk)
and **Hotcourses** (www.hotcourses.co.uk)

are available online or from most bookshops.

For living expenses while you are at University or College full-time in London, expect to pay between £7,000 and £9,000 per year. If you plan to have a heavy social life, however, these costs will greatly escalate. Thank heavens for cheap drinks at the student bar.

Universities and higher education

If you plan to attend a university full-time, you will obviously need to trawl through the course catalogues and decide which course and institution suit you the best.

Applications for all full-time university placements must be made through UCAS, the Universities and Colleges Admissions Service, which filters applications and matches students with the available places based on your study intentions and exam results.

For more information, contact UCAS on 01242 222 444 or see www.ucas.co.uk For shorter courses or part-time studies, contact the university admissions directly. Most universities have daycare facilities for students with small children.

Birkbeck College, University of London. Malet Street, WC1. Tel: 0845 601 0174. www.bbk.ac.uk Tube: Goodge Street or Russell Square.

City University, Northampton Square, EC1. Tel: 020 7040 5060. www.city.ac.uk Tube: Angel, Barbican or Farringdon.

Goldsmiths College, New Cross, SE14. Tel: 020 7717 2232. www.goldsmiths.ac.uk Tube: New Cross or New Cross Gate.

Heythrop College, Kensington Square, W8. Tel: 020 7795 6600. www.heythrop.ac.uk Tube: High Street Kensington.

Imperial College of Science, Technology and Medicine, South Kensington, SW7. Tel: 020 7594 8014. www.ic.ac.uk Tube: South Kensington.

Institute of Education, 20 Bedford Way, WC1. Tel: 020 7612 6104. www.ioe.ac.uk Tube: Russell Square.

King's College London, Strand, WC2. Tel: 020 7836 5454 www.kcl.ac.uk Tube: Temple or Charing Cross.

London Guildhall University, 133 Whitechapel High Street, E1. Tel: 020 7320 1616. www.lgu.ac.uk Tube: Aldgate, Aldgate East, or Liverpool Street.

London School of Economics and Political Science, Houghton Street, WC2. Tel: 020 7955 7124. www.lse.ac.uk Tube: Holborn or Temple.

Middlesex University, White Hart Lane, N17. Tel: 020 8411 5898. www.mdx.ac.uk Rail: White Hart Lane.

Queen Mary, University of London, Mile End Road, E1. Tel: 020 7882 5511. www.qmul.ac.uk Tube: Mile End or Stepney Green.

Royal Veterinary College, Royal College Street, NW1. Tel: 020 7468 5148. www.rvc.ac.uk Tube: Camden Town or Mornington Crescent.

South Bank University, 103 Borough Road, SE1. Tel: 020 7815 7815. www.sbu.ac.uk Tube: Waterloo.

Thames Valley University, St Mary's Road, W5. Tel: 020 8579 5000. www.tvu.ac.uk Tube: Ealing Broadway or South Ealing.

University College London, Gower Street, WC1. Tel: 020 7679 3000. www.ucl.ac.uk Tube: Warren Street

University of Greenwich, 30 Park Row, SE10. Tel: 0800 005 006. www.gre.ac.uk Tube: Cutty Sark DLR or Greenwich DLR.

University of North London, 166-220 Holloway Road, N7. Tel: 020 7753 3355. www.unl.ac.uk Tube: Holloway Road.

University of Westminster, 309 Regent Street, W1. Tel: 020 7911 5000. www.wmin.ac.uk Tube: Oxford Circus.

More than 3,000 bodies are believed to be buried in Westminster Abbey including Geoffrey Chaucer, Charles Darwin, Charles Dickens, George Frideric Handel, and Laurence Olivier.

Art and design colleges

Camberwell College of Art, Peckham Road, SE5. Tel: 020 7514 6302. www.camb.linst.ac.uk Rail: Peckham Rye.

Central St Martins College of Art and Design, Southampton Row, WC1.. Tel: 020 7514 7022. www.csm.linst.ac.uk Tube: Holborn

> The Sex Pistols got their first gig on November 6 1975 at St Martins College of Art in Charing Cross Road, as bassist Glen Matlock was a student there. Shocking the organizers, they were forced off the stage after only five songs. They went on to play at the 100 Club on 21 September 1976 along with The Damned, The Clash, The Vibrators, Siouxsie and the Banshees and others in the first ever Punk Festival. All the bands were unknown and all were unsigned. According to *Melody Maker*, "The 600-strong line that stretched across two blocks was undisputable evidence that a new decade in rock is about to begin." Thus, in a small underground club beneath Oxford Street, Punk was born. God Save The Queen.

Chelsea College of Art and Design, Manresa Road, SW3. Tel: 020 7514 7751. www.chelsea.linst.ac.uk Tube: Sloane Square.

Courtauld Institute of Art, Somerset House, Strand, WC2. Tel: 020 7848 2645. www.courtauld.ac.uk Tube: Charing Cross or Temple

London College of Fashion, 20 John Princes Street, W1. Tel: 020 7514 7400. www.lcf.linst.ac.uk Tube: Oxford Circus.

London College of Printing, Elephant and Castle, SE1. Tel: 020 7514 6569. www.lcp.linst.ac.uk Tube: Elephant and Castle.

Royal College of Art, Kensington Gore, SW7. Tel: 020 7590 4444 www.rca.ac.uk Tube: South Kensington.

Slade School of Fine Art, UCL (University College London), Gower Street, WC1. Tel: 020 7679 7772. www.ucl.ac.uk/slade Tube: Warren Street

Wimbledon School of Art, Merton Hall Road, SW19. Tel: 020 8408 5000. www.wimbledon.ac.uk Tube: Wimbledon.

Slap on those little red dancing shoes and cut some rug. You know what they say, dancing is a sensual form of foreplay.

Danceworks, 16 Balderton Street, W1. Tel: 020 7629 6183. Tube: Bond Street. www.danceworks.co.uk

Street dance, belly dancing, breakdancing, flamenco, tap, hip-hop. This school offers one of the most comprehensive ranges of dance classes in London. There's no excuse to dance like old Uncle Chester down at Turnmill's next weekend.

Music and drama colleges

Central School of Speech and Drama, Embassy Theatre, 64 Eton Avenue, NW3. Tel: 020 7722 8183. www.cssd.ac.uk
Tube: Swiss Cottage.

Guildhall School of Music and Drama, Silk Street, Barbican, EC2. Tel: 020 7628 2571. www.gsmd.ac.uk Tube: Barbican or Moorgate.

London College of Music and Media, Thames Valley University, Ealing Campus, St Mary's Road, W5. Tel: 020 8231 2304. www.elgar.tvu.ac.uk Tube: Ealing Broadway.

Royal Academy of Music, Marylebone Road, NW1. Tel: 020 7873 7393. www.ram.ac.uk Tube: Regents Park or Baker Street.

Royal College of Music, Prince Consort Road, SW7. Tel: 020 7589 3643. www.rcm.ac.uk Tube: South Kensington.

Trinity College of Music, King Charles Court, Old Royal Naval College, Greenwich, SE10. Tel: 020 8305 3888. www.tcm.ac.uk
Tube: Cutty Sark DLR.

If you think you are the next Madonna or Mick Jagger, then you can book a session at Brixton's Slap Studio and record a song on CD. Pre-order obscure tracks or choose from something on hand at the studio. Sing the song (up to twelve times) and they will edit it and burn the CD. Takes karaoke into the next realm. Call 01799 526 526 or visit www.activitysuperstore.com for information.

Envious of the acrobatic skills of the clowns at Cirque du Soleil? Ever wanted to make like Calamity Jane and lasso a bucking bronco? The Circus Space in Hoxton, housed in a gorgeous old power station, has a great range of courses to ensure that your party trick is always the best at every soiree.

The Circus Space, Coronet Street, N1. Tel: 020 7613 4141. www.thecircusspace.co.uk

Juggling, trapeze, acrobatics, tightrope, whip-cracking, lassoing, and knife throwing. What more could you want?

General colleges

City and Islington College, Marlborough Building, 383 Holloway Road, N7. Tel: 020 7700 9200. www.candi.ac.uk Tube: Holloway Road.

City of Westminster College, 25 Paddington Green, W2. Tel: 020 7723 8826. www.cwc.ac.uk Tube: Edgware Road or Paddington.

College of North East London, Tottenham Centre, High Road, N15. Tel: 020 8442 3055. www.conel.ac.uk Tube: Seven Sisters.

College of North West London, Dudden Lane, NW10. Tel: 020 8208 5050. www.cnwl.ac.uk Tube: Dollis Hill.

Ealing, Hammersmith and West London College, Gliddon Road, W14. Tel: 0800 980 2175. www.hwlc.ac.uk Tube: Barons Court.

Greenwich Community College, 95 Plumstead Road, SE18. Tel: 020 8488 4800. www.gcc.ac.uk Rail: Plumstead.

Hackney Community College, Shoreditch Campus, Falkirk Street, N1. Tel: 020 7613 9123. www.comm-coll-hackney.ac.uk Tube: Old Street.

Kensington and Chelsea College, Hortensia Road, SW10. Tel: 020 7573 5333. www.kcc.ac.uk Tube: Fulham Broadway.

Lambeth College, 56 Brixton Hill, SW2. Tel: 020 7501 5000. www.lambethcollege.ac.uk Tube: Brixton.

South Thames College, Wandsworth High Street, SW18.
Tel: 020 8918 7777. www.south-thames.ac.uk Tube: East Putney.

Southwark College, The Cut, SE1. Tel: 020 7815 1600.
www.southwark.ac.uk Tube: Southwark or Waterloo.

Tower Hamlets College, Poplar High Street, E14. Tel: 020 7510 7777.
www.tower.ac.uk Tube: Mile End.

Westminster Kingsway College, Vincent Square, SW1.
Tel: 020 7556 8001. www.westking.ac.uk Tube: Victoria.

Financial support

If you have been living in the UK for three years, or come from a European Union country, you may qualify for partial payment of fees and/or a local authority grant. Nationals of the European Economic Area, (Sweden, Norway, Iceland, Finland and Austria), may also be eligible. If not, you may qualify for a Commonwealth scholarship, British Council postgraduate fellowship, or an Overseas Research Student award.

Whatever you do, it is a good idea to sort out your finances before leaving your home country. To apply for a grant contact the UCAS offices at 01242 222 444 or see www.ucas.co.uk, or the British Council:

> NACPME, The British Council
> Bridgewater House
> 58 Whitworth Street
> Manchester
> M1 6BB
> 0161 957 7218, or fax on 0161 957 7029

Overseas students

If you are from a country outside of the European Union, you will need to show immigration officers proof of acceptance on a full-time course and proof of sufficient financial resources to pay tuition fees and living expenses. More information on this will be available from the British Embassy or High Commission in your home country. The British Council does not offer advice on visa matters. Keep in mind that if you have not been a resident of the EU for the three years immediately prior to the beginning of your course, you will be considered an international student and will face substantially higher fees. This will cost up to seven times as much as a home student will pay. Most university websites will be able to answer any status questions that you have.

Language schools

You don't need any qualifications to attend a language school, and due to the huge number of non-English speakers that arrive in London every day, there are numerous courses of varying prices and lengths from weeks to months. Shop around until you find a course that suits you.

Angloschool, 146 Church Road, SE19. Tel: 020 8653 7285. www.angloschoool.co.uk Rail: Crystal Palace.

ELS Language Centres, 3 Charing Cross Road, WC2. Tel: 020 7976 1066. Tube: Charing Cross.

International House, 106 Piccadilly, W1. Tel: 020 7518 6999. www.ihlondon.com Tube: Green Park.

Internexus Centre for Language Studies, Regent's College, Inner Circle, Regent's Park, NW1. Tel: 020 7487 7489. www.riscl.ac.uk Tube: Baker Street.

London City College, 15 Holland Park Gardens, W14. Tel: 020 7603 1656. Tube: Holland Park.

London Institute Language Centre, 65 Davies Street, W1. Tel: 020 7514 7261. www.linst.ac.uk Tube: Oxford Circus.

Twin English Centres, 24 Clarendon Rise, SE13. Tel: 020 8297 1132. www.twinschool.co.uk Rail: Lewisham.

Part-time and evening courses

There are scores of short courses available to anyone who wishes to sign up. Guitar, painting, accounting, writing, wine tasting, computer programing ... the list goes on and on. Browse through the courses in *Floodlight* (www.floodlight.co.uk) and *Hotcourses* (www.hotcourses.com), available from newsagents and bookshops. Alternatively, call a university, college or community center from the above list and ask for a prospectus or course listing.

Keep your eyes open for interesting courses. The *Hot Tickets*, free with the *Evening Standard* newspaper on Thursdays, *TNT*, free from bins outside of Tube stations on Mondays, and *Time Out*, available at newsagents on Wednesdays, all have some course listings and many highlight more obscure and interesting choices. Go on, try your hand at juggling, stock car racing, or street dance. You might even make some new friends while you're there; if not

at least you'll have an interesting CV.
Open University London, Parsifal College, 527 Finchley Road, NW3. Tel: 020 7431 1048. www.open.ac.uk Tube: Finchley Road.

For short courses that are slightly cheaper and have a range of interesting subjects, try:

The City Lit, Various locations throughout London, Tel: 020 7831 7831 www.citylit.ac.uk Nearly every subject you can think of.

The Mary Ward Centre, 42 Queen Square, WC1. Tel: 020 7831 7711. Tube: Russell Square. www.marywardcentre.ac.uk. Acupuncture, writing, art, history and more.

The Drill Hall, 16 Chenies Street, WC1E 7EX. Tel: 020 7307 5061. Tube: Tottenham Court Road. www.drillhall.co.uk. Writing, fitness, tango, photography, theatre and much more.

Chapter Six:
Communications and Media

Ah, independence. It feels so great to wander about your own flat, to eat whatever junk food you want and to leave the heating on all night just because you've passed out on the sofa. Before you've even unpacked your sheets you've probably rushed right out to fully stock the booze cupboard, because hell, who needs food.

But don't let all that freedom go to your head. I give you three days maximum before you're calling mom to ask her which compartment of the washing machine the powder goes into, or how long can you leave raw chicken in the fridge for. Better get a lifeline to the outside world ...

Telephone

Getting set up

London has two main telephone providers, BT (British Telecom) and Cable and Wireless. Both deliver a similar service, but rates vary. Check out their websites to see which one best suits your requirements, www.bt.com and www.cw.com, or ask friends for a recommendation.

You need to determine whether a line already exists in your new home. The provider can find out when you give them your address. If there is one, you simply need to set up your new account and give them your details. If you haven't got a line with one provider, you can check if it is with the other provider by calling them – or else arrange to have a line set up. Make the appointment for them to come to your house as soon as possible as there can be a wait of more than a week. There will be a charge for this.

Once you have the line and account sorted out, you will need to get a phone. Try Argos, a catalogue store located on many high streets (www.argos.co.uk) or just head around the department stores of Oxford Street, High Street Kensington or your local shops.

If you plan to call overseas frequently, it would be cheapest for you to purchase long distance phone cards from a local newsagent. You just buy the card in the denomination that you wish and follow the directions on the back of the card. This is normally considerably cheaper than either BT or Cable and Wireless's international rates.

International operator:	155
Local operator:	100
Directory enquiries:	192
Overseas directory enquiries:	153

Dialing

For emergency services, Ambulance, Police and Fire dial 999.

Most public telephones are operated by British Telecom (BT) and the traditional bright red boxes are easily spotted throughout the city, though some of the newer ones are made of glass and aren't quite so quaint looking. Payphones take either coins or phonecards, which are available from newsagents, post offices and supermarkets. Local calls cost 20 pence.

The phone code for London is 020. London is divided into two dialing areas. Central numbers begin with the prefix 0207 and outer numbers begin with 0208. You may still see the old phone codes of 0171 and 0181 around and these should be replaced with 0207 and 0208 respectively. Any number that begins with 0800 or 0500 is free to call, while 0345 and 0845 are charged at local rates and 0990 at the national rate. Beware of numbers that begin with 090 as these are premium rate numbers (usually smutty) and can cost your life savings if you linger on the phone for too long.

> To call overseas from London, dial 00 followed by the country code and the number (minus the first zero). Some country codes are: Ireland 353; France 33; Australia 61; USA and Canada 1; New Zealand 64; South Africa 27; Germany 49.

Mobile phones

There is a lot of choice in London for mobile (cellular) phones. There are numerous handsets, networks, plans and tariffs from Orange, O2, Virgin, Vodaphone, and T-Mobile.

You'll be faced with a wealth of information when trying to decide which phone and phone company to go with. For the most helpful and impartial advice, you can go to a general mobile shop such as Carphone Warehouse (www.carphonewarehouse.com) or The Link (www.thelink.com), which sell different phones from all the major networks. Branches are located on most high streets and throughout central London. It is also important to consider which network your closest friends are on, as it is much cheaper to call phones on the same network.

The major mobile networks are:

O2 (formerly BT Cellnet and Genie): www.o2.co.uk

Orange: www.orange.co.uk

T-Mobile (formerly One2One): www.t-mobile.co.uk

Virgin: www.virgin.net

Vodaphone: www.vodaphone.co.uk

Payment plans

You can choose to go on a monthly plan and receive monthly bills. The rates vary for monthly line rental and call charges from network to network so make sure that you shop around.

Pay-as-you-go

You will need to buy your own mobile phone from a mobile shop for a pay-as-you-go plan. Then instead of receiving bills, you can purchase top-up vouchers in various denominations. By calling the number on the card, your credit will be added and you can use your phone. The call charges are a bit more expensive than a monthly plan, but you will never be stuck with an unexpectedly high bill. Vouchers are available from mobile phone shops, supermarkets, and newsagents.

Post (Mail)

Your little brother's birthday is less than two weeks away and you want to make sure that Ninja T-shirt you picked up in Camden Market will reach him on time. The best way to ship packages overseas is to head down to your local post office, purchase a bubble-wrapped envelope, and send the small parcel by Parcelforce, which is the Royal Mail's delivery company. This may take anywhere from a few days to up to one and a half weeks to reach its destination, depending on the quality of the postal service in the other country.

If it is just a birthday card you are sending, however, post the letter by Airmail at the post office. This will reach most countries in Europe within three days, but allow for up to one week for it to get to Australia, New Zealand, Asia, the United States, Africa and Canada. Airmail will cost more than shipping it by boat, but takes considerably less time to get there. For example, a letter weighing around 60 grams (approx. 2 ozs.) sent to the United States by Airmail should cost £1.42 and arrive four days after you post it. Send it by surface mail and it will take around eight weeks but cost you only 61p. The difference gets bigger the heavier the item.

The Royal Mail's Parcelforce delivers to 239 countries and territories and its service is conveniently located at your local Post Office. See the list below for a list of courier companies available in London:

Parcelforce (part of Royal Mail), Tel: 0800 224 466.
www.parcelforce.co.uk
UPS, Tel: 08457 877 877. www.ups.com
Federal Express, Tel: 0800 123 800. www.federalexpress.com
TNT, Tel: 0800 100 600. www.tnt.com

Post offices are located on the high street and are sometimes inside other shops such as newsagents. Most post offices are open Monday to Friday 9 a.m. to 5.30 p.m. and Saturdays 9 a.m. to 12.30 p.m. Post arrives six days a week – all but Sunday. Stamps can also be bought from many newsagents, supermarkets and at vending machines outside of post offices. First-class letters cost 27p and should arrive the following day, while second-class stamps cost 19p and take two to three days.

Post offices do a lot more than just send mail these days. You can pay bills, purchase a TV licence, and pick up a driver's licence and motor vehicle registration forms.

> The Royal Mail has its own Tube line, the Mail Rail, which runs between Padddington and Whitechapel, carrying no passengers, just post, to ensure that your first-class letters really do arrive at their destination the very next day.

Internet

If you want to access the Internet from home, you will need to sign up with an ISP (Internet Service Provider). Many of them advertise in major newspapers. Free trial CDs are often given out at high street shops, and most ISPs offer competitive rates. Ask your friends and colleagues for recommendations about the best ISPs to suit your needs.

AOL	www.aol.co.uk
Freeserve	www.freeserve.co.uk
NTL	www.ntl.co.uk

Cybercafés

There are many Internet cafés in London. **Easyeverything** is the biggest and most inexpensive, but they are simple cafeteria-like shops that are distinctly lacking in atmosphere. The price changes due to the time of day and amount of current surfers. However, they are open 24 hours a day and are conveniently located:

456–459 Strand. Tube: Charing Cross
9–16 Tottenham Court Road. Tube: Tottenham Court Road
358 Oxford Street. Tube: Oxford Circus or Marble Arch
9–13 Wilton Road. Tube: Victoria

To surf and e-mail with a nice cold beer, try **Webshack** at 15 Dean Street, W1. Tel: not listed. Tube: Tottenham Court Road. It is fully licensed, has very helpful staff and pumps out loud music.

Most local libraries offer free Internet access, and there are lots of small cybercafés dotted around London. Take a look at *TNT* magazine (free from Tube stations on Mondays), which has an extensive listing of cybercafés in London.

Media

Whether you are into obscure art magazines, specialist model railway publications, or soft porn, you'll find it in London. There is a huge variety of national newspapers and more than 300 different magazines are available throughout the capital, meaning that you will never be short of choices. These can either be picked up at your local newsagent, from high street shops like WHSmith, or delivered directly to your door.

Newspapers

London's national daily newspapers are divided into two categories, broadsheet and tabloid. *The Times* and *The Daily Telegraph* are examples of broadsheet newspapers, which concentrate on delivering the political, international and business news. Most of the broadsheet newspapers have a conservative slant in their news and current affairs reporting, except for *The Guardian* and *The Independent,* which lean towards the left.

In contrast, easy-to-read tabloids like *The Daily Star* and the *Daily Express* tend to focus on celebrity gossip, sensationalist news stories and sports. The main tabloids include *The Sun* (notorious for its topless "Page 3 Girl"), *The Mirror*, the *Daily Mail*, the *Daily Express* and the *Daily Star*, all of which contain right-wing political views and offer sensational news stories. The city's only evening newspaper, *The Evening Standard*, has an excellent 'Just the Job' classified ads supplement on Mondays plus a good listings magazine titled *Hot Tickets*, out Thursdays.

Daily broadsheet newspapers

The Daily Telegraph	www.telegraph.co.uk
The Independent	www.independent.co.uk
The Guardian	www.guardian.co.uk
The Times	www.the-times.co.uk
The Financial Times	www.ft.com

Daily tabloids

Daily Mail	www.dailymail.co.uk
Daily Express	www.express.co.uk
The Sun	www.thesun.co.uk
Daily Star	www.dailystar.co.uk
Evening Standard	www.thisislondon.com
The Mirror	www.mirror.co.uk

Saturday papers

| The Guardian | www.guardian.co.uk |
| Financial Times Weekender | www.ft.com |

Sunday papers

Sunday Mirror	www.sundaymirror.co.uk
The Observer	www.observer.co.uk
News of the World	www.newsoftheworld.co.uk
Sunday Times	www.sunday-times.co.uk
The Mail on Sunday	www.dailymail.co.uk
Independent	www.independent.co.uk

Magazines

The women's market is literally saturated with choices, including *Cosmopolitan*, *New Woman*, *Zest* and *Marie Claire*, while the men's most popular publications include *Maxim*, *FHM* and *GQ*. A raft of art and street culture magazines for the trendy 18–35 year old generation are also prominent in London, including *Dazed and Confused*, *Sleazenation* and *ID*.

One of the best sources of clubbing, music, theatre, TV and radio listings is *Time Out*, an entertainment magazine out each Tuesday in central London and Wednesday outside of Zone 1. However, there are also specialist magazines for every interest, ranging from fashion to gardening or travel. For example, clubbing and music fans will want to pick *Mixmag, Ministry of Sound* or *NME* for their music listings and reviews.

Scanning the racks at WHSmith, it may take a few months before you find a couple of magazines that truly suit your tastes, but one thing is for sure: you will never have a shortage of options.

Let me peer into my crystal ball, my pretty.

College of Psychic Studies, 16 Queensberry Place, SW7. Tel: 020 7589 3292. www.psychic-studies.org.uk. Readings from £20.

Crystal Clear – psychic, palmist, clairvoyant, medium. Tel: 02392 665 117. £35 for a half-hour telephone reading, £25 for face to face, or send in a photograph of yourself to be read for £15.

Lee Catt – psychic, tarot reader, medium. Tel: 020 7635 6197. £25 for half-hour readings.

Mysteries, tarot, astrology and more, 9–11 Monmouth Street, WC2. Tel: 020 7240 3688. £20 for a basic reading.

Sharom Rimmer – clairvoyant. Tel: 020 7237 3429. £20 per reading.

Twelfth House – astrology, 35 Pembridge Road, W11. Tel: 020 7727 9620. Astrology charts from £4.80.

London publications

In addition to the monthly consumer magazines, there are a few London-specific street publications. Some of these are available from bins placed outside main Tube and train stations, others are sold on the street, and some can be purchased in the local newsagents. Each of these, however, are a good source of job ads and entertainment listings within the capital.

Time Out is a weekly entertainment and listings guide (out Tuesdays in Zone 1 and Wednesdays in outer zones) offering news, features and specialist articles focusing on clubbing, music, theatre, TV and radio listings. Tel: 020 7813 3000 or www.timeout.co.uk. Costs £2.20.

The Big Issue is a weekly street magazine sold by homeless people on the streets, with a portion of the proceeds going into their own pockets. This £1 publication covers entertainment, politics and the arts. Tel: 020 7526 3200.

The Evening Standard is London's only evening newspaper and publishes a useful *Hot Tickets* entertainment listings magazine each Thursday. Tel: 020 7938 6000 or see www.thisislondon.co.uk. This comes free with the newspaper (35p).

Girl About Town (*GAT*), *Midweek*, *Ms London* and *Nine to Five* are free weekly publications with entertainment or lifestyle features plus a good selection of recruitment ads mainly for secretarial and office jobs. These are distributed from bins outside major Tube and train stations. Tel: 020 7636 6651.

Loot is the best newspaper to pick up if you want to rent a flat, find a flatmate, sell or buy a property, or buy virtually anything under the sun. This can be picked up at any newsagent for £1.40. Tel: 020 7328 1771 or www.loot.com.

The Metro can be picked up each morning from distribution bins located at major Tube and train stations. Published by *The Evening Standard*, this free daily is a good source of daily gossip and news. Tel: 020 7651 5200 or www.metro.co.uk.

TNT Magazine provides weekly clubbing, theatre and music reviews plus travel and arts and entertainment features. While mainly directed towards expatriate Australians, New Zealanders and South Africans living in London, its content will interest anyone who is new to the capital. Published each Monday and distributed free from bins outside Tube and train stations. Tel: 020 7373 3377 or www.tntmagazine.com.

SX Magazine is similar to *TNT Magazine* in its content, although it is also targeted at Canadians living in London. This free weekly travel and entertainment magazine is distributed on Wednesdays outside Tube and train stations. Tel: 020 7373 3377 or www.sxmagazine.com.

TV

Depending on where your telly is positioned throughout the house, and the effectiveness of its antenna, most Londoners should be able to pick up five stations without having to sign up to a cable TV provider. This includes BBC1, the British Broadcasting Company's main channel, which offers daily news programmes and general programing, including one of London's most popular television programmes: *EastEnders*. The BBC's second channel, BBC2, offers similar programmes with a slant towards gardening, cooking, household DIY and driving programmes.

Channel 3, or ITV, offers a range of dramas, sitcoms, documentaries and films, while Channel 4 runs a lot of US imports such as *Sex and the City*, *Friends*, and other popular British programmes.

Channel 5, London's youngest station, has a reputation for running low-budgeted television programmes and soaps, plus its notorious late-night American soft porn flicks, but it often plays some good sitcoms and dramas as well.

If these are not enough choices, you may want to hook up to a satellite dish, which will give you access to a whole range of new channels including MTV, CNN and NBC Superchannel.

To hook up to cable, therefore widening your choices once again, call the Cable Television Association at 0800 300 750 to find out prices.

TV licence

Everyone who lives in Britain and owns a television must pay a TV licence fee. In return, the BBC provides two commercial-free television stations offering a good mixture of documentaries, soaps, dramas and comedies. The licence fee not only keeps the BBC commercial free, but it also allows them to fund quality programing from all sectors of society – not just the ones that produce high ratings. This keeps the Beeb (as it is known) free of bias and prejudice.

The annual cost for owners who use a color TV is approximately £115, while the fee for a black and white television is about half that. Many a horror story has circulated in the past decade about households being stung with a £1,000 penalty for not paying their annual fees, so unless you plan on taking the risk, don't forget to pay. This can be done online at www.tv-l.co.uk, by credit card over the telephone on 08705 22 66 66, at the post office with cash or a cheque, or by post to TV Licensing, Freepost (BS6689), Bristol, BS98 1TL.

Radio

Returning home from a hot date with the woman of your dreams calls for a little mood music. But the hot and heavy luvva luvva vibe will be spoiled if you snap on the stereo and Nirvana's "Smells Like Teen Spirit" belts out of the stereo at full throttle. Flick through the stations in search of some soft jazz, but it may be too late. The moment has been doused in cold water and no amount of pine-scented candles and cheap Chardonnay will be able to get her back into that Barry-White-walrus-of-love feeling. In the future, each radio station should be programmed into your stereo to ensure that you are prepared for those rare condom opportunities. Here is a list of the main FM channels to choose from in London:

BBC Radio 1	97.6–99.8	Pop, rock
BBC Radio 2	88–90.2	Light music & culture programmes
BBC Radio 3	90.2–92.4	Classical, jazz, drama, discussions
BBC Radio 4	92.4–94.6	Talk
Capital Radio	95.8	Pop
London Live	94.9	Pop, talk
GMR	95.1	Talk
Heart	106.2	Adult pop
Jazz FM	102.2	Jazz, blues
Classic FM	101.9	Classical
Kiss FM	100	Dance, pop
Magic	105.4	Light music
News Direct	97.3	News
Virgin	105.8	Pop, rock
XFM	104.9	Indie, rock

Pirate radio stations are alive and well in London, you just have to know where to look. Try these ones, or turn the dial until you find something you like.

Reggae

Groove	94.0
Power Jam	92.0
Vogue	90.4

Hip-hop

Itch	105.15

Garage and Drum 'n' Bass

Y2K	90.6
Flex	103.2
Flava	87.6
Rampage	87.5

Chapter Seven:
Shopping

London is a Mecca for hordes of credit card swiping shoppers. Oxford Street turns into a human pinball table on the weekends as punters part with their hard-earned savings and wrestle for the last blue spangly top in a size ten. From the more upmarket shops of High Street Kensington, to the dodgy market stalls on Brick Lane, you'll find more than what you are after in London. Just make sure you never succumb to the urge to purchase an oversized novelty Union Jack hat. Please. Don't.

Markets

London has lots of markets dotted about selling all manner of bizarre and banal wares. Many local areas turn into bustling farmers' markets on one day a week, and the weekends transform many normal streets into animated mayhem, with punters grappling over the price of an off-cut of leather, a packet of custard creams, or a 1970s mock-teak table. Leave the Manolos at home, put on some comfy trainers and be prepared to barter and banter.

Berwick Street Market

Berwick Street, W1
Tube: Oxford Circus or Piccadilly Circus
Mon–Sat, 9 a.m.–5 p.m.
Fruit and vegetable stalls are littered about the street in front of fantastic record shops.

Borough Market

Borough High Street, SE1
Tube: London Bridge
Friday 12 a.m.–6 p.m. Saturday 9 a.m.–4 p.m.
Hidden under the railway arches, Borough Market is a sight to behold with its Victorian architecture and cobbled streets. *Bridget Jones's Diary* and *Lock, Stock and Two Smoking Barrels* are amongst the many films that have shot scenes here. This farmers' market sells high quality fruits, veggies and cheeses. Things cost a bit more than a normal farmers' market, but at least it's central and the food is always tops.

Brick Lane

Brick Lane, Cheshire Street, and Slater Street, E1
Tube: Aldgate East or Liverpool Street
Sunday 8 a.m.–2 p.m.
A real cockney market selling fresh fruit, veggies, and fish, vintage clothing, cheap household basics such as bin liners, food, and shampoo, bric-a-brac, furniture, bicycles, tools. A market certainly worth getting up early on a Sunday for, and make sure you stop off at one of the two 24-hour bagel shops – an East London must.

Brixton Market

East of Brixton Road area, SW9
Tube: Brixton
Mon–Sat, 10 a.m.–sunset
Caribbean foods and specialist exotic fare. You can also find CDs, clothes, toiletries, and crafts.

Camden Market

Camden Lock Place, NW1
Tube: Camden Town
Saturday and Sunday 10 a.m.–6 p.m.
Camden is a frenetic place at the best of times with all the kids who hate their parents and rebel against them via pink hair and multiple face piercings, but as soon as the weekend hits the place becomes absolute anarchy. Thousands of people converge on this market on the lookout for retro clothing, techno club wear, new clothing, art, ethnic knick-knacks, jewelry, records, anything you can imagine. The market is huge and takes hours to explore. If you are looking for retro clothing though, you may want to skip the first half and head up past the overhead train bridge on Camden High Street, nip back into the market on your left and you'll find heaps of stands around the outside of the Stables selling old Levis and vintage clothes.

Columbia Road Flower Market

Columbia Road, E2
Tube: Liverpool Street, then bus 26 or 48.
Sunday 8 a.m.–2 p.m.
This is one of the most beautiful places in London on a Sunday morning in the springtime. The entire market is dedicated to flowers and plants and the smell is unbelievable. Whether you want plants for your house or flowers for your garden, you will find everything you could ever want here. There are some great pubs tucked away on cobbled streets around the market if you fancy a refreshment or you need to nurse your pollen allergy.

The Courtyard

St. Martin-in-the-Fields Church, WC2.
Tube: Charing Cross
Mon–Sat 11 a.m.–5 p.m., Sun noon–5 p.m.
This market is alongside the church and sells books, tourist tat, clothes and jewelry.

Covent Garden

The Piazza, Covent Garden, WC2
Tube: Covent Garden
Mon–Sun 10 a.m.–7 p.m.
www.coventgardenmarket.co.uk

The original vegetable market moved to Vauxhall in 1974, but the stalls have been preserved and are now filled with handicrafts, jewelry, and antiques.

Greenwich Market

Church Road, SE10
DLR: Cutty Sark or Island Gardens
Mon–Sun 9.30 a.m.–5.30 p.m.

This market is positively enormous, selling antiques, clothing, books, arts and crafts. Almost anything you could possibly want can be found at Greenwich and it is certainly worth the trek out on the Docklands Light Rail. There is a lot of great retro and vintage clothing, excellent sources of vinyl records, and heaps of kitsch furniture.

Petticoat Lane

Middlesex Street, and Wentworth Street, Aldgate, E1
Tube: Liverpool Street or Aldgate
Mon–Fri 10 a.m–2.30 p.m., Sun 9 a.m.–2 p.m.

Hundreds of stalls sell everything from fabrics and jewelry, to fairy-lights and clothes. This market has been around for over a hundred years, so get down there and haggle with a thick-necked cockney geezer for a toaster – it's tradition.

Portobello Market

Portobello Road and Portobello Green, W11
Tube: Notting Hill Gate or Ladbroke Grove
Saturdays 8 a.m.–5 p.m.

Antiques, art, vintage and retro clothes, records, books, fruit and veggies. Prices get lower as you head north away from Notting Hill Gate. This market has been trendy since the 60s and is still a great place to spend the weekend. Break up your wandering with a drink in one of the many great pubs in the area and discuss your lucky finds. Apparently Kylie Minogue bought the infamous gold hotpants from her 'Spinning Around' video here. I wish I could buy her arse.

Spitalfields Market

Commercial St, E1
Tube: Liverpool Street
Mon–Fri 11 a.m.–3.30 p.m., Sun 10 a.m.–3 p.m.

Organic fruit and veggies, clothing and accessories by upcoming designers, retro sportswear, trendy vintage home furnishings, art, records. A very posh market and a great way to spend the morning. Grab a fresh fruit drink and wander about the handicrafts.

Clothing

London is a shoppers' dream. Whether you want vintage jeans, the latest Prada skirt, or an inexpensive belt from the high street, you'll find it here. The main shopping areas are Oxford Street, Covent Garden (Neal Street), and High Street Kensington, while Bond Street caters for the upmarket platinum card crowd.

Women's Clothing Size Conversion

UK	Euro	USA
6	32	4
8	34	6
10	36	8
12	38	10
14	40	12
16	42	14

Women's Shoe Size Conversion

UK	Euro	USA
3.5	36	5.5
4	37	6
4.5	37.5	6.5
5	38	7
5.5	39	7.5
6	39.5	8
6.5	40	8.5
7	40.5	9
7.5	41	9.5

Men's Shirt Sizes

UK	Euro	USA
14	36	14
14.5	37	14.5
15	38	15
16	41	16
16.5	42	16.5
17	43	17

Men's Shoe Size Conversion

UK	Euro	USA
-	39	6.5
7	40	7
-	41	8
7.5	41	8.5
8	42	9
9	43	10
-	44	10.5
10	45	11
11	46	12

```
Discount Designer Clothes
Nicole Farhi/French Connection, 3 Hancock Road,
Bromley-by-Bow, E3. Tel: 0207 399 7125. Tube: Bow.
Samples, seconds and last season's stock at bargain prices.
```

Classy department stores

Harrods, Brompton Road, SW1. Tel: 020 7730 1234.
Tube: Knightsbridge
Harvey Nichols, 109–125 Knightsbridge, SW1. Tel: 020 7235 5000.
Tube: Knightsbridge
House of Fraser, 318 Oxford Street, W1. Tel: 020 7529 4700.
Tube: Oxford Street
Selfridges, 400 Oxford Street, W1. Tel: 020 7629 1234.
Tube: Bond Street
Liberty, 214–220 Regent Street, W1. Tel: 020 7734 123.
Tube: Oxford Circus
Dickens and Jones, 224–244 Regent Street, W1. Tel: 020 7734 7070. Tube: Oxford Circus
Fortnum and Mason, 181 Piccadilly, W1. Tel: 020 7734 8040.
Tube: Piccadilly Circus

General department stores
(all have other locations throughout London)

BHS, 252–258 Oxford Street, W1. Tel: 020 7629 2011.
Tube: Oxford Circus
Debenhams, 334–348 Oxford Street, W1. Tel: 020 7580 3000.
Tube: Oxford Circus
John Lewis, 278–306 Oxford Street, W1. Tel: 020 7629 7711.
Tube: Oxford Circus
Marks and Spencer, 458 Oxford Street, W1. Tel: 020 7935 7954.
Tube: Bond Street

Vintage shops

There are heaps of great vintage shops in London. More chic than a charity shop, they have done all of the hard work and normally offer only the best pieces. Go on, you know you want that blue and purple chevron print polyester leisure suit. It'll go great with the fondue set you got last week at Greenwich Market, and you can try out your new John Denver LP.

Blackout II, 51 Endell Street, WC2. Tel: 020 7240 5006.
Tube: Covent Garden
Steinberg and Tolkien, 193 Kings Road, SW3. Tel: 020 7376 3660.

Tube: Sloane Square
Cloud Cuckoo Land, 6 Charlton Place, N1. Tel: 020 7354 3141.
Tube: Angel
Pop Boutique, 6 Monmouth Street, WC2. Tel: 020 7497 5262.
Tube: Covent Garden

Salons

There are plenty of hairdressers to choose from. Here are the details of a few, most of which have branches throughout London:

Charles Worthington, 34 Great Queen Street, WC2.
Tel: 020 7831 5303. www.cwlondon.com Tube: Covent Garden
Coopers of Covent Garden, 27 Maiden Lane, WC2.
Tel: 020 7240 7170. Tube: Covent Garden or Charing Cross
Cuts, 39 Frith Street, W1. Tel: 020 7734 2171. Tube: Oxford Circus
Daniel Galvin, 42–44 George Street, W1. Tel: 020 7486 8601.
Tube: Baker Street
Nicky Clarke, 130 Mount Street, W1. Tel: 020 7491 4700.
Tube: Green Park
Essensuals, 34 Southampton Street, WC2. Tel: 020 7240 4090.
www.essensuals.co.uk Tube: Covent Garden.
Fish Hairdressing, 30 D'Arbley Street, W1. Tel: 020 7494 2398.
Tube: Oxford Circus
John Frieda, 4 Aldford Street, W1. Tel: 020 7491 0840.
Tube: Marble Arch
Toni and Guy, 4 Henrietta Street WC2. Tel: 020 7240 7342.
www.toniandguy.co.uk Tube: Covent Garden.

Budget salons

Getting your haircut in London can be a luxurious experience. You can get a massage, nibble on chocolates and sip champagne as your hair gets styled. But if you want all that you will have to pay upwards of £50 for a cut and style. You don't want to go without a haircut and you certainly can't let your flatmate attack your hair with the scissors.

Hairdressing schools

You're reading this, so you must have more balls than Batman in a leotard. You will have to put your precious hair in the hands of a greasy student, but as long as you are assertive, watch what is going on, and speak up as soon as you think something is amiss – then you should be fine. The students are watched like a hawk by their instructor, and if you're really lucky you'll get someone at the end of their course. The schools charge £8.50–£10 for a cut, but appointments are only during the day on weekdays and the petrified students often take hours so you will need to take the day off work. If you agree to come back and act as a model for the student to be graded on, then your cut or color may be free.

Vidal Sassoon School, 15 Davies Mews, W1. Tel: 020 7318 5202. Tube: Bond Street
Toni and Guy Hairdressing School, 75 New Oxford Street, WC1. Tel: 020 7836 0606. Tube: Tottenham Court Road

If you can't face having your locks trimmed by a student, the next cheapest option is Hair By Fairy. Bright paint job, dreadlocks flowing, and pounding bass. It's an experience.
Hair By Fairy, 8–10 Neals Yard, WC2. Tel: 020 7497 0776. www.hairbyfairy.co.uk Tube: Covent Garden

Or wander into the supermarket of hairdressers.
Supercuts, The Piazza, 120 Oxford Street, W1. Tel: 020 7637 0612. Tube: Tottenham Court Road or Oxford Circus. Prices from £15.

Inexpensive beauty treatments

Even if a girl is strapped for cash, she still needs to be pampered. There are a few places you can go to be aesthetically indulged without parting with too much cash …

London College of Beauty Therapy, 47 Great Marlborough Street, W1. Tel: 020 7208 1300. Tube: Oxford Circus. Book ahead for an appointment to let the students test their skills on a human.

Pure Beauty, 151 Oxford Street, W1. Tel: 0845 129 6604. Tube: Oxford Circus or Tottenham Court Road. This beauty emporium was set up by Boots, and offers inexpensive basic beauty treatments.

Groceries

You should have a major supermarket chain near your house. But to save yourself the bother of lugging bags of food home, you can always have them delivered.

Asda:	www.asda.co.uk
Tesco:	www.tesco.com
Sainsbury's:	www.sainsbury.co.uk
Waitrose:	www.waitrose.com
Marks and Spencer:	www.marksandspencer.com

For dented tins at unbelievably low prices, keep an eye out for a

Kwik Save, Lidl, or Netto near your home. Just make sure that you check the expiration dates. Whatever you do, don't indulge in the poorly labelled generic booze. Saving a quid or two just isn't worth a day of projectile vomiting.

> Fancy having milk delivered right to your door in a charming glass bottle? www.milkdeliveries.co.uk

Housewares

A new lamp? A duvet cover? How about a trash bin? From cheap and cheerful Argos to sleek and stylish Conran designs, you'll be able to find all the housewares you need. You can find much of it on your local high street, or just wander into the department stores on Oxford Street. Central shops are listed below; call them or see the website for shops in your area.

For basics
Argos, 80–110 New Oxford Street, WC1. Tel: 020 7637 1869. www.argos.co.uk Tube: Tottenham Court Road
Robert Dyas, 97 St Martin's Lane, WC2. Tel: 020 7836 0611. www.robertdyas.co.uk
Ikea, 255 North Circular Road, NW10. Tel: 020 8233 2300. www.ikea.co.uk Tube: Stonebridge Park, then bus 112
John Lewis, Oxford Street, W1. Tel: 020 7629 7711. www.johnlewis.com Tube: Oxford Circus
Woolworths, 115–119 Camden High Road, NW1. Tel: 020 7485 3932. www.woolworths.co.uk Tube: Camden Town

For classier items
General Trading Company, 2 Symons Street, SW3. Tel: 020 7730 0411. Tube: Sloane Square
Habitat, 26–40 Kensington High Street, W8. Tel: 020 7795 6055. www.habitat.co.uk Tube: High Street Kensington
Heal's, 196 Tottenham Court Road, W1. Tel: 020 7631 3880. www.heals.co.uk Tube: Tottenham Court Road

Spend more than a penny

If nature calls during an Oxford Street shopping trip, don't even think about sneaking into a nearby pub or fast food chain without buying a drink. They're on to you and a hefty security guard will swiftly turf you out before you get a chance to do your business. Instead, just go shopping in Topshop at Oxford Circus as they have toilets on the lower ground floor for customers. While you're there, ladies, be sure to pick up some of their hipster knickers – the best cotton pants in town.

DIY and decorating

B&Q DIY Supercentre, 524 Old Kent Road, SE1. Tel: 020 7252 0657. www.diy.co.uk Tube: Elephant & Castle

Homebase, O2 Centre, 255 Finchley Road, NW3. Tel: 020 7435 5173. www.homebase.co.uk Tube: Finchley Road

Robert Dyas, 123 Tottenham Court Road, W1. Tel: 020 7388 0183. www.robertdyas.co.uk Tube: Warren Street

Electronics

Dixons, 493–497 Oxford Street, W1. Tel: 020 7408 0890. www.dixons.co.uk Tube: Oxford Circus

Comet, Unit 2a, Cantium Retail Park, 522 Old Kent Road, SE1. Tel: 08546 007 002 www.comet.co.uk Tube: Elephant & Castle

Currys, 268 North End Road, SW6. Tel: 020 7381 5289. www.currys.co.uk Tube: Putney Bridge or Parsons Green

Gultronics, 52 Tottenham Court Road, W1. Tel: 020 7323 9188. www.gultronics.co.uk Tube: Goodge Street

PC World, Unit 1 Geron Way, Staples Corner, NW2. Tel: 020 8450 0909. www.pcworld.co.uk Tube: Brent Cross or Hendon Central

Richer Sounds, 29 Bloomsbury Way, WC1. Tel: 020 7831 2888. www.richersounds.com Tube: Holborn

Music

From The Clash's infamous "London Calling", to The Jam's "Going Underground" and The Kinks' "Waterloo Sunset", there is no better music scene than London's. If you think you are the next Robbie Williams, Noel Gallagher, or Mick Jagger, then you'll need some suitable paraphernalia.

The following are the major CD shops with locations all over London (central shops listed):
HMV, 150 Oxford Street, W1. Tel: 020 7631 3423. www.hmv.co.uk Tube: Oxford Circus

Tower Records, 1 Piccadilly Circus, W1. Tel: 020 7439 2500. www.towerrecords.co.uk Tube: Piccadilly Circus

Virgin Megastore, 14–16 Oxford Street, W1. Tel: 020 7631 1234. www.virgin.net Tube: Tottenham Court Road

For vinyl records, peruse one of these shops:
Black Market Records, 25 D'Arblay Street, W1. Tel: 020 7287 1932. Tube: Oxford Circus

Disque Records, 11 Chapel Market, N1. Tel: 020 7833 1104. Tube: Angel

MSM, 17 Chalk Farm Road, NW1. Tel: 020 7284 2527. Tube: Camden Town

Ray's Jazz Shop, 180 Shaftesbury Avenue, WC2. Tel: 020 7240

3969. Tube: Covent Garden
Reckless Records, 79 Upper Street, N1. Tel: 020 7359 0501.
Tube: Angel.
Rough Trade, 16 Neals Yard, WC2. Tel: 020 7240 0105.
Tube: Covent Garden.
Selectadisc, 34 Berwick Street, W1. Tel: 020 7734 3297.
Tube: Tottenham Court Road
Small Fish Records, 372 Curtain Road, EC1. Tel: 020 7739 2252.
Tube: Old Street

If it's drumsticks and guitar picks that you're after, then head for Denmark Street, London's Tin Pan Alley. Located just off Charing Cross Road, WC2, Tube: Tottenham Court Road, you'll find a glut of instruments from bongos and bagpipes, to violins and Fender Stratocasters in shops all along the street. All the musical greats have trodden upon the cobbles; the Beatles, the Rolling Stones, the Kinks and Jimi Hendrix recorded on this street. David Bowie set up a campervan to be close to his studio, Elton John wrote "Your Song" on the rooftops and Bob Marley bought his first guitar here.

Andy's Guitar Centre and Workshop, 27 Denmark Street, WC2.
Tel: 020 7916 5080
Bass Cellar, 22 Denmark Street, WC2. Tel: 020 7240 3438
Gigwear, 28 Denmark Street, WC2. Tel: 020 7240 3438
Helter Skelter (music bookshop), 4 Denmark Street, WC2.
Tel: 020 7836 1151
Hank's Acoustics, 24 Denmark Street, WC2. Tel: 020 7379 1139
London Drum and Percussion Centre, WC2. Tel: 020 7240 3438
London PA Centre, 23 Denmark Street, WC2. Tel: 020 7836 4656
Rhodes Music Company, 21 Denmark Street, WC2.
Tel: 020 7379 3398
World of Pianos, 8 Denmark Street, WC2. Tel: 020 7497 1139

Books

There are bookshops all over the high street, but Charing Cross Road is the spiritual home to all things literary. The legendarily chaotic Foyles bookshop anchors the top of the street, but all along the full length are tiny new and used booksellers. You never know what you'll find, from a first edition of Truman Capote's *In Cold Blood*, to the latest fad diet manual.

The largest bookshops in London are:
Borders, 203 Oxford Street, W1. Tel: 020 7292 1600.
Tube: Oxford Circus. www.borders.co.uk
Books Etc, 26 James Street, WC2. Tel: 020 7379 6947.
Tube: Covent Garden. www.booksetc.co.uk
Foyles, 119 Charing Cross Road, WC2. Tel: 020 7437 5660.

Tube: Tottenham Court Road. www.foyles.com
Waterstone's, 203–206 Piccadilly, W1. Tel: 020 7851 2400.
Tube: Piccadilly. www.waterstones.co.uk
WHSmith, 218–219 Tottenham Court Road, W1. Tel: 020 7636 4078.
Tube: Tottenham Court Road. www.whsmith.co.uk

Films

If you're looking to rent videos and DVDs, then you'll have to look around for your local rental shop. The main chain is Blockbuster (www.blockbuster.co.uk), but you'll probably find many smaller chains and independent shops in your neighborhood. If you're looking to buy that box set of *The Godfather* or if you've worn out that much-loved copy of *Withnail and I*, then shop around in major music shops, bookstores, and even supermarkets.

Erotic

Sex. It's such a fun pastime. I'm sure we've all called in sick at one time or another in order to spend another amorous and primal day romping with a new partner and discovering their favorite little perversions. If you haven't, then you should, it's far more interesting than e-mail innuendo or taking notes. Whether you like to partake in wife-swapping over a cheese fondue on the weekends, enjoy batteries with your love-life, or have a cupboard full of gimp-suits and a bondage rack for a coffee table, then London certainly comes up trumps with all sorts of fun and games to keep you busy. And my, what busy little beavers you will be ...

Strip bars

There are plenty of strip joints in London. One stroll through the depths of Soho and you'll be spoilt for choice, peep shows, lap-dances, erotic films ... But one word of warning: make sure you keep your wits about you. Stories go around about guys who go into these small clubs, only to have a lovely lady come up for a chat. Don't believe your luck, lads. That small chat will definitely cost you. You probably won't be able to leave without parting with a few hundred quid – and chances are you won't even catch a glimpse of nipple for your trouble. And the largest, most gladiator-esque bouncers that you've ever seen will walk you to the cash point to make sure they get it. You've been warned. Try one of the places listed below for an, erm, credible establishment.

For Your Eyes Only, 11 White Horse Street, W1. Tel: 020 7499 6816. Tube: Green Park
Raymond's Revue Bar, Walkers Court, W1. Tel: 020 7734 1593.

Tube: Piccadilly Circus
Spearmint Rhino Gentleman's Club, 161 Tottenham Court Road.
Tel: 020 7209 4488. Tube: Tottenham Court Road
Stringfellows, 16–19 Upper St Martin's Lane, WC2.
Tel: 020 7240 5534. Tube: Leicester Square

Prostitutes

If prostitutes are your thing, then they have made life easy for you. Marketing and advertising haven't escaped the world's oldest profession, and prostitutes place their, and I use this term loosely, business cards in telephone booths across the city. In Soho, pretty girls stand outside in their brothel doorways to entice the punters. Just be aware of the old bait and switch ploy. Now, I don't have to warn you to be careful ... condoms, condoms, condoms.

Randy retailers

Ann Summers, 95 Oxford Street, W1. Tel: 020 7494 0379.
Tube: Oxford Circus
Sexy knickers, rubber nurse uniforms, a wide variety of sex toys and all sorts of tacky hen night paraphernalia. One-stop sex toy shop.

Clone Zone, 64 Old Compton Street, W1. Tel: 020 7287 3530.
Tube: Leicester Square
A mainstream, mildly titillating ground floor veils the more fetish-erotic delights of the eyebrow-raising basement. If you are after equipment that would petrify the gimp in *Pulp Fiction*, this would be a good bet.

Coco de Mer, 23 Monmouth Street, WC2. Tel: 020 7836 8882.
Tube: Covent Garden
Classy yet sexy, and certainly not demure. For ladies who lunch, but like a kinky session on a Sunday morning before brunch.

Expectations, 75 Great Eastern Street, EC2. Tel: 020 7739 0292.
Tube: Old Street
A vast cavernous burrow rammed with all sorts of leathery rubbery charms to revel in.

Harmony, 167 Charing Cross Road, WC2. Tel: 020 7439 6261.
Tube: Tottenham Court Road
Massive sex emporium catering for all needs, mainstream fetishes, and preferences.

Little Shoe Box, 89 Holloway Road, N7. Tel: 020 7607 1247.
Tube: Highbury & Islington

If you're into large patent thigh-high stilettos and lashings of leather then you've found retail heaven. Foot fetishists' delight. **Prowler Camden**, 283 Camden High Street, NW1. Tel: 020 7284 0537. Tube: Camden Town
Sex toys beyond your most perverse fantasies, and videos and magazines for your multimedia pleasure.

RoB London, 24 Wells Street, W1. Tel: 020 7735 7893.
Tube: Oxford Circus
Arousal accoutrements loom from every angle.

SH!, 39 Coronet Street, N1. Tel: 020 7613 5458. Tube: Old Street
Vibrators, vibrators, vibrators ... who needs men anyway? This shop is ladies only, so unless curious blokes are accompanied by a damsel, they'll have to make do with dribbling outside the window. Everything a modern gal could want.

Need some sexy knickers for that lovely lady?
Agent Provocateur, 6 Broadwick Street, W1. Tel: 020 7439 0229.
Tube: Tottenham Court Road or Leicester Square
La Senza, 162 Oxford Street. Tel: 020 7580 3559. Tube: Oxford Circus
La Perla Boutique, 163 Sloane Street, SW1. Tel: 020 7245 0527.
Tube: Sloane Square

Clubbing that oozes sex

If you believe that your wild side should not be restricted to the bedroom, Torture Garden is the club night for you. Take an erotic adventure into the S&M world of PVC, whips, leashes and chains. The dress code is fantasy, fetish and cyber. So don't be turning up in a pair of jeans, unless they're crotchless. Splash about in a puddle of drum 'n' bass, ska, nu-skool breaks, hard house and sleazy rock 'n' roll. The venue is always changing so take a look at www.torturegarden.com.

Cheap or free

London is notoriously expensive. But that doesn't mean that you have to stay indoors like a hermit with the lurgy. There's plenty to do that won't cost you your meager life savings.

Cinemas

The Prince Charles Cinema, 7 Leicester Place, WC2. Tel: 020 7437 7003. Tube: Leicester Square. Second run and cult films at low prices. From £1.50–£3.50.

The Tricycle Cinema, 269 Kilburn High Road, NW6. Tel: 020 7328 1000. Tube: Kilburn. Holds a 'Pay what you can' night on Mondays at 8 p.m.

Happy hippy stuff

Auricular Acupuncture and Indian Head Massage, Chelsea Methodist Church (opposite Habitat) at 155a Kings Road, SW3. Tel: 07946 705 657. Free every Thursday from 11.30 a.m. to 4 p.m. Ear acupuncture can help many conditions such as high blood pressure, stress, addictions and PMT.

Healing, The White Eagle Lodge, 9 St Mary Abbots Place, Kensington High Street, W8. Tel: 020 7603 7914. This service of spiritual healing is free at 6.15 p.m. every Wednesday in the chapel. Cope with the stress of everyday living and forget about how broke you are after paying for those tickets to Glastonbury.

Forgotten your anniversary? Guilty conscience? All loved up? Say it with flowers.

Beryl Williams, 71 Heath Street, NW3. Tel: 020 7435 3876

Floraldesign, www.floraldesign.co.uk

Floral Direct, 25b Crawford Street, W1. Tel: 0870 743 7386

House of Flowers, 34 Brunswick Centre, WC1. Tel: 020 7278 4233

My Fair Lady, 6 The Market, The Piazza, WC2. Tel: 020 7379 9130

Teleflorist, www.teleflorist.co.uk or call 0800 111 800

Vayle Spring Flowers, 40 St Lukes Road, W11. Tel: 020 7792 8232

Theatre

To get cheaper tickets to most major shows, try the discount ticket booths around Leicester Square on the day of the performance.

The TKTS booth is the only official half-price and discount theatre ticket booth in London. It is located in the clocktower building on the south side of the garden in the middle of Leicester Square. You can only book tickets on the day of the performance and it's best to get there early. Open Mon–Sat 10 a.m.–7 p.m., Sun noon to 3.30 p.m. www.tkts.co.uk

Filming

You can get free tickets to watch television programmes being filmed. The details of the show are usually a bit vague, but you could end up at something spectacular or the next big sitcom.

Avalon – www.tvrecordings.com or 0700 22 22 111

BBC – www.bbc.co.uk/tickets or 020 8576 1227

Channel 4 – www.channel4.com/tickets

Chortle – www.chortle.co.uk

Hat Trick Productions – www.hattrick.co.uk or 0207 434 2451

Powerhouse Film and TV – www.powerhousetv.co.uk 0207 240 2828

Standing Room Only – 0208 870 0111

or e-mail: freetvtix@standroom.com

Pound shops (Dollar Stores)

Pound shops are all over London selling cheap household cleaners, Christmas decorations, and stationery. These are normally independently run and are on most high streets. Get most things for a pound or less.

Need some impartial consumer advice? Don't let the big companies get away with bad service.

Government consumer advice: www.consumer.gov.uk

Legal service for info on any legal problem: www.justask.org.uk

National Consumer Council: www.ncc.org.uk

Government Office of Fair Trading: www.tradingstandards.gov.uk

Independent consumer advice and testing: www.which.net

Chapter Eight:
Gay and Lesbian

London is very cosmopolitan. Every race, religion and sexuality is represented and whether you're in the closet or out, there are plenty of bars and events in London to keep you busy. The gay community is mainly centerd around Soho, and Old Compton Street in particular. Around here the most narrow-minded right-wing Nazi is used to seeing forays into the flamboyant, so even if you're an overtly camp ten-foot fully tattooed drag queen who enjoys stapling pink goose feathers to your arse, then by all means go ahead. But chances are you're just a normal Joe who needs to know where to head for a night out.

Try the following magazines and newspapers, available at most newsagents or free from Soho bars, for listings of clubs, bars, and events: *The Gay Times, Time Out, Boyz, Pink Voice, Outcast Magazine, Rainbow Tickets.*

Top club nights

G-A-Y @ The Astoria
Charing Cross Road, WC2
Tel: 020 7734 6963
Tube: Tottenham Court Road
Mon, Thurs, Fri and Sat 10 p.m.–3 a.m.
Over the top and camp-tastic, this is the biggest gay club in the country. Put on your dancing shoes because the music is pop, pop, pop.

DTPM @ Fabric
77a Charterhouse Street, EC1
Tel: 020 7439 9009
Tube: Farringdon
www.dtpm.net
Sundays
Hard house, soul and R&B.

Trade @ Turnmills
63 Clerkenwell Road, EC1
Tel: 020 7700 5352
Tube: Farringdon
www.tradeuk.net
From 5 a.m. Sunday mornings.
Up-for-it crowd of muscle boys and hard house. Seriously serious.

Heaven

The Arches, Villiers Street, WC2
Tel: 020 7930 2020
Tube: Embankment or Charing Cross
www.heaven-london.com
An institution with three floors of house, pop, and techno. Something for everyone.

Accommodation

If you want to be sure that you won't be sharing an apartment with any raving homophobics, then take a look in the *Time Out* magazine's accommodation listings, or the *Pink Voice*. An excellent gay and lesbian accommodation agency is **Outlet**, 32 Old Compton Street, W1. Tel: 020 7287 4244. Tube: Leicester Square

---

Traditional pubs and bars

Mixed

The Admiral Duncan

54 Old Compton Street, W1. Tel: 020 7437 5300.
Tube: Leicester Square

Bar Fusion

45 Essex Road, N1. Tel: 020 7688 2882. Tube: Angel

The Box

Seven Dials, 32–34 Monmouth Street, WC2. Tel: 020 7240 5828.
Tube: Leicester Square

The Brewery Tap

78 Lingham Street, SW9. Tel: 020 7738 6683. Tube: Stockwell

The Champion

1 Wellington Terrace, Bayswater Road, W2. Tel: 020 7243 9531.
Tube: Notting Hill Gate or Queensway

The Chapel

29a Penton Street, N1. Tel: 020 7833 4090. Tube: Angel

City of Quebec

12 Old Quebec Street, W1. Tel: 020 7629 6159. Tube: Marble Arch

Compton's of Soho
53–55 Old Compton Street, W1. Tel: 020 7479 7961.
Tube: Piccadilly Circus

The Edge
11 Soho Square, W1. Tel: 020 7439 1313.
Tube: Tottenham Court Road

First Out
52 St Giles High Street, WC2. Tel: 020 7240 8042.
Tube: Tottenham Court Road

Freedom Bar/Club
60–66 Wardour Street, W1. Tel: 020 7734 0071,
Tube: Piccadilly Circus

Friendly Society
Basement, 79 Wardour Street (entrance Tisbury Court), W1.
Tel: 020 7434 3805. Tube: Piccadilly Circus

Ku Bar
75 Charing Cross Road, W1. Tel: 020 7437 4303.
Tube: Leicester Square

Retro Bar
2 George Court, WC2. Tel: 020 7321 2811. Tube: Charing Cross

The Shadow Lounge
5 Brewer Street, W1. Tel: 020 7287 7988. Tube: Leicester Square

Men Only

Brief Encounter
42 St Martin's Lane, WC1. Tel: 020 7557 9851. Tube: Charing Cross

Brompton's
corner of Old Brompton Road and Warwick Road, SW5.
Tel: 020 7370 1344. Tube: Earl's Court

Kudos
10 Adelaide Street, WC2. Tel: 020 7379 4573. Tube: Charing Cross

Manto
30 Old Compton Street, W1. Tel: 020 7494 2756.
Tube: Leicester Square

Rupert St
50 Rupert Street, W1. Tel: 020 7734 5614. Tube: Piccadilly Circus

79 CXR
79 Charing Cross Road, WC2. Tel: 020 7734 0769.
Tube: Leicester Square

The Yard
57 Rupert Street, W1. Tel: 020 7437 2652. Tube: Piccadilly Circus

Female Only

Candy Bar
4 Carlisle Street, W1. Tel: 020 7494 4041.
Tube: Tottenham Court Road

Glass Bar
West Lodge, Euston Square Gardens, 190 Euston Road, NW1.
Tel: 020 7387 6184. Tube: Euston

Vespa Lounge
Under Centre Point House, St Giles Circus, WC1. Tel: 020 7836 8956. Tube: Tottenham Court Road

---

London Pride March and Mardi Gras. Held in late June/early July, this colorful march starts at Hyde Park and finishes with a huge party in Finsbury Park

---

Cabaret

Mixed

BJ's Black Swan
556 Commercial Road, E14. Tel: 020 7780 9870. Tube: Aldgate East

The Black Cap
171 Camden High Street, NW1. Tel: 020 7428 2721.
Tube: Camden Town

Central Station
37 Wharfdale Road, N1. Tel: 020 7278 3294. Tube: King's Cross

Men Only

The Block

28 Hancock Road, E3. Tel: 0909 464 6804. Tube: Bromley By Bow.
Dress code (club): leather, rubber, uniform ...

The Hoist

Railway Arch 47c, South Lambeth Road, SW8. Tel: 020 7735 9972.
Tube: Vauxhall. Dress code (bar): leather, rubber, uniform ...

The 2 Brewers

114 Clapham High Street, SW4. Tel: 020 7498 4971.
Tube: Clapham Common

London websites:

www.gaytimes.co.uk

www.gay.uk.net

www.queenscene.com

www.gaybritain.co.uk

www.rainbownetwork.com

www.gaypride.co.uk

24-hour gay and lesbian switchboard: 020 7837 7324

Chapter Nine:
Sightseeing

Chances are that by the time mom, dad, and little sis come to London to lounge on your sofas and pretend that they miss you, you won't have visited many of the capital's major attractions. You could put the family on a tour bus for a few hours and head to The Olde Abbot's Fjord pub with some friends, or you could take them to these mouth-gaping wonders and pretend that you've already marvelled at them. Even better, go now and by the time they've found someone to look after the puppy, you'll be able to act all worldly and knowledgeable about your new city.

Bus tours

Big Bus Company, Tel: 020 7233 9533. www.bigbus.co.uk Costs £15

Original London Sightseeing Tour, Tel: 020 8877 1722. www.theoriginaltour.com Costs £14

London Pride, Tel: 020 8877 1722. www.londonpride.co.uk Costs £12.50

London landmarks

Big Ben and the Houses of Parliament

Parliament Square, SW1
Tel: 020 7219 3000
Tube: Westminster
Entrance: £7 adults, £3.50 concessions

Built in neo-Gothic style in 1840, the Houses of Parliament are a remarkable sight. They are best known for Big Ben, which has rung in the New Year since 1924. Head to the area at noon to hear the bells in all their glory. The House of Commons is where Members of Parliament meet to discuss legislation. The public can watch debates when parliament is in session. You don't need tickets in advance, but may have to wait a while to get in.

British Airways London Eye

Jubilee Gardens, York Road, SE1
Tel: 0870 500 0600
Tube: Waterloo
Tickets: £10.50 / £8.50 disabled
www.ba-londoneye.com

Take a half-hour ride on one of the Eye's 32 hi-tech silver pods for unrivalled views over London. Soaring 135 meters in the air, you will be flying high in slo-mo in the world's largest Ferris wheel. Be sure to book ahead online or over the telephone to avoid the queues.

Buckingham Palace

At the end of The Mall
Tel: 020 7321 2233
Tube: St James Park
Admission: £11.50

Built in 1705, this mansion became the official London residence of the royal family in 1837. Some of its 661 rooms are open to the public from mid-August until late September, when you can visit the magnificent State Rooms, which have been used over the centuries to entertain the wealthy and powerful.

Millennium Bridge

Open 24 hours and free
Links the South Bank to the City of London

It will forever be known to Londoners as "The Wobbly Bridge", thanks to those humorous first days when the swaying metallic platform was revealed to the world. But since its latest multimillion-pound renovation, not even the fattest troublemakers have been able to force much movement out of it. All the same, this futuristic pedestrian walkway is worth a photo in the album.

St Paul's Cathedral

St Paul's Churchyard
Tel: 020 7246 8348
Tube: St Paul's
www.stpauls.co.uk
Costs £6 for a guided tour

Destroyed in the Great Fire of London, Sir Christopher Wren was commissioned to rebuild the great cathedral in 1675. Its impressive dome dominates the skyline and the surrounding gardens are a great place to sit with a sandwich during your lunch hour. It's open for sightseeing Monday to Saturday but closed for services on Sundays.

Tower Bridge

Tel: 020 7403 3761
Tube: Tower Hill
www.towerbridge.org.uk
Admission: £6.50 (no charge just to walk across)

The famous bridge, built in 1894, offers amazing views from high walkways perched 140 feet above the Thames. You will have to pay an entrance fee to enter the exhibition section, but if you simply want to get your picture taken on the bridge, save yourself the money by walking along the South Bank and taking a photo from street level.

Tower of London

Tower Hill, EC3
Tel: 020 7709 0765
Tube: Tower Hill
www.hrp.org.uk
Admission: £11.50

The Tower of London was built 1078, and the stunning castle has been used over the years as a prison, palace, place of execution, and a showcase for the Crown Jewels. Today, it is one of London's most popular visitor attractions and you may have to wait about 20 minutes to see the infamous crown in the height of summer.

> The last execution in the Tower of London took place on Thursday, August 14, 1941, when Josef Jakobs, a German spy, was shot by an eight-man firing squad. Because he suffered a broken ankle when he parachuted into England on the night of 31 January 1941, he could not stand before the firing squad and was instead seated in an old Windsor chair and tied up. Five of the eight shots pierced his heart.

Westminster Abbey

Dean's Yard, SW1.
Tel: 020 7222 7110
Tube: Westminster
www.westminster-abbey.org
Admission: £6

Dating back to the eleventh century, this cathedral is one of Europe's finest Gothic buildings, and the scene of coronations, marriages and burials of many British monarchs. With the exception of Edward V and Edward VIII, every sovereign has been crowned here since William the Conqueror in 1066. Unsurprisingly then, Westminster Abbey is one of the most visited churches in history. Closed on Sundays for services.

Walking tours

Beatles Walks, £5 / £3.50. Tel: 020 7624 3978. www.walks.com

Jack the Ripper Mystery Walk, £5. Tel: 020 8558 9446. www.mysterywalks.co.uk

Sherlock Holmes Walk, £5. Tel: 020 7624 3978. www.walks.com

Riverside Pubs Walk, £5. Tel: 020 7624 3978. www.walks.com

Museums and galleries

British Museum
Great Russell Street, WC1
Tel: 020 7636 1555
Tube: Tottenham Court Road
www.thebritishmuseum.ac.uk
Admission: free

The best tip we have for visiting this vast museum is to do it on a few separate visits, otherwise you certainly won't get to see everything. Admission is free, so you can return as often as you like to visit the rooms you are most interested in. Don't miss the Egyptian mummies in rooms 62 and 63 on the upper floor.

London Transport Museum
Covent Garden Piazza, WC2
Tel: 020 7565 7299
Tube: Covent Garden
www.ltmuseum.co.uk
Admission: £5.95 (no entry fee for gift shop only)

If the story of the Tube fascinates you, this exhibition will teach you all you need to know about London's transportation system. This is the place to go if you'd like to pick up a 'Mind the Gap' T-shirt or pencil case for your little sister back home.

Museum of London
London Wall, EC2
Tel: 020 7600 3699
Tube: Barbican
www.museumoflondon.org.uk
Admission: free

Walk through the epochs that London progressed through from the Ice Age to modern day. This is one of the best museums for Londoners because you can chart out where you live on the maps and check whether prehistoric people used to bury their meat nearby. Fascinating.

National Gallery
Trafalgar Square, WC2
Tel: 020 7747 2885
Tube: Charing Cross
www.nationalgallery.org.uk
Admission: free

Attracting nearly 5 million visitors each year, it will be nearly impossible to avoid the tourists while taking in the display of 2,000 Western European paintings from the thirteenth century to 1900 – but don't let that put you off. This museum has one of the best collections in the world, so be sure to chart out a plan of attack before going in to make sure you visit the wings that are the most important to you. You can see works by da Vinci, Botticelli, Raphael, Michelangelo, Titian, Goya, Turner, Cézanne, and Velázquez, among others.

National Portrait Gallery

St Martin's Place, WC2
Tel: 020 7312 2463
Tube: Charing Cross or Leicester Square
www.npg.org.uk
Admission: free

The gallery houses a collection of some 9,000 pieces on five floors, including oil paintings, watercolors, charcoal drawings, sculptures and photographs. See works from Van Dyck, Hogarth, Joshua Reynolds, and photographs from Helmut Newton, among others.

Natural History Museum

Cromwell Road, SW7
Tel: 020 7942 5000
Tube: South Kensington
www.nhm.ac.uk
Admission: £7.50 / £4.50 concessions

A giant robotic T-Rex is one of the main attractions at this impressive museum, which has more than 68 million items on display. Learn about volcanoes, earthquakes, and peer at those creepy crawlies up close. This is as close to nature as it gets in London.

Photographer's Gallery

5 and 8 Great Newport Street, WC2
Tel: 020 7831 1772
Tube: Leicester Square
www.photonet.org.uk
Admission: free

Head here for some of the best contemporary photography exhibitions from world-class artists. There's also a bookshop and sales area to pick up those prints you've always wanted to get your hands on.

Tate Britain

Millbank, SW1
Tel: 020 7887 8000
Tube: Pimlico
www.tate.org.uk
Admission: free

The Tate Britain is nominally dedicated to ancient and

contemporary British Art, from 1500 to the present. Now that some works have been moved to the Tate Modern, this gallery is able to offer a lot more than previously possible. The short list of the prestigious and controversial Turner Prize is displayed at the gallery, as well as other constantly changing exhibitions. See works in the permanent collection by William Blake, Hogarth, Constable, Rossetti, Singer Sargent, Bacon, Gilbert and George, and Hockney.

Tate Modern

25 Sumner Street, SE1
Tel: 020 7887 8000
Tube: London Bridge or Waterloo
www.tate.org.uk
Admission: free; some exhibitions £3–£10

Here you will be treated to some of the best Dali, Picasso, Matisse and Warhol originals spanning from 1900 to the present day. Housed in the former Bankside Power Station, the immense brick building is in itself a breathtaking sight.

Strange Museums

Bethnal Green Museum of Childhood, Cambridge Heath Road, E2. Tel: 020 8980 2415. Tube: Bethnal Green. Closed Fridays. www.museumofchildhood.org.uk

Clink Prison Museum, 1 Clink Street, Bankside, SE1. Tel: 020 7403 6515. Tube: London Bridge

Dickens House Museum, 48 Doughty Street, WC1. Tel: 020 7405 2127. Tube: Russell Square

Elvisly Yours, 223 Baker Street, NW1. Tel: 020 7486 2005. Tube: Baker Street. More of a shop than a museum, but where else can you get Elvis music all day long and heaps of memorabilia?

The Old Operating Theatre and Herb Garrett, 9a St Thomas's Street, SE1. Tel: 020 7955 4791. Tube: London Bridge. www.thegarret.org.uk

Pollock's Toy Museum, 1 Scala Street, W1. Tel: 020 7636 3452. Tube: Goodge Street. www.pollocksweb.co.uk

Vinopolis: The City of Wine, 1 Bank End, SE1. Tel: 0870 241 4040. Tube: London Bridge. Find all things vino-related. Admission: £11.50

Zandra Rhodes' Fashion and Textile Museum, 83 Bermondsey Street, SE1. Tel: 020 7403 0222. Tube: London Bridge. www.ftmlondon.org

Outdoor London

Hampstead Heath

Tube: Hampstead

This 790-acre plot of woodland, hills and meadows is home to a surprising abundance of wildlife, including more than 100 bird species. Some sections of the heath are laid out as sports fields, while acres of roaming forest – perfect for walking and exploring – lie untouched. The park also has several ponds for swimming, and an excellent lookout point on Parliament Hill.

Hyde Park

Tube: Hyde Park Corner

First opened to the public by King James I, this park has a history of hangings, duels and was host to the Great Exhibition of 1851. Each Sunday, Speaker's Corner moves into Hyde Park for an afternoon of screaming matches. Hecklers, religious extremists, and proper loony bins gather here to stand on proverbial soapboxes and speak their mind to whoever passes by.

London Zoo

Regent's Park, NW1

Tel: 020 7722 3333

Tube: Baker Street or Camden Town

www.londonzoo.co.uk

Admission: £11

It's funny how lethargic sloths, fidgety marmosets, and cowarding lizards can remind you of some of the people you've met during your travels. Home to 12,000 animals, you can spend all day here wandering from the aquarium to the elephant house, penguin pool and the new Web of Life exhibition.

Royal Botanic Gardens of Kew

Richmond, Surrey

Tel: 020 8332 5000

Tube: Kew Gardens

Admission: £5

Have a civilized afternoon perusing the gardens of this 300-acre plot with over 40,000 varieties of plants. The Palm House is world famous and has a delightful collection of tropical, alpine and temperate plants. This is a great place to take your mom when she's in town.

221b Baker Street was the fictional home, between 1881 and 1904, of the world's most famous detective, Sherlock Holmes, and his companion Dr Watson. The house, which played an important illusionary role in the novels by Sir Arthur Conan Doyle, was built in 1815 and was used as a lodging house until 1936. The study on the first floor remains as it was then and is open to the public. Elementary.

Sherlock Holmes Museum, 239 Baker Street, NW1. Tel: 020 7935 8866 Tube: Baker Street. The museum is housed on the four levels of a Georgian townhouse and is recreated to specifications described in the books. Admission: £6

Tourist traps

London Aquarium

County Hall, Westminster Bridge Road, SE1
Tel: 020 7967 8000
Tube: Westminster or Waterloo
www.londonaquarium.co.uk
Admission: £8.50 / £6.50 concessions
Visit the massive shark tank and watch the piranha attack during fishing time if you've got a macabre taste for blood. For the non-psychopathic, go coo at the seahorses.

London Dungeon

28–34 Tooley Street, SE1
Tel: 020 7403 7221
Tube: London Bridge
www.thedungeons.com
Admission: £10.95
Listen to Henry VIII's wife Anne Boleyn scream as her head is axed off, relive Thomas Becket's murder, and brace yourself for the scary man in dark robes to jump out of the corner and scream in your face. Prepare to endure long queues in July and August.

London Trocadero

1 Piccadilly Circus, W1
Tel: 09068 881 100
Tube: Piccadilly Circus
www.troc.co.uk
Admission: free, pay extra for games and rides
Overpriced rides, high-tech games and enough car simulators to remind you of how you screwed up parking in your driving test.

Madame Tussaud's

Marylebone Road
Tel: 0870 400 3000
Tube: Baker Street
www.madame-tussauds.com
Admission: £14.95

The one thing your photo album is missing is some tacky photos of you chumming it up with David Beckham and the Beatles. If you aren't cool enough to meet them in the flesh, then head here – where you can stand next to a wax replica and pretend it's the real thing. Only they don't move. And they're made of wax.

Free stuff

You can't visit London without seeing for yourself the legendary Changing of the Guard procession. Afterwards, you'll probably be wondering what all the fuss was about, but at least you can tell your friends back home that you saw it. The ceremony takes place outside Buckingham Palace at 11.30 a.m. daily, at which time the old guard – decked out in the legendary bright red uniforms and bearskin hats – comes off duty to be replaced by the new guard.

Take a walk on a sunny day along the Thames-side footpath in the South Bank leading from Waterloo rail station towards London Bridge. Stop to take a look at the used books on offer at the stalls or sit down at an outdoor table for a pint in Gabriel's Wharf.

Hold up traffic while sauntering across the zebra crossing at Abbey Road Studios. It's absolutely legendary, and you know you want to do it. Go to 3 Abbey Road, NW8. Tube: St Johns Wood.

Day trips from London

When the fast pace of city life starts to catch up to you, there is no better way to escape than to hop on the next train to the countryside. Nearby are a number of must-see historical sights and attractions that not only draw tourists from all over the world, but also Londoners looking to unwind after a hectic week. On a sunny day, head down to the south-east coast of England to lie on a pebbled beach or take in the summer nightlife. For a spot of culture, hop over to Canterbury, Oxford, Bath or Cambridge. Contact National Rail on 08457 48 49 50 for train times and prices or travel by coach with National Express by calling 08705 80 80 80.

Brighton

A hedonist's paradise, Brighton is the place to be for soaking in the sun on its pebbled beach, gambling for 10p coins on the pier, and living large in its raging nightclubs. Popular due to its seafront,

Brighton was also the scene of the notorious battle between Mods and Rockers, as immortalized in the film Quadrophenia. Today, it is home to big-time DJ Fatboy Slim who is amongst the dozens of famous spinners who head to the seaside town to grace its nightclubs.

Brighton is about 50 miles from London and is easily reachable by road and rail. Trains leave frequently from Victoria station and the journey takes about one hour. Contact the Brighton and Hove Tourist board on 09067 112 255 or see www.visitbrighton.com for tourist information.

Canterbury

This ancient cathedral town, which is the home of the Church of England, has been attracting adoring visitors since pilgrimage began in the twelfth century. It all started with the murder of Britain's famous archbishop, Thomas Becket, who was stabbed by four crazed knights in 1170 while praying in Canterbury's renowned cathedral. This time in history has been immortalized forever thanks to Geoffrey Chaucer and his much-read collection of stories, *The Canterbury Tales*. Loved by English teachers around the world, this book was based on the lives of 24 pilgrims who entertained themselves by telling stories while on their way to visit the tomb. Today, the downtown area is a mecca of timber-framed houses roofed in the traditional Kent-style clay tiles and magnificent flint churches keeping in tune with its medieval flavor.

Canterbury is located in the southeast of England and travel time is about one hour by train from Victoria station. Contact the South East England Tourist Board on 01892 540 766 or see www.seetb.org.uk for further details.

Oxford

Most famously known for its university, Oxford is actually made up of dozens of spectacular colleges, halls and courtyards. Settlement in Oxford began in the early eighth century along the tranquil riverside and today its economy mainly relies on tourism and its university population. If you plan on visiting, be sure to go during term-time if you want a glimpse at what student life is like. This may sound obvious, but during the summer months, Oxford tends to be home to little else other than tourists.

This famous city is located one hour from London by train from Paddington rail station. Coaches are also available from Victoria Coach Station. Call the Oxford Tourist Information Centre at 01865 726 871 or go to www.visitoxford.org to learn more.

Cambridge

This university town is thankfully less touristy than Oxford and shows how student life has been in England for the past 700 years. King's College Chapel swarms with thousands of students frantically rushing off to lectures or heading down to the River Cam for a lazy sunny afternoon. And just outside of the city is some of the most relaxing and unspoilt countryside in England, home to peaceful villages and riverside pubs.

Get there by train from King's Cross or Liverpool Street stations. The journey takes just over an hour. Coaches are also available from Victoria Coach Station. For further details, contact Tourism Cambridge on 01223 322 640 or see www.tourismcambridge.com.

Bath

Viewed throughout the ages as being an ideal place to retreat from the rigors of London life, Bath is home to the famous hot spring Roman baths, a showcase of ancient buildings constructed of the typical honey-colored stone, and countless Georgian squares, crescents and terraced houses. If you head here on a sunny day, be sure to hire a canoe or rowboat to cruise down its lush canals. Relax, soak up the history, and take the legendary ghost walk for a spine-tingling thrill.

The train from London Paddington takes 1½ hours, or take the coach for a more leisurely (and cheaper) journey. Contact the Bath Tourist Information Centre on 01225 477 101 or go to www.visitbath.co.uk.

> The British royal family changed their surname from Saxe-Coburg-Gotha to Windsor in 1917. George V was king of England from 1910 to 1936. Son of Edward VII, King of England, and Princess Alexandra of Denmark, he married Queen Mary of Teck in 1893. World War I broke out in 1914 and was in full rage in 1917. In protest, King George V renounced all the German titles belonging to him and his family and adopted the name Windsor, after that of his castle.

Windsor Castle

High Street, Windsor
Tel: 01753 831 118
Entrance: £11.50

London became the Royal capital of Great Britain in 1066 when William the Conqueror used Westminster Abbey for his coronation during the same year. At that time, the king chose to build a castle at Windsor to defend the capital's western approach. Today, visitors marvel at the architecture of Windsor Castle and its lavishly furnished State Apartments. It was here where Prince Edward and Sophie Rhys-Jones were married in June 1999.

Catch the train from Waterloo to Windsor Riverside to see it for yourself. The journey takes one hour. For further information, see www.royalresidences.com.

Leeds Castle

Maidstone, Kent
Tel: 01622 765 400
Admission: £10

Perched on two small islands in a lake surrounded by wooded hills, this impressive castle is not only visually stimulating, but its illustrious past includes being a Norman stronghold, a royal residence for six of England's medieval queens, and a palace of Henry VII. Firework displays here during the summer are absolutely spectacular and worth the journey out of London.

For an up-to-date listings of events or further information, check out the website at www.leeds-castle.com

PART TWO

ENTERTAINMENT

Chapter One:

Clubbing

Looking back on those first forays into clubland back in my hometown, it is hilarious to think that my idea of hitting the town involved downing cheap tequilas in a tacky dive named The Kats Klub. Reeking of vomit, strong cologne, and cheap local cigarettes, I willingly strutted the two-step to AC/DC on the beer-stained floor, thinking that must be what clubbing is all about.

When the time came to venture on into the nearby city, suddenly there were a dozen clubs to choose from, and the clubbing world appeared to be as vast and uncharted as Antarctica.

And then there was London. Home to at least one nightclub at every Tube stop, a game of Russian roulette could find you sitting next to Mussolini's greatest modern day supporter. Worse, you could find yourself stumbling into a glitzy celebrity party, wearing a mud-caked pair of trainers and a stained T-shirt not even fit for a hobo. It happens.

Having jiggled and diva'd my way throughout the best and worst of London's nightclubs over the years, I've put together a list of the top ones you should certainly try, and a few others you will probably be led into at one point or another.

Since the birth of acid house and the rise of dance music in the early 90s, Britain has been at the forefront of rave and club culture. Whether you are into house music, breakbeat, hip-hop, drum 'n' bass or garage, there are countless numbers of clubs catering to your musical and lifestyle tastes.

As a basic guideline, if you are into Fatboy Slim, Chemical Brothers or Underworld, go to clubs that play breaks or big beat. Similarly, progressive house DJs like Sasha or John Digweed may also be your style.

On the other hand, if Ministry of Sound compilations or happy dance tracks that you can sing to are what you like, go to a club that plays house or funky beats.

For those of you who are looking for a full-on, glowsticks-and-whistles warehouse rave-style party, hard house and trance should get you gurning.

Get down and dirty with some moody drum 'n' bass, jungle, or UK garage music, which is a mixture of rap and R&B with a repetitive bassline.

As you can see, the London club scene is as colorful and varied as a Balinesian seafood platter. From exclusive hideaway dancing dens to 4,000-capacity multi-level nightclubs, there are clubs that suit all tastes.

When it comes to choosing your club for the evening, be sure to check whether the club has a dress code. Most house clubs, for example, require that men wear nice shoes (no trainers) and shirts, while women should dress up in skirts or sexy partywear. On the other hand, clubs that play breakbeat, hip hop or progressive house will have a more relaxed dress code, so you will certainly feel more comfortable in a pair of Diesel jeans than a miniskirt.

Keep your eye on magazines like *Time Out*, the *Evening Standard*'s *Hot Tickets*, or the *Guardian*'s Saturday *Guide*, for their weekly club listings. Also, a good London clubbing e-zine to keep your eye on is www.burnitblue.com.

Think you might be the next Paul Oakenfold, but haven't got a clue how to mix, scratch or even turn on a set of decks? Time for a lesson in DJing.
Point-Blank, 23–28 Penn Street, N1. Tel: 020 7729 4884. Tube: Angel.

Top Clubs

Cargo

Kingsland Viaduct, 83 Rivington Street, EC2
Tel: 020 7739 3440
Tube: Old Street
Open noon–1 a.m., costs £5–£8
www.cargo-london.com

A playground for your Shoreditch artsy types, afrocentrics, 45-year-old mullet-chopped club throwbacks and spotty Playstation addicts. An eclectic mix of people for a harmonious blend of music. Mixing up experimental beats, rare grooves and world music, Cargo has a bit of something for everyone. One of the newest clubs on the scene and certainly one of the best.

Egg

5-13 Vale Royal, off York Way, King's Cross, N1
Tel: 020 7428 7574
Tube: Kings Cross
Open weekends
www.egglondon.net

Not only does this impossibly hip venue host the dazzling electro-clash new wave night Nag Nag Nag, but it also doubles up as a live music venue. Simply one of the hottest clubs in town, this three-story Victorian warehouse sends the cognoscenti drooling into their Asahi lager. Head here for Sean McClusky's Sonic Mook Experiment and club nights programmed by the multi-talented DJ Andrew Weatherall.

Fabric

Charterhouse Street, EC1
Tel: 020 7336 8898
Tube: Farringdon
Open 10 p.m.–6 a.m., costs £12–£15
www.fabric-london.com

Although its heydey may have dipped somewhat in the past two years, this subterranean drinking cave (which was once a nineteenth century meat cellar) continues to enlist podium-cracking lineups, including The Chemical Brothers, Adam Freeland and Sasha. Fabric opened in 1999 and immediately became the place to be, judging by the four-hour queues it attracted of impatient ravers tottering in high heels and skimpy clothing. Today, Fabric continues to recruit world-class acts that never fail to please the masses.

The Key & Canvas

Goods Way, Kings Cross, N1
Tel: 020 7833 8301
Tube: Kings Cross
Open every Friday and Saturday night

Bye, bye Bagleys Warehouse. May you rot in the stale depths of rundown clubbing hell. Okay, so the interior of this old warehouse was about as charmless as a wet fart from the Queen's bum, but now clubbers have a reason to return. New owners have pumped £35 million into refurbishing this new venue into Canvas, conceived as a space that will provide a blank canvas for theatre, art, live music, clubbing and multimedia events. Downstairs is a 400-capacity Key venue for fans of indie, hip-hop, house and funk.

333

333 Old Street, EC1
Tel: 020 7739 5949
Tube: Old Street
Open 10 p.m.–5 a.m., costs £5–£10

Picture a dancefloor packed to the hilt with an intimate crowd of fashionable, street-smart types getting down to a brazen mash of funky trax without giving a toss about messing up their hair. Taking an anti-superclubbing stance, this non-commercialized venue caters to an up-for-it crowd just looking to have a good dance with likewise people. Head to Off Centre for a blend of jazz house and hip hop or Mènage a Trois for some hedonistic beats and breaks. Unbeatable.

Turnmills

121 Clerkenwell Road, EC1
Tel: 020 7250 3409
Tube: Farringdon
Open 11 p.m.–5 a.m., costs £5–£12
www.turnmills.co.uk

Stepping down the stairs into this underground abyss is like stumbling upon Batman's hideaway lair. Beneath the shaking cobblestones, you become part of a secret world, dissected by rainbow stabs of lasers and hugging packs of strangers. For a spot of dancefloor mayhem, go to the Gallery on Friday nights, as long as you don't miss its blinding Saturday nights. And for those of you who can stick it out, Turnmill's famous gay club night, Trade, kicks off at 5 a.m. on Sunday morning. Five stars.

The End

West Central Street, WC1
Tel: 020 7419 9199
Tube: Tottenham Court Road or Holborn
Open 11 p.m.–5 a.m., costs £8–£10
www.the-end.co.uk

This purpose-built club, slotted into the converted vault of a nineteenth-century post office, is full of the kind of people you want to make friends with. Its relaxed door policy, retro-cool crowd and good sound system make this club one of the best in London. The music sways heavily towards techno, breakbeat, drum 'n' bass and UK garage, so trance-heads will want to steer clear.

Heaven

Charing Cross Arches, Villiers Street, WC2
Tel: 020 7930 2020
Tube: Embankment or Charing Cross
Open 10 p.m.–5 a.m., costs £6–£12
www.heaven-london.com

Made up of a myriad of dance floors and hideaway bars, this venue has received international recognition as being one of the world's top gay clubs. Home to John Digweed's massive progressive house night on Thursdays, Bedrock attracts a mèlange of students, music industry types and open-minded 20-somethings. It is also the new venue to the storming Big Beat Boutique versus Bugged Out! night.

Ministry of Sound

Gaunt Street, SE1
Tel: 020 7378 6528
Tube: Elephant & Castle
Open 11 p.m.–8 a.m., costs £12–£15
www.ministry.co.uk

You've read the magazine, bought the T-shirt, and listened to the compilation CDs. Since 1991, when the club opened with much-trumpeted fuss, the brand has gone global and the nightclub has forged its way into every travel guide to London. The Ministry has now become an older brother to a host of new superclubs, but the atmosphere is still electric. Saturday's Rulin' serves up a sublime mix of house and garage, while Smoove delivers slick garage tracks in UK style.

93 Feet East

Brick Lane, E1
Tel: 020 7247 3293
Tube: Liverpool Street
Open 8 p.m.–2 a.m., costs £5–£10
www.93feeteast.co.uk

It may not have the exposed-brick-and-silver-pipe theme that seems to typify most London clubs, but this school hall-like venue can really kick. Free of the pretention and commercialism of British superclubs, 93 Feet East has an experimental style of its own. Set in Brick Lane, it is populated by an older and less fashion-conscious type than nearby Cargo and Herbal, playing host to the storming Haywire Sessions nights featuring Andrew Weatherall.

The Cross

Goods Way Depot, York Way, N1
Tel: 020 7837 0828
Tube: Kings Cross
Open 10.30 p.m.–6 a.m., costs £10–£15.
www.the-cross.co.uk

The second home to hedonistic creatures, this decadent venue – complete with an outdoor courtyard, comfy sofas and fairy-lights – packs 'em in under three arches for Renaissance, its house party extravaganza night, and hard house nights Serious and Fiction.

24-hour restaurants

Hungry? It's 3 a.m. and your stomach won't stop rumbling. Don't stop for a dodgy kebab, try one of these: **Tinseltown**, 44–46 St John Street, EC1. Tel: 020 7689 2424. Tube: Farringdon. Milkshakes, burgers and comfort food.

Brick Lane Beigel Bake, 159 Brick Lane, E1. Tel: 020 7729 0616. Tube: Aldgate East or Liverpool Street. Fresh bagels for mere pennies.

Café Boheme, 13–17 Old Compton Street, W1. Tel: 020 7734 0623. Tube: Leicester Square. Food and people-watching 24 hours on the weekends.

Old Compton Café, 34 Old Compton Street, W1. Tel: 020 7439 3309. Tube: Leicester Square. Grab a sandwich and watch the drunks stumble around looking for a taxi.

Bar Italia, 22 Frith Street, W1. Tel: 020 7437 4520. Tube: Leicester Square. Well-known round the clock grub.

Other goodies to try

Bridge 'n' Tunnel

4 Calvert Avenue, E2
Tel: 020 7739 5451
Tube: Old Street
Open 7 p.m.–12 a.m., costs up to £3

This two-floor DJ bar and restaurant is creating quite a stir since opening its doors in 2002, raking in globally-famous DJs including Groove Armada, Fatboy Slim and Andrew Weatherall. Get it while it's hot.

CherryJam

58 Porchester Road, W2
Tel: 020 7727 9950
Tube: Royal Oak
Open 6 p.m.–2 a.m., costs £5–£8, free before 8 p.m.
www.cherryjam.net
Disco-flavored shenanigans and deep house for a groovy crowd.
Take in the art exhibitions while you're at it.

Herbal

12–14 Kingsland Road, E2
Tel: 020 7613 4462
Tube: Old Street
Open 7.30 p.m.–2 a.m., costs £3–£5
www.herbaluk.com
Listen to DJs in the upstairs New York-esque relaxed bar then move
downstairs for a dance to anything from house and funky beats to
electronica. You'll know you're at Herbal when you see the fake
grass strapped to the outside of this otherwise unassuming building.

Pacha

Terminus Place, SW1
Tel: 020 7834 4440
Tube: Victoria
Open 10 p.m.–5 a.m., costs £15–£20
www.pachalondon.com
Hailing from its mothership in Ibiza, London's newest superclub
delivers a mish-mash of funky house and sexy beats. But the
novelty does not come cheap.

The Fridge

1 Town Hall Parade, Brixton Hill, SW2
Tel: 020 7326 5100
Tube: Brixton
Open 10 p.m.–6 a.m., costs £8–£12
Notorious for its popular gay nights and psychedelic trance events
like Escape from Samsara. Heavy on uplifting house, trance and
hard house.

Dogstar

389 Coldharbour Lane, SW9
Tel: 020 7733 7515
Tube: Brixton
Open 9 p.m.–4 a.m., costs £4–£6, free before 10 p.m.
www.dogstarbar.com
More like a late bar, but with a mental crowd and nightly DJ
sessions specialising in breaks and house.

Mass

St Matthew's Church, Brixton Hill, SW2
Tel: 020 7737 7616
Tube: Brixton
Open 10 p.m.–6 a.m., costs £8–£10
For regular knees-up events of heavenly proportions, including breakbeat, hip hop and house nights. Freakily, the club is housed in an old crypt. Blaspheme at your peril.

Scala

Pentonville Road, N1
Tel: 020 7833 2022
Tube: Kings Cross
Open 10 p.m.–5 a.m., costs £5–10
www.scala-london.co.uk
For that intravenous dose of deep house or breaks with a laid-back crowd without the large superclub mentality. Some good ol' back-to-basics anti-commercial fun.

Madame JoJo's

Brewer Street, W1
Tel: 020 7734 3040
Tube: Piccadilly Circus
Open 9 p.m.–3 a.m., costs £5
Well-heeled professionals meld with students, Dieselites and could-be fashion models at this unpretentious late bar/club/theatre for a spot of deep funk.

Meanfiddler

165 Charing Cross Road, WC2
Tel: 020 7344 0044
Tube: Tottenham Court Road
www.meanfiddler.com
Opening times and prices vary
Its decor may look slightly dated, but this venue hosts many notorious gigs and popular club nights.

The Velvet Room

143 Charing Cross Road, WC2
Tel: 020 7734 4687
Tube: Tottenham Court Road
Open 10 p.m.–4 a.m., costs £6–£10
Recreating the intimate vibe of a house party with its attitude-free crowd, lush interior and small dancefloor. Promises quality house sessions.

Camden Palace

1a Camden High Street, NW2
Tel: 09062 100 200
Tube: Camden Town

Open 10 p.m.–6 a.m., costs £10–£15

Neon glowsticks, horns and whistles come out in full force for this hedonistic clubber's haven. Cranks up the hard house and trance.

Hanover Grand

Hanover Street, W1
Tel: 020 7499 7977
Tube: Oxford Circus
Open 10 p.m.–late, costs £12

A glamorous setting for the well heeled and silver polished. Dress up and be prepared to pose.

Tattoo parlors

If your flesh is in need of inking, check out www.tattoo.co.uk or try these top tattoo parlors:

Into You, 144 St John Street, EC1. Tel: 020 7253 5085

Evil from the Needle, 232 Camden High Street, NW1. Tel: 020 7482 2412

Liquid Art, Old Brompton Road, SW5. Tel: 020 7373 0047

Creative Hand, 37 Camden High Street, NW1. Tel: 020 7387 3253

Diamond Jacks, 5 Walkers Court, Soho W1. Tel: 020 7437 0605

Club nights

In addition to the nightclubs listed previously, there are countless independently-promoted club nights that often float between clubs. Below is a list of some of the most popular – and unique – nights on offer. Check your weekly club listings guides to find out where and when they will be running.

Nag Nag Nag

Simply one of the coolest club nights in London, boasting queues around the block and a formidable door-picker. It's bisexual, heavily ironic and achingly cool, as the many lingering celebrities and new wave trendies will tell you. The party normally takes place at The Egg, a futuristic new venue on York Way. Email: contact@nagnagnag for details.

Carwash

A seventies to noughties funky disco party with soul and breaks and other groovy tunes. Dress up disco diva or risk not getting in. Tel: 020 7287 1010 or see www.carwash.co.uk

School Disco

Relive those teeny-bopper fantasies of snogging your classmate by dusting off those school uniforms and dancing to your favorite cheesy tunes. Tel: 020 8699 9983 or see www.schooldisco.com

Big Beat Boutique versus Bugged Out!

Guaranteed to be one of your best nights out in clubbing history. Previous guests have included Fatboy Slim, The Chemical Brothers and Adam Freeland. Likely to either be running at Fabric or Heaven, so check the websites for both nightclubs for further details.

Bedrock

A serious night for the discerning clubber. The monthly DJ list looks like the track listing of a compilation CD, with top names like Sasha, Digweed, Danny Tenaglia and Darren Emerson all wanting to play here. Tel: 020 7930 2020 or see www.bedrock.org.uk

Torture Garden

Take an erotic adventure into the S&M world of PVC, whips, leashes and chains. The dress code is fantasy, fetish and cyber, so don't be turning up in a pair of jeans – unless they're crotchless. Lather up with sex, and splash about in a puddle of drum 'n' bass, ska, nu-skool breaks, hard house and sleazy rock 'n roll. See it for yourself at www.torturegarden.com

Return to the Source

Neon props, lasers and tribal art set the scene for these fantastically adorned psychedelic trance and acid techno parties. It's swarming with a mixture of dreadlocked hippies and wide-eyed Aussies. Tel: 020 7346 8488 or see www.rtts.com

Worldwide Live

Sunday night extravaganza spinning experimental beats and rare grooves, some *Boogie Nights*-style 70s porn music, smooth grooves with jazzy beats. A good way to wind up the weekend. See www.cargo-london.com

Serious

Dive into a full-on hedonistic night of sexy music, sinful people and one seriously shaking dancefloor. With Judge Jules usually headlining the show, you are guaranteed an extra-sweet broth of deep progressive house. Sure to be a sweaty, down and dirty, packed-to-the-hilt night. Tel: 020 7837 0828 or see www.the-cross.co.uk

Haywire Sessions

Andrew Weatherall hits the decks, spinning some irresistible sessions of what he refers to as "the sound of deep mentality". The Haywire Sessions began at 93 Feet East in early 2001, marking the spinmeister's first London residency since the mid-90s. See www.haywire.co.uk

KHz
Serving up a tasty platter of progressive beats and breaks to a crowd boasting a high hip quotient. Likely to play at The End. (www.the-end.co.uk)

Fevah
Prepare to drown in a sea of horns and neon glow sticks because this is guaranteed to be one lunatic hard house and trance party that will carry on until kick-out time. These times call for Red Bull. See www.fevah.co.uk.

Elements
Get down and dirty with some deep and filthy progressive house with a splash of tribal flavor. See www.elementslondon.com.

Keep it Unreal
Featuring marathon vinyl sets from Manchester wunderboy Mr Scruff. Tunes progress from jazzy house to hip hop and skipping about with heavy electro. Go to www.mrscruff.com to see it for yourself.

Dance albums and vinyl shops:

Selectadisc, 34 Berwick Street, W1. Tel: 020 7734 3297. Tube: Tottenham Court Road.

Black Market Records, 25 D'Arblay Street, W1. Tel: 020 7287 1932. Tube: Oxford Circus.

MSM, 17 Chalk Farm Road, NW1. Tel: 020 7284 2527. Tube: Camden Town.

Disque Records, 11 Chapel Market, N1. Tel: 020 7833 1104. Tube: Angel.

Small Fish Records, 372 Curtain Road, EC1. Tel: 020 7739 2252. Tube: Old Street.

Gay club nights

DTPM, Fabric, 77a Charterhouse Street, Clerkenwell, EC1. Tel: 020 7439 9009 or see www.dtpm.net Tube: Farringdon. A Sunday night hard house affair blowing the doors off with a bit of soul and R&B in the chill-out room.

G-A-Y, Astoria and LA2, 157 Charing Cross Road, Soho, WC2. Tel: 020 7734 6963. Tube: Tottenham Court Road. Feel free to dress up in drag, shake your sweet thang, and get ready for some hardcore action. This is one of London's biggest gay parties.

Heaven, The Arches, Villiers Street, Charing Cross, WC2. Tel: 020 7930 2020 or see www.heaven-london.com Tube: Embankment or Charing Cross. Three floors of tri-sexual fun with a mixture of house, pop and techno music.

Trade, Turnmills, 63 Clerkenwell Road, Clerkenwell, EC1. Tel: 020 7700 5352 or see www.tradeuk.net Tube: Farringdon. Known around the world for its up-for-it crowd of muscle boys and hard house. Gets going at 5 a.m. Sunday morning, so it's not for the lazy or faint-hearted.

London clubbing websites:

www.burnitblue.com

www.spaced.co.uk

www.jockeyslut.com

www.trustthedj.com

www.bbc.co.uk/radio1/dance

Clubbing isn't always about gurning to banging dance music

Virginia Creepers

If rockabilly music is your underground scene, then one of the best nights in London is Virginia Creepers held every first Saturday of the month at the Water Rats, Islington. Live bands and retro DJs get the minxy sex-kittens and kitsch rock n' roll greasers sweating on the dance floor. See www.virginiacreepersclub.com for details. Start growing that quiff, this nights a swingin'.

Coast to Coast

Coast to Coast keeps the spirit of the swinging sixties alive with rare ska, reggae, motown, boogaloo, and northern soul. This unique club night in Shoreditch attracts a cult following, from throwback teddy boys pulling off moves in talc on the floor, to mini skirted mod birds and local trendy Hoxton-ites. For details of the next bi-monthly event, see www.coasttocoast.org.uk.

Club Montepulciano

Kitsch as a plastic-flower adorned shower cap, Club Montepulciano is all about retro glamour and tongue-in-cheek sophistication. For the most over-the-top lounge and cabaret night in London, check out www.clubmontepulciano.com and see what the next themed event will be. Cruise Trip? Hawaii Five-o? Bond? Whatever the night, make sure you dress outrageously for it – or you won't be getting in.

Chapter Two:
Live Music Venues

From the first time the Sex Pistols thrashed on the stage at the 100 Club, to the Brit Pop heyday of Oasis and Blur, London has always been the place to be for major bands. Camden and Islington are the best places to check out gigs from up and coming groups, but if it's Madonna or Radiohead you are hoping to see, chances are that you will be heading to larger venues like Earls Court exhibition center or Brixton Academy. Check the weekly listings guides for updated gig information.

Astoria

157 Charing Cross Road, WC2
Tel: 0207 434 0403
Tube: Tottenham Court Road or Leicester Square
Huddling precariously amongst seedy sex shops and tacky tourist stalls, this London landmark is one of the main venues for clubs and gigs, having some of the world's most photographed musicians gracing its stage.

Brixton Academy

211 Stockwell Road, SW9
Tel: 020 7771 3000
Tube: Brixton
www.brixton-academy.co.uk
Everyone from the Rolling Stones and The Clash to Underworld and The Chemical Brothers has played here. Today, the 1930s art deco building is the scene to many all-nighter trance parties as well as world-class live gigs.

Shepherd's Bush Empire

Shepherd's Bush Green, W12
Tel: 020 8354 3300
Tube: Shepherd's Bush
www.shepherds-bush-empire.co.uk
Opened in 1903, this glamorous old building saw its heyday in the 60s, when everyone from the Beatles to Lulu appeared there. Today, it is still going strong, roping in some of the world's biggest bands.

Earls Court Exhibition Centre

Warwick Road, Earls Court, SW5
Tel: 020 7385 1200.
Tube: Earls Court
If you've always wanted to see Radiohead or Oasis playing in a cozy, intimate venue, you'd better be prepared to wait until your pension plan kicks in. All the best acts hit the stage in this massive auditorium monstrosity, which can pack in 40,000 people under one roof. As you would expect, tickets for shows can cost the equivalent of putting a down payment on a new house, but at least you'll be rocking out to one of the biggest musical acts of your generation.

Forum

9–17 Highgate Road, Kentish Town, NW5
Tel: 020 7284 1001
Tube: Kentish Town
A mid-sized venue with a great atmosphere, good crowds, and class-A bands. Go to www.meanfiddler.com for the latest gig information.

London Arena

Limeharbour, Isle of Dogs, E14
Tel: 020 7538 1212
Tube: Crossharbour DLR
www.londonarena.co.uk
Poor acoustics, a massive seating space, and more kids wearing Limp Bizkit T-shirts than you can handle – this is another musical monster for hosting gigs that are sure to fill the 10,000-seat capacity.

Wembley Arena

Empire Way, Wembley, Middlesex
Tel: 020 8902 0902
Tube: Wembley Park
Another big venue with crappy acoustics. Say no more. But there's not a whole lot you can do about it, especially if it's Radiohead or Robbie Williams that you want to see. Bring your binoculars or prepare for a flea-circus.

In 1985, Wembley Stadium hosted Live Aid, a hugely successful concert organized by Bob Geldof to help victims of the famine in Ethiopia. The concert was a worldwide effort with bands and singers playing in countries all over the world to raise money for the cause. More than 1.4 billion people in 170 countries around the world watched the concert on television. Huge stars such as Spandau Ballet, Sting, Phil Collins, U2, Queen, The Who, Elton John, David Bowie and Paul McCartney came together for the London leg of the concert. Live Aid raised over $100 million worldwide.

The concert was a follow up to Band Aid, the name given to the group of famous singers who all got together to record "Do They Know it's Christmas/Feed the World" in 1984. Geldof hoped that this would raise £72,000 for Ethiopian famine relief, but the single surpassed this sum and went on to raise over £8 million worldwide.

For his selfless efforts Bob Geldof was given an honorary knighthood in 1986.

Ocean

270 Mare Street, Hackney, E8
Tel: 020 8986 5336
Rail: Hackney Central, or see website for the numerous bus routes.
www.ocean.org.uk
This £23 million purpose-built contemporary music venue has three performance stages, including a main stage with a 2,100-capacity, good air circulation, decent bar prices, and a fantastic sound system. It plays host to everything from jazz and soul to rock concerts or poetry readings.

> In the early 1960s, journalist William F. Buckley, Jr wrote the following about the Fab Four: "The Beatles are not merely awful, I would consider it sacrilegious to say anything less than that they are godawful ... They are so unbelievably horrible, so appallingly unmusical, so dogmatically insensitive to the magic of the art, that they qualify as crowned heads of anti-music." Regret is a terrible thing ...

Others to try

Borderline

Orange Yard, Manette Street, W1
Tel: 020 7734 2096
Tube: Tottenham Court Road
www.borderline.co.uk
Blur, Pulp, Oasis, Pearl Jam, PJ Harvey, REM. Not a bad list for a venue that has just barely been around for more than a decade. With a capacity of only 275, you'll be sure to see the blood, sweat and tears. The last time I was at the Borderline, I saw a band whose bass player had his arm in a plaster cast. Now that's dedication.

100 Club

100 Oxford Street, W1
Tel: 020 7636 0933
Tube: Oxford Circus
www.the100club.co.uk
When they say that they've had some of the biggest talent over the years, they're not kidding. The Sex Pistols, Muddy Waters, The Clash, Travis, The White Stripes, Nico, the Rolling Stones, Paul Weller. It's exhausting just thinking about it.

Union Chapel

Compton Terrace, N1
Tel: 020 7226 1686
Tube: Highbury & Islington
www.unionchapel.org.uk

Set in a grade II listed Victorian building, this working chapel still holds church services, but also hires out rooms for concerts and events. Major artists are now playing at this gorgeous venue, and you can hire out a room for parties, exhibits and shows. Stunning. Keep an eye on their website, they've got some great musicians scheduled.

> More than 2,500 cover versions of The Beatles' "Yesterday" exist, making it the most recorded song in history.

The Monarch

49 Chalk Farm Road, NW1
Tel: 020 7916 1049
Tube: Camden Town or Chalk Farm

Dig out your finest mod garments and head to Casino Royale on Friday nights, playing a mixture of retro tunes from the 60s to modern floorshakers. Or head upstairs to check out some live gigs by up-and-coming bands.

12 Bar Club

Denmark Place, Denmark Street, WC2
Tel: 020 7916 6989
Tube: Tottenham Court Road or Leicester Square

With live music every night of the week, ranging from acoustic and folk to blues and rock, this intimate venue is said to be a popular spot amongst the likes of David Gray and the Gallagher brothers.

> **Work is the curse of the drinking classes**
>
> The phrase "on the wagon" can be traced back to London in the middle ages. Condemned prisoners had to walk three miles from the old Newgate Prison on The Strand to be hanged at the Tyburn Tree, near Marble Arch. It was customary for the Bow Tavern to give a pint of ale to the ill-fated prisoner, who would then sit, drink, and be cheered on by all the morbidly curious vagrants and vagabonds. If the executioner rode to the hanging in a cart, he would stay aboard to drink his pint. Thus, he was "on the wagon".

Jazz clubs

Jazz might conjure up images of the New Orleans scene, but the soulful craze didn't pass London by. You can still hear it live on most nights, and if you're lucky you'll catch a well-known jazz hero, or a ram-jam group of old gents giving it their all in a smoky subterranean dive. Jazz flute? Hell, why not? As long as you feel the music, anything goes.

Ronnie Scott's

47 Frith Street, W1
Tel: 020 7439 0747
Tube: Leicester Square or Tottenham Court Road
www.ronniescotts.co.uk
Open 8.30 p.m–3 a.m. Monday to Saturday, costs £15–£25.

This place is an absolute legend. Opened by the late Ronnie Scott in 1959, the venue has since become world famous, having attracted jazz big wigs such as Miles Davis and Tom Waits. An absolute must-see.

Jazz Café

5 Parkway, NW1
Tel: 020 7916 6060
Tube: Camden Town
Open 7 p.m.–1 a.m. Monday to Thursday and Sunday, 7 p.m.–2 a.m. Friday and Saturday, costs £12–£20

Who'da guessed it? A jazz dance club combining soulful tunes with a packed-out dancefloor? Well, it works. Really well. Attracting some of the biggest jazz and soul acts from around the world, the youthful crowd of musical enthusiasts packs it in every night of the week.

Pizza Express Jazz Club

10 Dean Street, W1
Tel: 020 7439 8722
Tube: Tottenham Court Road
Open 7.45 p.m.–midnight, costs £10–£20

Another well-known underground intimate jazz basement joint pulling in many of the big named jazz greats. Book a table and sit back with a bottle of wine for a night you'll never forget.

Smollensky's on the Strand

105 The Strand, WC2
Tel: 020 7497 2101
Tube: Embankment or Charing Cross
Admission: free Monday to Saturday or £4.50 on Sunday
www.smollenskys.co.uk

For a spot of jazz, soul or blues along with a bite of American-style cuisine, this central venue is worth a visit.

606 Club

90 Lots Road, SW10
Tel: 020 7352 5953
Tube: Earls Court or Fulham Broadway

A small club with a mixture of jazz and R&B. On weekends, non-members must pay for a dinner to gain admission. A meal costs around £30 per head and is delightfully worth every penny.

Jazz After Dark

9 Greek Street, W1
Tel: 020 7734 0545
Tube: Leicester Square
Open noon–2 a.m. Monday to Thursday, noon–3 a.m. Friday and Saturday
www.jazzafterdark.co.uk

A nice little drinking den to chill out after work with some easy listening jazz and blues. The late licence and cheap admission make this a popular night spot with the after work crowd. Entrance free if you have a bite to eat from Monday to Thursday, £3 Monday to Thursday and Sunday if you're just drinking, and £5 Friday and Saturday.

Swing

If you're bored of the usual aural melodies in the clubs and DJ bars, then hark back to the 40s, paint on some scarlet lipstick, get suited and booted, and go for a different night out. There are lots of lindy hop and swing dance classes around London and plenty of clubs that put on Big Band nights where you can show off your new found toe-tapping skills. For details look on www.swingland.com, www.swinginter.net, or www.mogoboogie.com

Chapter Three:
Theatres

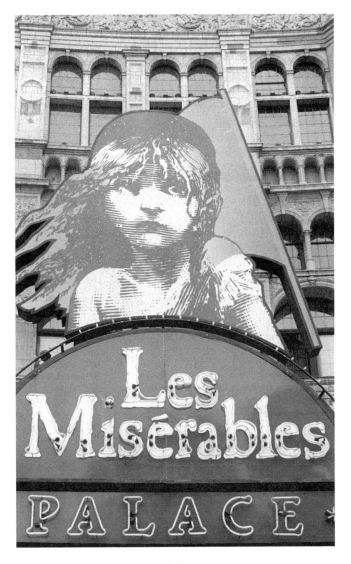

London's West End is second only to Broadway for its outstanding performances. Whether you want to see a blockbuster musical, a Hollywood celebrity like Madonna treading the boards, or a small independent production at your local theatre, you can do it all in London. If you've never had the chance to see a major musical production such as Les Misèrables or Phantom of the Opera, there is no better time than the present. With more than 100 venues, countless numbers of musical, dance and theatre performances, plus reasonably priced tickets, it would be silly not to go. To find out what's playing, be sure to pick up *Time Out* from your local newsagent or contact Ticketmaster at 020 7344 4444 (www.ticketmaster.co.uk). Tickets can also be purchased through the theatre's box office, or head down to the Leicester Square ticket booths on the day of the show to buy a ticket at half the normal price. For smaller performances in West End and fringe theatre, keep your eye out for weekly events listings guides such as the *Guardian*'s *Guide*, *Time Out* and *The Evening Standard*'s *Hot Tickets*.

Below are the major theatres showing blockbuster West End musicals. Chicago, Fame, Les Misèrables, The Lion King, and the infamously long-running Agatha Christie's Mousetrap, have all graced these elegant and opulent stages.

> During a stage revival of the musical *The King and I*, star Yul Brynner reportedly acted like a prima donna, making frustrating demands of the cast and crew. One incident that escalated the friction was the London Palladium's backstage pay phone. Brynner said the phone's ringing woke him during naps, so he requested a private phone be installed in his newly-redecorated dressing room. He then had the public phone disconnected. Reportedly, cast members retaliated by pouring glue on his dressing room doorknob.

Adelphi Theatre
Strand, WC2. Tel: 020 7344 0055. Tube: Charing Cross

Cambridge Theatre
Earlham Street, WC2. Tel: 020 7494 5080. Tube: Covent Garden

Criterion Theatre
Piccadilly Circus, W1. Tel: 020 7413 1437. Tube: Piccadilly Circus

Dominion Theatre
Tottenham Court Road, W1. Tel: 020 7413 1713. Tube: Tottenham Court Road

Her Majesty's Theatre
Haymarket, SW1. Tel: 020 7494 5400. Tube: Piccadilly Circus

London Palladium
Argyll Street, W1. Tel: 020 7494 5020. Tube: Oxford Circus

Lyceum Theatre
Wellington Street, WC2. Tel: 0870 243 9000. Tube: Charing Cross

Palace Theatre
Shaftesbury Avenue, W1. Tel: 020 7434 0909. Tube: Piccadilly Circus

Phoenix Theatre
Charing Cross Road, WC2. Tel: 020 7369 1733. Tube: Leicester Square

Prince of Wales Theatre
Coventry Street, W1. Tel: 020 7839 5972. Tube: Leicester Square

St Martin's Theatre
West Street, WC2. Tel: 020 7836 1443. Tube: Leicester Square

Theatre Royal Drury Lane
Catherine Street, WC2. Tel: 020 7494 5060. Tube: Covent Garden

Victoria Palace
Victoria Street, SW1. Tel: 020 7834 1317. Tube: Victoria

For smaller running productions, the following theatres host some outstanding performances:

Aldwych Theatre
Aldwych, WC2. Tel: 0870 400 0805. Tube: Holborn

Apollo Theatre
Shaftesbury Avenue, W1. Tel: 020 7494 5070. Tube: Piccadilly Circus

Donmar Warehouse
Earlham Street, WC2. Tel: 020 7486 2431. Tube: Covent Garden

Garrick Theatre
Charing Cross Road, WC2. Tel: 020 7494 5085. Tube: Leicester Square

Gielgud Theatre
Shaftesbury Avenue, W1. Tel: 020 7494 5065. Tube: Piccadilly Circus

Lyric Theatre
Shaftesbury Avenue, W1. Tel: 0870 890 1107. Tube: Piccadilly Circus

National Theatre
South Bank, London, SE1. Tickets: 020 7452 3000 or see www.nationaltheatre.org.uk Tube: Waterloo

New Ambassadors Theatre
West Street, London, WC2. Box office: 020 7369 1761 or see www.theambassadors.com Tube: Leicester Square

Open Air Theatre
Inner Circle, Regent's Park, NW1. Tel: 020 7486 2431 or see www.open-air-theatre.org.uk Tube: Baker Street

Royal Court Theatre
Sloane Square, SW1. Tel: 020 7565 5000 or see www.royalcourttheatre.com Tube: Sloane Square

Theatre Royal
Haymarket, Haymarket, SW1. Tel: 0870 901 3356. Tube: Piccadilly Circus

Vaudeville Theatre
Strand, WC2. Tel: 020 7836 9987. Tube: Charing Cross

The Venue
Leicester Place, WC2. Tel: 0870 899 3335. Tube: Leicester Square

Whitehall Theatre
Whitehall, SW1. Tel: 020 7369 1735. Tube: Charing Cross

Wyndham's Theatre
Charing Cross Road, WC2. Tel: 020 7369 1736. Tube: Leicester Square

Young Vic
Belvedere Road, The Cut. SE1. Tel: 020 7928 6363 or www.sbc.org.uk. Tube: Waterloo

Fancy a bit of Shakespeare?

Shakespeare's Globe
New Global Walk, SE1. Tel: 020 7902 1500 or see www.shakespeares-globe.org Tube: Waterloo

Fans of Mozart, Beethoven and Bach won't want to miss the world's biggest celebration of classical music, The Proms. This yearly music event is held from July until September and most concerts are held in the gloriously opulent Royal Albert Hall. The months of music culminate in The Last Night of the Proms, where the mood is suitably relaxed. If you can't make it, a massive screen is erected in Hyde Park so you can enjoy the best that classical music has to offer over a picnic with your lover on a hot summer night.

Opera, ballet, and classical

London Coliseum
St Martin's Lane, Covent Garden, WC2. Tel: 020 7632 8300. Tube: Leicester Square

Royal Opera House
Bow Street, Covent Garden, WC2. Tel: 020 7240 1200 or see www.royaloperahouse.org Tube: Covent Garden

Barbican Centre
Silk Street, EC2. Tel: 020 7638 4141 or see www.barbican.org.uk Tube: Barbican

South Bank Centre
Belvedere Road, SE1. Box office: 020 7960 4242 or recorded information: 020 7921 0682. Tube: Waterloo

Sadler's Wells
Rosebery Avenue, Islington, EC1. Tel: 020 7863 8000 or see www.sadlers-wells.com Tube: Angel

Top five places to hear classical music:

South Bank Centre, Royal Festival Hall, Queen Elizabeth Hall and Purcell Room, South Bank, SE1. Tel: 020 7960 4242 or see www.rfh.org.uk Tube: Waterloo.

Wigmore Hall, 36 Wigmore Street, W1. Tel: 020 7935 2141 or see www.wigmore-hall.org.uk Tube: Bond Street

Barbican, Silk Street, EC2. Tel: 020 7638 8891 or see www.barbican.org.uk Tube: Barbican

Royal Albert Hall, Kensington Gore, SW7. Tel: 020 7589 8212 or see www.royalalberthall.com Tube: South Kensington

Kenwood House, Hampstead Lane, NW3. Tel: 020 7413 1443. Tube: Hampstead

Film locations

Stanley Kubrick converted Gallions Reach, the site of the old Beckton Gas Works into the Vietnam set for *Full Metal Jacket* in 1987 and shot on locations around the Isle of Dogs.

Lock, Stock and Two Smoking Barrels was shot in the Bethnal Green Town Hall, Repton Boys Club, and St John Street, Smithfields in 1998.

Pierce Brosnan as 007 filmed *The World Is Not Enough* in the Docklands and on the Thames in 1999.

Many of Alfred Hitchcock's films were shot in the Gainsborough Studios, now converted into luxury flats, on New North Road, N1.

In the old cobbled lanes south of the Thames in the Shad Thames area, many scenes in *Oliver Twist* were filmed in 1967, and *The Elephant Man* in 1980.

The haunting scenes in *A Clockwork Orange* where Alex and his Droogs attack a tramp below a bridge were filmed in the subway behind the Tavy Bridge Shopping Centre, Thamesmead, SE28.

Chapter Four:
Art

Since the whirlwind hysteria of the YBA (Young British Artist) days in the early 90s, when the names of Gavin Turk, Sarah Lucas, Tracey Emin and Damien Hirst were made, London has been the art-world leader. Its scene may not have the financial zeal of New York or various Euro-art fairs, but as a multifarious and innovative force, it is unrivalled. If your work shows in London, it's going to sell globally.

Though the formaldehyde and red-top headline days are now over, the capital is as industrious as ever. The new century brings a more serious slant as the creative forces try to push themselves beyond the rhetoric of postmodernist thinking.

Whether you are an art consumer, observer, would-be curator, or closet creator, if London doesn't satisfy you then nowhere will.

Harking back farther, London as an environment was inseparable to the developing works of such luminaries as Francis Bacon, David Hockney, Gilbert and George, and Lucien Freud – all of whose works are still on display at various non-commercial exhibition spaces, but your only chance of a purchase would come at a pricey Christie's auction re-sale.

Many budding young artists come to London to mold their talents in some of the world's finest colleges and academies, including the Royal College of Art and Goldsmiths College, whose summer degree shows are not to be missed. Artists come to London to immerse themselves in the scene, to work with peers who share their passion, and to get their work under the noses of the galleries that one day might represent them.

Highlights

Anthony Wilkinson

242 Cambridge Heath Road, E2
Tel: 020 8980 2662
Tube: Whitechapel or Aldgate East
www.anthonywilkinson.com
Open Thurs–Sat, 11 a.m.–6 p.m., Sun noon–6 p.m.

This is a slightly more established (commercial) East End space that still manages to show some of the best new graduate artists and the more established. Bob and Roberta Smith (real name Patrick Brill) and BANK (art collective), Jessica Voorsanger, and Matthew Higgs, a more intellectual strand of artists paralleling the YBA generation have been featured. The gallery has a video project space with a rolling program showing rare early video and performance work by the pioneers of the genre, such as Joseph Beuys and Marcel Broodthears.

The Approach

Above The Approach Tavern, 47 Approach Road, E2
Tel: 020 8983 3878.
Tube: Bethnal Green
Open Wed–Sun, noon–6 p.m.
The former function room of this traditional pub was turned into a non-profit gallery space in 1997. Since then The Approach has exhibited shows by artists such as Liz Arnold, Jane Simpson, and Kerry Stewart. Host curators have included Peter Doig, and Matthew Higgs. The Approach has become more commercial, yet has remained edgy, in recent years and now represents Emma Kay, Michael Raedecker, Daniel Coombs, Enrico David, Tim Stoner, amoung others.

Neon Gallery

117 Commercial Street, E1
Tel: 020 7247 1444.
Tube: Liverpool Street
Open Fri–Sun noon–6 p.m.
Go to Neon to see a mixture of established names Like Mat Collishaw, Tracey Emin, and other Young British Artists as well as up-and-coming London artists working in a variety of media. It is set up like a shop, selling art objects and books, and curated exhibitions show the big names of the London art scene along side unknowns (who will certainly not be unknown for long). Informal.

Nylon Gallery

10 Vyner Street, E2
Tel: 020 8983 5333
Tube: Bethnal Green
www.nylongallery.com
Open Thurs–Sat 10 a.m.–6 p.m., Sun noon–6 p.m.
Tucked away in a side street you'll feel like you have discovered a secret art world. The shows are exciting and young, with artists that are not obviously commercial, from all media: painters, sculptors and video installation. Past exhibits include Twentieth Century – an art collective, painter Paul Housley, and the outstanding fantasy fabric costume/sculptures of Craig Fisher.

Saatchi Gallery

County Hall, South Bank, SE1
Tel: 020 7823 2363
Tube: Waterloo or Westminster
www.saatchi-gallery.co.uk
Open Sun – Thurs 10 a.m.-6 p.m., Fri – Sat 10 a.m. – 10 p.m.
The newly opened Saatchi Gallery houses a permanent contemporary art collection with some of the biggest names in

British and internationally renowned art. Invited guests will also curate major exhibitions. Expect to see works such as Damien Hirst's dead animals in formaldehyde, Tracey Emin's raunchy unmade bed, Jake and Dinos Chapman's nude sculptures hanging from a tree, and Sarah Lucas's erotically placed everyday objects. Not for the faint hearted.

Vilma Gold

66 Rivington Street, EC1
Tel: 020 7613 1609
Tube: Old Street
www.vilmagold.com
Open Thurs–Sun noon–6 p.m.

Named after an imaginary art dealer called Vilma Gold, this gallery is one of the finest spaces in London. Past shows have included Colin Thompson and Roddy Doyle, the hyped Sophie Von Hellermann and the hobbypopMUSEUM art collective. Showcasing mostly young and promising talent, the gallery has a non-commercial feel, and regularly shows performance and video installations as well as canvases. The Bedroom Bar is part of the same building and acts as the private view bar.

White Cube

44 Duke Street, SW1
Tel: 020 7930 5373
Tube: Green Park
Open Tue–Sat 10 a.m.–6 p.m.
www.whitecube.com

In 1993, director Jay Jopling set up White Cube as a temporary project space for contemporary art. The gallery has since evolved into an extensive venture, and played a major role in the 1990s boom for Brit Art. White Cube has an impressive range of now-established artists including, Tracey Emin, Damien Hirst, Angus Fairhurst, Antony Gormley, Mona Hatoum, Marc Quinn and Sam Taylor-Wood.

Recommended public galleries and museums

Barbican Art Gallery, Level 3 Concourse Gallery, Barbican Centre, Silk Street, EC2. Tel: 020 7638 8891. Tube: Barbican. www.barbican.org.uk

Camden Arts Centre, Arkwright Road, NW3. Tel: 020 7435 5224. Tube: Finchley Road

Chisenhale Gallery, 64 Chisenhale Road, E3. Tel: 020 8981 4518. Tube: Mile End. www.chisenhale.org.uk

Hayward Gallery, South Bank, SE1. Tel: 020 7960 5226. Tube:

Waterloo. www.hayward-gallery.org.uk

Institute of Contemporary Arts (ICA), The Mall, SW1. Tel: 020 7930 3647. Tube: Charing Cross. www.ica.org.uk

Matt's Gallery, 42–44 Copperfield Road, E3. Tel: 020 8983 1771. Tube: Mile End or Stepney Green

The Photographer's Gallery, 5 and 8 Newport Street, WC2. Tel: 020 7831 1772. Tube: Leicester Square. www.photonet.org.uk

Royal Academy of Arts, Burlington House, Piccadilly, W1. Tel: 020 7300 8000. Tube: Piccadilly Circus. www.royalacademy.org.uk

Serpentine Gallery, Kensington Gardens, W2. Tel: 020 7402 6075. Tube: South Kensington. www.serpentinegallery.co.uk

The Showroom, 44 Bonner Road, E2. Tel: 020 8983 4115. Tube: Bethnal Green

South London Gallery, 65 Peckham Road, SE5. Tel: 020 7703 6120. Tube: Oval, then bus 36. www.southlondonart.com

Tate Britain, Millbank, SW1. Tel: 020 7887 8008. Tube: Pimlico. www.tate.org.uk

Tate Modern, Bankside, SE1. Tel: 020 7887 8008. Tube: Southwark or Blackfriars. www.tate.org.uk

Whitechapel, Whitechapel High Street, E1. Tel: 020 7522 7888. Tube: Aldgate East. www.whitechapel.org

Recommended commercial galleries

asprey jacques, 4 Clifford Street, W1. Tel: 020 7287 7675. Tube: Green Park. www.aspreyjacques.com

Dominic Berning, 1 Hoxton Street, N1. Tel: 020 7739 4222. Tube: Old Street

Entwistle, 6 Cork Street, W1. Tel: 020 7734 6440. Tube: Green Park

Gagosian, 8 Heddon Street, W1. Tel: 020 7292 8222. Tube: Oxford Circus

Hales, 70 Deptford High Street, SE8. Tel: 020 8694 1194. Tube: New Cross

Interim Art, 42 Herald Street, E2. Tel: 020 7729 4112. Tube: Bethnal Green

Lisson, 52–54 Bell Street, NW1. Tel: 020 7724 2739. Tube: Edgware Road. www.lisson.co.uk

Robert Sandelson, 5a Cork Street, W1. Tel: 020 7439 1001. Tube: Green Park

Sadie Coles HQ, 35 Heddon Street, W1. Tel: 020 7434 2227. Tube: Oxford Circus. www.sadiecoles.com

Essor, 1 America Street, SE1. Tel: 020 7928 3388. Tube: Southwark or Borough

Rhodes + Mann, 37 Hackney Road, E2. Tel: 020 7729 4372. Tube: Old Street

Saatchi Gallery, 30, 34, 36 Underwood Street, N1. Tel: 020 7336 7365. Tube: Old Street

Vertigo, 62 Great Eastern Street, EC2. Tel: 020 7613 1386. Tube: Old Street
White Cube², 48 Hoxton Square, N1. Tel: 020 7930 5373. Tube: Old Street

Recommended artist-run project spaces

Cubitt, 2–4 Caledonia Street, N1. Tel: 020 7278 8226. Tube: Angel
www.cubittartists.org.uk
291 Gallery, 291 Hackney Road, E2. Tel: 020 7613 5676. Tube: Liverpool Street or Old Street

Funders and Facilitators

The Arts Council of England, 14 Great Peter Street, SW1. Tel: 020 7333 0100. www.artscouncil.org.uk

London Arts Board, Elme House, 133 Long Acre, WC2. Tel: 020 7240 1313. www.arts.org.uk/lab

The British Council, Visual Arts Department, 11 Portland Place, W1. Tel: 020 7930 8466. www.britishcouncil.org

Contemporary Art Society, 17 Bloomsbury Square, WC1. Tel: 020 7831 7311. www.contempart.org.uk

Patrons of New Art, Tate Britain, Millbank, SW1. Tel: 020 7887 8743. www.tate.org.uk

Chapter Five:
Sports

The only sport that really counts in London, as with anywhere else in Great Britain, is football. A mighty fine way to upset a Briton is to call any sport other than association football "football", and using the term "soccer" is especially liable to earn unsettling disdain, unless you're being ironic. However, for the joy of spectatorship, football is not necessarily a visitor's best choice. In fact, delving a little deeper into London's sporting life is the perfect route to learn more about London, its history and Londoners themselves.

Sports to watch

Hockey: London Knights, London Areana, Limeharbour, E14. Tel: 020 7536 2626. Tube: Crossharbour (DLR). Tickets £7–£18

Basketball: London Towers, Crystal Palace National Sports Centre, Ledrington Road, SE19. Tel: 020 8776 7755. Rail: Crystal Palace. Tickets £6–£8

Hot rod and stock car racing, Wimbledon Stadium, Plough Lane, SW17. Tel: 020 8946 8000. Tube: Wimbledon Park. £5–£9

Football (Soccer)

Having said all of the above, it's probably best to start with Britain's national obsession.

The Premiership

The fancy names, massive wage packets, huge crowds, and impressive stadia of England's top league make for a marvellous concoction. In London, you can find Fulham, Chelsea, Arsenal, Charlton Athletic, West Ham United and Tottenham Hotspur all plying their trade in the Premiership. Arsenal are in especially high spirits having won the league and cup double, much to the chagrin of bitter North London rivals Tottenham, and the other big London club, Chelsea, who Arsenal beat in the 2002 FA Cup Final to gain one half of said double. Fulham by contrast are small fish, despite being owned by Harrods boss and all round nice guy Mohammed Al Fayed.

However, for the potential spectator of games at the home grounds of these teams, opportunities are rare. The only games for which there are spare tickets involve the lowlier clubs in the division and often provide unexciting fare. Attendance at these games is crucial for those attempting to understand just what a faithful football fan goes through for the cost of around £30 per ticket. But for those seeking thrills and spills, there are better choices. In fact, the only way to secure a ticket for the big games is to strike up a friendship with a fan that already has access. Should an opportunity present itself, jump at it. Otherwise, there are better ways to spend your hard-earned cash. Try the ticket lines of these clubs, just in case.

Arsenal
Ticket Line: 0207 413 3366
Tube: Arsenal
www.arsenal.com

Charlton Athletic
Ticket Line: 020 8333 4010
Rail: Charlton
www.charlton-athletic.co.uk

Chelsea
Ticket Line: 0207 386 7799
Tube: Fulham Broadway
www.chelseafc.com

Fulham
Ticket Line: 020 8336 7451
Tube: Putney Bridge
www.fulhamfc.com

Tottenham Hotspur
Ticket Line: 08700 112222
Tube: Seven Sisters or Tottenham Hale
www.spurs.co.uk

West Ham United
Ticket Line: 020 8548 2700
Tube: Upton Park
www.whufc.com

Sports bars

Shoeless Joe's, 555 King's Road, SW6. Tel: 020 7610 9346 or see www.shoelessjoes.co.uk Tube: Fulham Broadway

The Sports Cafe, 80 Haymarket, SW1. Tel: 020 7839 8300 or see www.sportscafe.com Tube: Piccadilly Circus

Terry Neill's Sports Bar, Bath House, 53 Holborn Viaduct, EC1. Tel: 020 7329 6653. Tube: Chancery Lane

Non-league

A fuller appreciation for just how deep football runs through the blood of so many Brits, Londoners included, is available at England's non-league club grounds. A prime example in London is Barnet FC, which can be found at the far tip of the Northern Line. Barnet can typically expect crowds of about 2,000 people to watch its squad of semi-professional players take on other sets of semi-professional players in the chase for a coveted place in the Football League proper and professional status. Barnet were only recently relegated from the League and are desperate to get back in by winning the Conference – the name given to the foremost non-league division. The winners of the Conference in each season are promoted to the football league at the expense of the bottom-placed League team. Games to decide these places are among the fiercest on offer due to the significance upon a club's status and its bank balance. However, it is the sheer fact that teams such as Barnet can command loyal away support numbering in the hundreds that does most to give a flavor of the country's love for the game. It might be worth making the trip on a spare Saturday to experience football in its most shabby gloriousness.

Barnet FC

Barnet Football Club
Underhill, Fairfield Way/Barnet Lane
High Barnet
Tube: High Barnet
www.barnetfc.com

Hackney Marshes

The Saturday and Sunday league amateur games enjoyed by thousands of ordinary Joes that should know better are a fantastic way to enjoy the full-blooded excitement of terrible football. In particular, Hackney Marshes in North East London on either day is an incredible spectacle. The area holds 87 full-size football pitches and each will have a game of varying standards on display. A stroll around the Marshes on a weekend is a great way to increase one's swearing vocabulary, learn a new way to injure somebody, and truly understand just how seriously even the worst footballer can treat the game. Well worth the trip.

Hackney Marshes

Rail: Hackney Wick. Follow the Lee Valley Walk to the recreation grounds.

In October 1980, West Ham United played a crucial European game to a completely empty stadium. During the first leg of a tie against Castilla, hooliganism erupted. To punish the guilty, all fans were turned away from the second leg at Upton Park. West Ham won the match 5–1, but all goals were met by silence from the empty stands.

Cricket

England's second national sport – supposedly a summer one, although much of the time is spent ruing the climate's strange sense of humor – is cricket. It is another game, like football, that England invented and promptly became poor at. However, England's national side is enjoying half a revival and international test matches still provide a fascinating day's entertainment.

London can boast both the Oval in the south and Lord's in the north, two of the world's most famous cricket grounds. Ordinarily, the two grounds are home to the Surrey and Middlesex county teams respectively. However, when England are in town, test series will usually take place on both grounds. Tickets can usually be had on the day and don't forget to bring the following items: sunglasses, umbrella, anorak, your own beers, money for more beers from the bar, and a funny hat. All the above are musts as is the recognition that watching the cricket only comes about halfway down the list of things to do when attending a cricket match.

For information on ticket availability at the Oval and Lord's, contact the English Cricket Board website, www.ecb.co.uk or call 0870 533 8833.

Village cricket

Much like football's Sunday leagues, village cricket is part of the lifeblood of English existence. Again, the fare is provided by generally poor exponents of the game and, again, it is this, combined with those players' evident love for their sport, that makes it worth the effort. There are grounds all over outer London, and it's always pleasant to stumble across one near a cracking country pub. But you can start at Pesthouse Common, Richmond-upon-Thames, bordering which are several top traditional pubs.

Pesthouse Common
Richmond-upon-Thames
Tube: Richmond

Greyhound racing

Greyhound racing is London's most accessible live betting experience. Without the snobbery of horse racing, nor the often prohibitive costs, going to the dogs is invariably a giggle. There is little value in form or odds since the races are so short, bumps and scrapes so common, and previous knowledge so unhelpful. Instead, it is more fun and often more successful to pick a name you like, favorite color trap – the separate gates the greyhounds emerge from – or lucky number, than try and make an educated guess based on the form guides. Entry is cheap, usually around £10, and food equally cheap and hearty. In London, the two best known dog tracks are at Wimbledon stadium in the South West, and Walthamstow in the East, the latter of which, in case one is interested, was the spiritual setting for the Blur album Parklife.

Walthamstow Stadium
General Enquiries: 020 8498 3300
www.wsgreyhound.co.uk

Wimbledon Stadium
Enquiries: 020 8946 8000
Tube: Wimbledon
www.wimbledondogs.co.uk

Tennis

The Wimbledon Championships, held in late June and early July each year, is one of the most prestigious tournaments in the world. More than 500,000 spectators head down to the sacred lawns of SW19 to cheer on their nation's heroes, while millions more around the world will catch the two weeks of action on the telly. Battling it out at the Wimbledon Championships are the world's top tennis athletes, competing for more than £8 million in prize money and the top rankings.

After years of seeing the excitement unfold over the telly, here is your chance to head down to the courts to soak up the atmosphere first-hand. To purchase tickets ahead of time, applications must be sent to the All England Lawn Tennis Club before the end of December in the year before the competition.

A limited supply of tickets are also available on the day, costing anywhere from £8 to wander the grounds to £30 for center court, but beware that the best seats go first. If you want good tickets, you're going to have to queue well before 7 a.m. For further information on the matches, visit the official Wimbledon Championship website at www.wimbledon.org.

Or to try your own hand at the game, tennis courts are available in Hyde Park, Hampstead Heath, Battersea Park, Wandsworth Common, Regent's Park.

Log onto www.londontennis.co.uk to find a court near you or call the Lawn Tennis Association at 020 7381 7000 for a list of places to play. Otherwise, try the courts at the following two tennis clubs.

All England Lawn Tennis Club
Church Road, Wimbledon, SW19. Tel: 020 8944 1066. Tube: Wimbledon

Islington Tennis Centre
on Market Road, N7. Tel: 020 7700 1370. Tube: Caledonian Road

Sports to play

Climbing: The Castle Climbing Centre, Green Lanes, N4. Tel: 07957 605 632. Tube: Manor House

In-line skating: Mill Hill School Sports Hall, The Ridgeway, NW7. Tel: 01438 721 435. Tube: Mill Hill East

Kickboxing: Mornington Sports Centre, Arlington Rd, NW1. Tel: 07713 638 233. Tube: Camden Town

Judo: Tokei Judo Club, 28 Magdalen St, SE1. Tel: 0207 403 5979. Tube: Victoria

Trampolining: Canalside Activity Centre, Canal Close, W10. Tel: 0208 968 4500. Tube: Ladbroke Grove

Fitness centers

Gyms and fitness centers are located all throughout London, so the first thing you must consider is whether you should sign up with a facility near your home or your workplace. Flip through your local Yellow Pages for a list of clubs near you or check out their websites. You will be required to pay a registration fee plus a monthly membership price, so it is worth your while to shop around. Be aware that gyms located in the city will be more costly than those in the suburbs. Here are a few central gym locations to try, most of which have individual branches scattered all over London.

Cannons Health Club, 27–28 Kingly Street, W1. Tel: 08707 582 612. Tube: Oxford Circus. www.cannons.co.uk
Central YMCA, 112 Great Russell Street, WC1. Tel: 020 7343 1844. Tube: Tottenham Court Road. www.centralymca.org.uk
Christopher's Squash and Fitness Club, Plough Lane, Wimbledon, SW17. Tel: 020 8946 4636. Tube: Wimbledon
Curzon Fitness Club, 1 Embankment Place, WC2. Tel: 020 7839 5411. Tube: Embankment
The Chelsea Club, Chelsea Village, Fulham Road, SW6. Tel: 020 7915 2200. Tube: Fulham Broadway
Fitness First, Coram Street, WC1. Tel: 020 7833 1887. Tube: Russell Square. www.fitnessfirst.co.uk

Holmes Place Health Clubs, 188a Fulham Road, Chelsea, London, SW10. Tel: 020 7352 9452. Tube: South Kensington. www.holmesplace.com
LA Fitness, Lacon House, Theobalds Road, WC1. Tel: 020 7841 1130. Tube: Holborn. www.lafitness.co.uk
LivingWell, 32 Woburn Place, WC1. Tel: 020 7291 6500.
Tube: Russell Square. www.livingwell.co.uk
Soho Gyms, 12 Macklin Street, WC2. Tel: 020 7242 1290.
Tube: Holborn. www.sohogyms.com
The North Pole School of Tai Chi Chuan, 83 St Quintin Avenue, W10. Tel: 020 8960 2141. Tube: Ladbroke Grove

Swimming pools

Most boroughs have their own inexpensive swimming pools and recreation centers open to the public. Look in the Yellow Pages under Swimming Pools or Leisure Centres to find the one nearest you. Otherwise, try one of the few listed here.

Brockwell Park Lido (outdoor), Dulwich Road, SE24. Tel: 020 7274 3088. Rail: Herne Hill
Camberwell Leisure Centre, Camberwell Church Street, SE5. Tel: 020 7703 3024. Rail: Denmark Hill
Greenwich Arches Leisure Centre, 80 Trafalgar Road, SE10. Tel: 020 8317 5000. DLR: Maize Hill
Hampstead Heath Ponds (outdoor), Hampstead Heath, NW3. Tel: 020 7485 4491. Tube: Hampstead
Oasis Sports Centre, 32 Endell Street, WC2. Tel: 020 7831 1804. Tube: Covent Garden
Tooting Bec Lido (outdoor), Tooting Bec Common, SW16. Tel: 020 8871 7198. Tube: Tooting Bec

Splurge at **The Sanctuary** on Floral Street, WC2. Tel: 020 7420 5151 or see www.thesanctuary.co.uk
One day of bliss costs anywhere from £40–£225, depending on the treatments you desire. These include an exercise pool, whirlpools, relaxation lounges and steam rooms.

Speciality activities

Indoor climbing
Castle Climbing Centre, Green Lanes, N4. Tel: 020 8211 7000. Tube: Wood Green. www.castle-climbing.co.uk
Mile End Climbing Wall, Haverfield Road, E3. Tel: 020 8980 0289. Tube: Mile End

Golf

Chingford Golf Club, 158 Station Road, E4. Tel: 020 8529 2107. Rail: Chingford

Richmond Park Golf Course, Roehampton Gate, Priory Lane, SW15. Tel: 020 8876 3205. Tube: Richmond. www.gemgolf.com

Horse riding

Hyde Park Stables, 63 Bathurst Mews, W2. Tel: 020 7723 2813. Tube: Lancaster Gate. www.hydeparkstables.com

Ice skating

Broadgate Ice Rink at Broadgate Circus, Eldon Street, EC2. Tel: 020 7505 4068. Tube: Liverpool Street. This open-air rink is only open from October to April.

Somerset House, The Strand, WC2. Tel: 020 7413 3399. Tube: Charing Cross. During winter months.

Streatham Ice Rink, 386 Streatham High Road, SW16. Tel: 020 8769 7771. Rail: Streatham. www.streathamicearena.co.uk

Watersports

Rent boats in Hyde Park. Bluebird Boats, Tel: 020 7262 1330

Docklands Watersports Club, Gate 14, King George V Dock, Woolwich Manor Way, E16. Tel: 020 7511 7000. DLR: Crossharbour and London Arena

Docklands Sailing and Watersports, 235a Westferry Road, Millwall Docks, E14. Tel: 020 7537 2626. DLR: Crossharbour and London Arena. www.dswc.org

Shoot pool

Brixton Snooker Centre, 36–38 Acre Lane, SW2. Tel: 020 7207 6762. Tube: Brixton

Camden Snooker Centre, 16 Delancey Street, NW1. Tel: 020 7485 6094. Tube: Camden Town

Clerkenwell House, 23–27 Hatton Wall, EC1. Tel: 020 7404 1113. Tube: Farringdon

The Elbow Rooms, 89–91 Chapel Market, N1. Tel: 0207278 3244. Tube: Angel

The Pool, 104–108 Curtain Road, EC2. Tel: 020 7739 9608. Tube: Old Street

Suzy Q's, 16 Semley Place, SW1. Tel: 020 7824 8261. Tube: Sloane Square

Cultural centers and religious groups

Brent Sikh Centre, 241 Stag Lane, NW9. Tel: 020 8206 1231

Catholic Communications Services, 39 Eccleston Square, SW1. Tel: 020 7901 4800

Chinese Community Centre, 2nd Floor, 28-29 Gerrard Street, WC2. Tel: 020 7439 3822

Goethe Institute (Germany), 50 Princes Gate, Exhibition Road, SW7. Tel: 020 7596 4000

Hackney Congolese Community Support Group, Metropolitan Business Centre, Enfield Rd, N1. Tel: 020 7923 4703

Hong Kong Society, Swire House, 59 Buckingham Gate, SW1. Tel: 020 7963 9447

Institut Français, 17 Queensberry Place, W7. Tel: 020 7838 2144

International Student Christian Services, 3 Crescent Stables,139 Upper Richmond Road, SW15. Tel: 020 8780 3511

Jewish Information Bureau, 37 Hallswelle Rd, NW11. Tel: 020 8455 5586

Jewish Lads and Girls Brigade, 3 Beechcroft Rd, E18. Tel: 020 8989 8990

London Chinatown Chinese Association, 12 Newport Place, WC1. Tel: 020 7734 5161

Parkside Christian Fellowship, 173 Upper Richmond Rd, SW14. Tel: 020 8878 7252

Salam Bhano Asian Girls and Young Women's Group, Aylesbury Youth Club, Inville Rd, SE17. Tel: 020 7252 4616

Southwark Vietnamese Youth, Bellenden Old School, Bellenden Road, SE15. Tel: 020 7732 6114

Sri Lanka Islamic Association, 7 Broadway Building, Boston Road, W7. Tel: 020 8840 3270

The Sternberg Centre for Judaism, Manor House, 80 East End Road, N3. Tel: 020 8349 5700

The Trinity Foundation, Holy Trinity Church, Sloane Street, SW1. Tel: 020 7730 8830

West Indian Women's Association, William Morris Community Centre, Greenleaf Road, E17. Tel: 020 8521 4456

Chapter Six:
Festivals and Events

Field of dreams

The start of the English summer months can only mean one thing: time to immerse yourself in waist-high farmland mud amongst a field of grinning Goth tribes, spotty kids with green hair, and fat naked men doing the funky chicken in mounds of green slop.

Music festival season grabs ravers by the balls with its world-class live DJ and band sets, performance art shows, neon glow sticks and tantric massages. It has become a British tradition, of sorts, since the glorified days of Glastonbury, when 1,500 love-bead-wearing hippies paid the £1 entrance fee in 1970 to see some of the biggest musicians of its day trip out in live action on-stage.

These days, Londoners have literally dozens of summer festivals to choose from across the UK, including everything from intimate outdoor park concerts to massive 12 arena dance music all-nighters and weekend camping extravaganzas.

The festivals listed below are the biggest, but if you'd prefer a lesser-known and more exclusive affair, be sure to scan *Time Out*, *Mix Mag*, *Ministry*, *TNT* and *SX* magazines in May and June for the most updated festival line-up details.

Homelands

The Bowl, Matterley Estate, near Winchester, Hampshire
At the end of July/early June, costs £49
www.meanfiddler.com

Pack 40,000 ravers into a giant paddock near Winchester and what do you get? One helluva party. This dance festival goes all out with more than 10 dance stages and arenas pulling in all the big-hitting DJs. The tents get rammed – especially if it's raining – so don't forget that umbrella.

Gatecrasher

Turweston Aerodrome, Brackley, Northamptonshire
In late June, costs £49
www.gatecrasher.com

The glowsticks, fog horns and spiked orange hair is out in full force for this hyperactive all-nighter featuring the world's most-loved spinners such as the Chemical Brothers, Carl Cox and Paul Oakenfold. Carnival rides, laser shows and skimpy costumes only brush the surface of the goodies on offer. Be sure to book ahead.

Glastonbury

Worthy Farm, Pilton, Somerset
On the last weekend in June, costs £105
www.glastonburyfestivals.co.uk

Since it's glory days in the 70s, this weekend camping mudfest sensation was forced to take a year off in 2001 to put an end to its ongoing fence-hopping problems. It's now back up and running, but don't expect to get in unless you fork out for the ticket. Those tree-hugging and ladder carrying days are over, sadly. See more acts here than any other festival, but don't forget to check out the tumbling midgets in the circus tents, the Miniscule of Sound – a club only big enough for two people, and the roller derby, heck, you can even go ballroom dancing, join the Hare Krishnas, or get married if you'd like. Music and more.

Essential Festival

Hackney Marshes, London
In the first week of August, costs £37.50 for a one-day ticket
www.essentialfestival.com

This festival has got a little something for everyone. Head to the dance stage for some groovy tunes, or opt for a mid-afternoon head banging session. Even better, strap yourself to a bungy rope or show off your stunts on the skateboarding half-pipe. It's all here.

V Festival

Hylands Park, Chelmsford
In mid-August, costs £67.50 for the weekend or £39.50 per day
www.vfestival.com

Some of the world's biggest bands are helicoptered in for this world-class weekend festival. This attracts your yuppy-ish, clean and well-manicured crowd. A world apart from your I-ran-out-of-toilet-roll-two-days-ago Glastonbury crusties.

Creamfields

Old Liverpool Airfield, Speke Road, Liverpool
At the end of August, costs £46
www.cream.co.uk

The great outdoors never felt so good. For wide-eyed musical fantasia, don't miss this dance raver's heaven, mixing up everything from rock and hip-hop to dance anthems. Guaranteed to book big-named DJ headliners such as Underworld or Judge Jules.

Reading Festival

Rivermead Leisure Complex, Reading
Held in late August, costs £90 for the weekend or £39 per day
www.meanfiddler.com or www.readingfestival.com

Pulsate to techno in the mud? No thanks. And send all those pop-tastic bands back to nursery school for nap-time. Reading is about rock. Not death-metal thrashing, but good tunes by bands who know how to play instruments. Expect a huge line-up of bands like Jane's Addiction, Ash, The Hives, The Strokes, or maybe Offspring.

Notting Hill Carnival

At Latimer Road or Royal Oak Tube stations
Held in late August, free event
A vibrant affair of bright colors, spicy foods and the sounds of the
Caribbean. The streets come alive with food stands, floats, and
stalls flogging everything under the sun. You can't beat this huge
free street party.

Other events

Keep your eye out in London's weekly events listings magazines
and look out for the London Tourist Board's bimonthly *Events in
London* pamphlet for the most up to date listings of current events.
Also go to www.londontouristboard.com or call its events
information line 09068 663 344. Below is a selection of some of the
hottest annual events you won't want to miss.

London Marathon

Late April
Tel: 020 7620 4117
www.london-marathon.co.uk
More than 35,000 runners take to the streets to compete in this 26-
mile road race.

Derby Day

Second Saturday in June
Tel: 01372 470 047
www.epsomderby.co.uk
Splash out on an eccentric hat and a bottle of champagne for the
most important horse race of the season.

London Pride March and Mardi Gras

Late June / early July
This colorful march starts from Hyde Park and comes to one
orgiastic triumph at the massive festival in Finsbury Park.

Wimbledon Tennis Championships

Last week of June & first week of July
Tel: 020 8946 2244
www.wimbledon.org
See all the biggest tennis players of the day fight it out on the
courts. Watched on the telly by millions worldwide.

Henley Royal Regatta

Early July
Tel: 01491 572 153
www.hrr.co.uk
The British upper classes take to the water for this annual rowing
race along the Thames.

Thames Festival

Mid-September
Tel: 020 7928 8998
www.thamesfestival.org
A riverside festival with food stalls and a fireworks display.

Regus London Film Festival

November
www.rlff.org.uk
Held at cinemas throughout London, this is your chance to see a huge variety of films before they go on general release. The celebrities and filmmakers descend on the capital and this is your chance to try for tickets to a film and director question and answer session. Film fever hits London.

Bonfire Night

Every year on 5 November, the skies come alive all over London in bursts of colorful fireworks, to celebrate the defeat of Guy Fawkes's plot to blow up Parliament and King James I in 1605.

Christmas Light Ceremony

Mid-November
Head down to Regent Street and Oxford Street for the ceremonial switching on of the Christmas lights, by a celebrity. Stop on the street for some roasted chestnuts and have a peek at the outstanding festive window displays of the major department stores.

New Year's Eve

31 December
Crowd into Trafalgar Square for the mayhem, or Parliament Square to hear Big Ben ring in the New Year.

Chinese New Year Festival

Late January
Tel: 020 7439 3822
Head down to Chinatown for this street party with flags, food stalls, and dragons skirting through the streets.

Oxford and Cambridge Boat Race

6 April each year
This grueling 4 1/4-mile race from Putney to Mortlake is three times the length of an Olympic course with competitors often struggling against choppy waves to claim the much-coveted title. Following six months of sweat and tears, the two universities battle it out to the bitter end. Pack a blanket, a picnic hamper of sandwiches, and a bottle of champers before claiming a prime vantage point along the river in Putney, south London, for this famed event.

PART THREE:

AREAS

West End

Avoided by Londoners at all cost, Leicester Square is a gaudily over-hyped pit of cinemas, naff bars, and overpriced shops flogging silly tourist tat. In the summertime, people drain through the square slower than water passing through a blocked drain, and unless you are armed with a shopping bag filled with tins to swing at peoples' knees, or are accompanied by a thick-necked Austrian bodyguard named Biff, you are not going to get anywhere fast.

The West End is the first place newcomers to London head to, drawn in by its notorious 24-hour energetic atmosphere, bright lights, and street performers. Whether you are a beetroot farmer from Shropshire, a prom queen from Texas, or an art history student from Stockholm, tourists who stumble upon the glaring neon lights of the square for the first time experience its full unadulterated glory.

But for those of us who've seen it too many times to count, unless you join the giddy masses by popping on a velveteen Union Jack top hat, or pausing mid-stride to take a picture of a clown juggling painted tennis balls, your nerves will suffer. Leicester Square is not for the fiery-tempered or those on the go.

Your average Londoner will only visit the square to pass onwards to Covent Garden, Soho or Chinatown. Some, however, are drawn to the screenings of blockbuster world premieres, which draw in the biggest celebrity heart-throbs from all over the world.

Just steps away is the much-photographed Piccadilly Circus, seething with traffic as vehicles and people pass by the neon advertising and statue of Eros to get to their next destination.

Carry on through the rambling seedy streets leading through Soho and you'll stumble upon Chinatown, a collection of Chinese restaurants and shops circling around one main pedestrian-only road. A few good bars can also be found here, although tucked away secretly from the stampede of camera-toting visitors.

Also within the boundaries of the West End is the most expensive place on the British Monopoly board: Mayfair. Swanky, snobby, and reeking of old money, this area is home to luxurious hotels, fine cuisine, and wealthy residents.

If you have a few thousand quid to spare, head down to Saville Row to have a bespoke suit tailored to fit. Or if you'd prefer to just do a little window shopping, take a peek in the arcades throughout Mayfair and the shops along New Bond Street; or twitch and fiddle your way through an auction at Sotheby's to see where the better half pick up their antiques.

But unless you were born into a family fortune, you will probably not be able to live in Mayfair. The price of renting a flat here is incredibly steep, and although some technology heads may be able to live here temporarily, the novelty will quickly wear off as rent day comes around. Around the rest of the West End, housing is sparse, and even if you manage to find a small loft apartment above a shop, the cost would be so outrageous that you could get an entire house in Kilburn for the same price.

Pubs and bars

Dive Bar

48 Gerrard Street, Chinatown, W1
Tel: no phone listed
Tube: Leicester Square

There's something to be said for the subterranean depths of London. Sure, it's where the plague spread between filthy vermin, but now that the deceased are dead and buried in Blackheath, the rat-runs of London have become a tomb of fabulous bars. Descend into the dimly lit Dive Bar, made up of a large room with two tunnels branching off at the back like streams of drunken piss in a Soho alley. Sit. Drink. Snog if the mood takes you. If you're lucky, the ambience will be set off by the sweet soul sounds of crooning swing troubadours and big band divas.

The Imperial

5 Leicester Street, WC2
Tel: 020 7437 6573
Tube: Leicester Square

Bypass the silver-painted buskers standing still on milk crates, sidestep the mock-mariachi band, and whatever you do, don't go into the Hippodrome. If you've headed for Leicester Square because you haven't yet worn out your shiny new Travelcard and you think that it's a cool place to be, well all is not yet lost. One word of advice: The Imperial. Your basic, average pub. Have a pint, maybe a bowl of chips, if you're feeling peckish. The Imperial is the last bastion of normalcy tucked in the gaudily bejewelled Pandora's box that is Leicester Square.

Fitzroy Tavern

16 Charlotte Street, W1
Tel: 020 7580 3714
Tube: Oxford Circus

Those literary greats were naughty wee lushes, weren't they? What we now quaintly refer to as alcoholism, they called genius back in Olde London Towne. The Fitz was another popular tavern for Dylan Thomas, George Orwell, and others. A verbose past, which can be read about on the walls, in clippings, and even in the pub's book. If you ain't much fer readin' dem books 'n such, then perhaps the large outdoor area will entice you.

Bradley's Spanish Bar

42–44 Hanway Street, W1
Tel: 020 7636 0359
Tube: Tottenham Court Road

Simple blond oak, glass-fronted shells of Hoegaarden-serving chain bars serve only to extinguish London's finest traditional public houses. Screw minimalist. I want over-the-top kitsch and some great tunes when I sit down to a relaxing pint. Bradley's is the best place to overload your numbed senses with gaudy Spanish mementos while you rest your pert rump on a velvet banquette. With the best jukebox in Britain playing vinyl singles from the 50s and 60s, you'll never want to leave.

Also in the area

Beaujolais, 25 Litchfield Street, WC2. Tel: 020 7836 2955. Tube: Leicester Square. Varied and sensual wine list.

The Salisbury, St Martin's Street, WC2. Tel: 020 7836 5863. Tube: Leicester Square. A fabulously gaudy old pub.

Waxy O'Connors, 14–16 Rupert Street, W1. Tel: 020 7287 0255. Tube: Piccadilly Circus. A massive Irish pub stuffed with tourists and office workers.

Jerusalem, 33–34 Rathbone Place, W1. Tel: 020 7255 1120. Tube: Tottenham Court Road. A Gothic-looking bar, without the kids in white facepaint.

Studio Lounge, Waterstone's, 203–206 Piccadilly, W1. Tel: 020 7851 2400. Tube: Piccadilly Circus. Oh, what amazing views …

> The famous statue of Eros at Piccadilly Circus is not actually a statue, but a fountain. It is not a tribute to the god of love, but the Angel of Christian Charity. It was unveiled in 1893 to commemorate Anthony Ashley Cooper, 7th Earl of Shaftesbury, who was a nineteenth-century philanthropist and social reformer.

Late bars

Mash

19–21 Great Portland Street, W1
Tel: 020 7637 5555
Tube: Oxford Circus

Drug-induced hues of hippy orange and green set off against chrome make for a groovy modern-day 70s theme that has proved to be popular amongst suited accountants, recruitment consultants, and sales people in need of a little color in their lives. Pervy backlit pictures of men in disco mustaches and a video screen in the ladies loo showing the view into the gents just goes to show that this modernistic microbrewery likes to provoke a smile. Just don't pick up anyone's keys off the table: they may like the seventies, but wife swapping is just going too far.

Match

37–38 Margaret Street, W1
Tel: 020 7499 3443
Tube: Oxford Circus

Media darlings and advertising execs become as excitable as children in a paddling pool when new cocktail bars like this open up within a five-minute radius of their glare-resistant computer screens. Sink into a leather sofa and spend the night supping away on Manhattans and Cosmopolitans for a sophisticated night out.

The Social

5 Little Portland Street, W1
Tel: 020 7636 4992
Tube: Oxford Circus

Dodge the vinyl hacks lugging their record collections to play it cool amongst swathes of Dieselites and Jarvis Cocker lookalikes. When the upstairs just gets too hot and crowded to handle, head to the pit, a dark and spacious room, to groove to DJ sets pumping funk and house trax.

Also in the area

Long Bar, Sanderson Hotel, 50 Berners Street, W1. Tel: 020 7300 1400. Tube: Oxford Circus. Posh bar for those with well-endowed wallets.

The Warwick, 1–3 Warwick Street, W1. Tel: 020 7734 4409. Tube: Piccadilly Circus. Drink until you vomit till 3 a.m. on the weekends.

Restaurants

Mr Wu's

6–7 Irving Street, WC2
Tel: 020 7839 6669
Tube: Leicester Square

Stacked up like a wedding cake in the front window are layers of plates heaped high with Chinese food set out for the daily all-you-can-eat buffet deal. Get all your classic dishes – noodles, soups, sweet and sour pork balls, curried chicken and vegetable chop suey – at this good value gorge-fest for just £4.50.

Café in the Crypt

St Martin-in-the-Fields, Trafalgar Square, WC2
Tel: 020 7839 4342
Tube: Charing Cross

Step into the deepest netherkens of this eighteenth-century church to mingle with the dead over a glass of wine and a live violin concerto. This refurbished crypt has all the design elements of a swanky café, albeit with worn tombstones under your feet. Eerily satisfying.

Rasa Samudra

5 Charlotte Street, W1
Tel: 020 7637 0222
Tube: Goodge Street

Never mind the pink exterior, beneath the vivid façade lies an outstanding Indian seafood restaurant. The waiting staff are all very pleasant and are more than happy to offer suggestions. Or try the set menu so that you can sample a few dishes. The food can be a bit spicy for someone with a tender palate such as mine, so order plenty of beer. I made the mistake of downing my partner's water, only to find out seconds later that it was her gin. I hate gin.

Better than a steak in the eye. Top steakhouses.

Arkansas Café, Unit 12, 107B Commercial St, Old Spitalfields Market, E1. Tel: 020 7377 6999. Tube: Liverpool Street. Cheap and cheerfully scruffy grill house in the mêlée of the market.

El Gaucho, 88 Ilfield Road, SW10. Tel: 020 7823 3333. Tube: West Brompton. Steak, steak and more high quality steak.

The Gaucho Grill, 19 Swallow Street, W1. Tel: 020 7734 4040. Tube: Piccadilly Circus. Top quality Argentinian steakhouse.

Planet Hollywood, Trocadero, 13 Coventry St, W1. Tel: 020 7287 1000. Tube: Piccadilly Circus. Tacky, yes, but still has great steak if you don't mind being surrounded by film tat.

Smiths of Smithfield, 67–77 Charterhouse St, EC1. Tel: 020 7236 6666. Tube: Farringdon. A pancake stack of restaurants with the most posh restaurant at the top serving amazing Welsh Black beef.

Also in the area

Palms of Goa, 12 Charlotte Street, W1. Tel: 020 7636 1668. Tube: Goodge Street. Cheap and lively Indian.

Gaby's, 30 Charing Cross Road, WC2. Tel: 020 7836 4233. Tube: Leicester Square. Spicy food from around the Med.

Café Fish, 36–40 Rupert Street, W1. Tel: 020 7287 8989. Tube: Leicester Square. Strap on your bib, this seafood extravaganza is gonna be messy.

Clubs

Bar Rumba, 36 Shaftesbury Avenue, W1. Tel: 020 7287 6933. Tube: Piccadilly Circus. A lot of booty wagging, drum 'n' bass nights for unsuspecting tourists and men who like to shine their Reebok trainers.

Café de Paris, 3 Coventry Street, W1. Tel: 020 7734 7700. Tube: Leicester Square. As horny as a brothel closed for a fortnight after an outbreak of the clap. Sleazy blokes on the prowl with more cash than your average leaches.

Entertainment

Handel Museum

23–25 Brook Street, W1
Tel: 020 7495 1685
Tube: Oxford Circus
Admission: £4.50

Although composer George Friederic Handel (1685–1759) was born in Germany, he lived at No 25 from 1723 until his death 36 years later. This museum has early editions of his works, plus portraits and letters charting his life. In more recent years, the house at No 23 became home to American guitarist Jimi Hendrix, who lived there from 1968 until his death.

Comedy Store

1a Oxendon Street, SW1
Tel: 020 7344 0234
Tube: Piccadilly Circus
Admission: £11–15

If the old whoopie cushion routine is getting a little stale amongst your mates, brush up your comedy skills by taking in a show at this world-renowned venue, known to be the stomping ground of some of the best comedians in the world. Book well in advance.

Crabtree Tree Fields

This park, just off the old mews of Colville Place, is a popular lunch spot among local office workers.

Cinemas

Odeon Leicester Square, Leicester Square, WC2.
Tel: 0870 5050 007. Tube: Leicester Square
Odeon Mezzanine, WC2.
Tel: 0870 5050 007. Tube: Leicester Square
Odeon Tottenham Court Road, Tottenham Court Road, W1.
Tel: 0870 5050 007. Tube: Tottenham Court Road
Odeon West End, Leicester Square,WC2. Tel: 0870 5050 007.

Tube: Leicester Square

Prince Charles Cinema, 7 Leicester Place, WC2. Tel: 0901 272 7007.

Tube: Leicester Square

UCI Empire Leicester Square, 5–6 Leicester Square, WC2. Tel: 0870 010 2030. Tube: Leicester Square

UGC Haymarket, 62–65 Haymarket, W1. Tel: 0870 907 0712. Tube: Piccadilly Circus

UGC Shaftesbury Avenue at The Trocadero, Coventry Street, W1. Tel: 0870 907 0716. Tube: Piccadilly Circus

Warner Village West End, Cranbourne Street, Leicester Square, WC2. Tel: 0870 240 6020. Tube: Leicester Square

---

Taxis

Swift and Safe Minicab Service, 34 Cranbourne Street, WC2. Tel: 020 7278 0000

British Car Service, 15 Little Newport Street, WC2. Tel: 020 7734 6555

Euro Cars Taxis, 136 George Street, W1. Tel: 020 7724 9990

Soho

Sex. Gay or straight, kinky or missionary: in Soho you'll always be able to find what you're after and learn things that would make a nymphomaniac dominatrix blush. This is where excess and debauchery take over. Soho is the alcohol-ridden liver, the throbbing genitals, and the newly-opened eyes of all things seedy in London.

Scantily-clad pretty ladies in loads of makeup get a near full body tan as they stand on the pavement to lure onlookers into the brothels like a suspicious wife drawn to a mobile phone bill. Brothels lie behind dark doors, porn-video shops lurk shiftily behind multicolored ribbons that hang over thresholds. Pink neon signs hum, blinking on and off: XXX, Girls, Peepshows.

Old Compton Street is gay central, and is one of the best streets in London for a continuous strip of buzzing action, regardless of sexual preference. Bars and cafés spill outside as tourists, gay couples, disco dollies and office workers strut up and down the street being watched by those sitting drinking strong coffees and stronger lagers.

If you do a bit of searching, you'll be able to live in Soho. It will probably be an overpriced grotty flat above a brothel or kebab shop, but if you want to live amidst the squalor and immorality, go right ahead. However, people don't often stick around for long, eventually growing tired of the constant river of piss, blood and vomit on their doorstep. You'll probably also be on first-name terms with local prostitutes. It will be a bit embarrassing if you are trying to walk a client to Quo Vadis for a posh business lunch and a load of hookers in latex minidresses and spiked stilettos call you by name. But then again, there are still plenty of Soho old-timers who are proud of their lively neighborhood. If you think you can handle it, start looking for a flat through *Loot*. Good luck to you, you'll need it.

> John Logie Baird, a Scottish inventor, gave the first public demonstration of the television in Soho in 1926.

Pubs and bars

The Coach and Horses
29 Greek Street, W1
Tel: 020 7437 5920
Tube: Leicester Square or Piccadilly Circus
A few old rogues who remember rations and tuppence can usually be found propping up the bar at this pub. They've been around since the beginning of forever and they've done it all without

missing an afternoon of smoke and ale down at the Coach and Horses. This pub is fermented in history and is more than a local institution: it's a landmark.

The French House
49 Dean Street, W1
Tel: 020 7437 2477
Tube: Tottenham Court Road

This pub was run by local character Gaston – and subsequently his son – and was where Charles de Gaulle met with the French Resistance during the war. In the 50s, the bohemians moved in and drank themselves into a jovial stupor on most nights. Irish painter Francis Bacon was one of the significant arty imbibers at The French and he spent the afternoons drinking with photographer John Deakin and a huge entourage before stumbling out into the gutter. Nowadays the pub is filled with ageing Soho intellectuals, thespians and literati, a considerable amount of tweed, and young media kids who are desperate to soak up some of the illustrious character of this treasure.

No 28 Dean Street was home to Karl Marx. He lived with his family in the dingy attic rooms and three of his children died here.

The John Snow
39 Broadwick Street, W1
Tel: 020 7437 1344
Tube: Oxford Circus

As a very dull man told me, The John Snow is named after the doctor who realized that people would avoid contracting cholera if they drank beer instead of water. I think we should all take this lesson with us as we go about our daily activities. Water is bad. Beer is good. As part of the inexpensive Sam Smiths brewery pubs, a round in here certainly does come cheap. Don't expect to recognize the names on any of the pumps as it's all from Smith's brewery, but you won't be disappointed with your pint, or your surroundings.

The Toucan
19 Carlisle Street, W1
Tel: 020 7437 4123
Tube: Tottenham Court Road

This pub is affectionately grubby from years of long happy nights enjoyed by heaps of Soho drinkers. The Toucan has been a place to meet, drink and relax for years. With the slightest tinge of sunshine on an evening, the nearby offices empty into the street outside the pub, allowing locals to happily suck up the smog and exhaust as only Londoners can.

Phoenix Artists' Club
1 Phoenix Street, off Charing Cross Road, WC2
Tel: 020 7836 1077
Tube: Tottenham Court Road

Although officially a member's bar, if you come before 8 p.m. on a weekend, you can get in. It's open late, so it may be worth your while to wander down early. It's not a Goth bar, but the upstairs Phoenix Theatre has been playing *Blood Brothers*, so it must be for that reason that this bar hosts the monthly meetings of the Vampire Society. Odd? Yes. Just make sure you don't walk in with your new garlic necklace lightly grazing the scabby puncture wounds on your neck. The people of the night get randy when they see a pricktease.

Two Floors
3 Kingly Street, W1
Tel: 020 77349 1007
Tube: Oxford Circus or Piccadilly Circus

There's a lot of trashy mock style bars in Soho. Luckily there are some bastions of normalcy such as Two Floors. It would fit in perfectly in Hoxton, with the leather sofas, wooden floors … you get the idea. The scarlet-hued basement is a cozy refuge from the pounding bass upstairs: it's a bit like being back in the womb. Only you're with mates. And you have a fully formed cranium.

Also in the area
Sun and Thirteen Cantons, 21 Great Pulteney Street, W1. Tel: 020 7734 0934. Tube: Oxford Circus. Young and trendy but traditional pub full of mee-ja types.

Old Coffee House, 49 Beak Street, W1. Tel: 020 7437 2197. Tube: Oxford Circus or Piccadilly Circus. Relaxed mixed crowd, this pub holds regular poetry and comedy nights.

The Crown and Two Chairmen, 31 Dean Street, W1. Tel: 020 7437 8192. Tube: Tottenham Court Road. A time-honoured pub with moldy old regulars and trendy young things.

The Dog House, 187 Wardour Street, W1. Tel: 020 7434 2116. Tube: Oxford Circus or Tottenham Court Road. Pounding basslines, cave enclosures, and crystals on the bar. No suits allowed.

The Rolling Stones played one of their first gigs at the Flamingo Jazz Club, which used to be at 33 Wardour Street, on January 14, 1963. This performance earned band members about 25 pence each after expenses, and it was the first time that all five Rolling Stones – Mick Jagger, Keith Richards, Brian Jones, Bill Wyman and Charlie Watts – appeared on stage together.

Late bars

Jazz After Dark

9 Greek Street, W1
Tel: 020 7734 0545
Tube: Leicester Square
www.jazzafterdark.co.uk

A nice little drinking den to chill out after work with some easy listening jazz and blues. The late licence and cheap admission make this a popular nightspot with the after-work crowd. Entrance is free if you have a bite to eat from Monday to Thursday, £3 Monday to Thursday and Sunday if you're just drinking, and £5 Friday and Saturday.

The Player

8 Broadwick Street, W1
Tel: 020 7494 9125
Tube: Tottenham Court Road

This underground bar was once members-only, but now they have relaxed the policy and as long as you aren't with a group of snakebite-drinking hooligans, they'll let you in. Plunge down the dark steep staircase next to the panty emporium, Agent Provocateur, and pop through the doors into the blackness of The Player. It's lounge-tastic and as dark as a David Lynch film, so relax with a martini, sink into a molded sofa, and loaf until dusk turns to night. Then, hell, loaf some more and look gorgeous.

Seville Mia

22 Hanway Street, W1
Tel: 020 7637 3756
Tube: Tottenham Court Road

Everyone is normally so paralytic here that they look like pale rows of connected paper dolls with oversized heads grotesquely misshapen due to an unfortunate slip of the scissors. This is a tapas bar, but after the witching hour the emphasis here is drink, and plenty of it. Entering the dodgy doorway on this peculiar little alleyway, your mates will probably protest with fear that they're about to be stabbed in the neck with a biro. But once you get down the stairs, they'll find London's young nutters singing, dancing, and being as merry as a clown on Prozac.

Also in the area

Pop, 14 Soho Street, W1. Tel: 020 7734 4004. Tube: Tottenham Court Road. Retro-kitsch bright late bar.

Lab, 12 Old Compton Street, W1. Tel: 020 7437 7820. Tube: Leicester Square or Tottenham Court Road. Cocktails are the speciality in this tiny sweat box.

Café Lazeez, 21 Dean Street, W1. Tel: 020 7434 9393. Tube: Tottenham Court Road. It's always good to know of a late bar that doesn't charge an entry fee. Here's a rather dull one, if you're desperate.

Amber, 61–63 Beak Street, W1. Tel: 020 7439 2190. Tube: Oxford Circus or Piccadilly Circus. Suited media late bar.

Yo! Below, 52 Poland Street, W1. Tel: 020 7439 3660. Tube: Oxford Circus or Piccadilly Circus. Japanese bar with beer pumps on the tables.

The best views in London

Vertigo 42, Tower 42, 25 Old Broad Street, EC2. Tel: 020 7877 2424. Tube: Bank.

Studio Lounge, Fifth Floor, Waterstones, 203–206 Piccadilly, W1. Tel: 020 7851 2400. Tube: Piccadilly Circus.

Bridge House, 218 Tower Bridge Road, SE1. Tel: 020 7407 5818. Tube: Tower Hill.

Windows Bar, London Hilton, Park Lane, W1. Tel: 020 7493 8000. Tube: Green Park.

If you want a truly fantastic view, then just you wait until the day that someone introduces you to a towerblock with an unlocked door to the roof. A magical secret that every Londoner should know. But I'm not telling you where mine is.

Clubs

Form, 4–6 Greek Street, W1. Tel: 020 7434 3323. Tube: Tottenham Court Road. Eclectic DJ music in a retro atmosphere.

Ronnie Scott's, 47 Frith Street, W1. Tel: 020 7430 0747. Tube: Tottenham Court Road. The best jazz club in London.

Restaurants

Kettner's

29 Romilly Street, W1
Tel: 020 7734 6112
Tube: Leicester Square or Piccadilly Circus

Kettner's made its name as the stomping ground for Soho's creative nutters and drinkers for decade after decade. It has always been popular with writers and artists living the champagne lifestyle whether or not it was within their means. This is where Oscar Wilde used to frolic with his young lovers in the upstairs bedrooms, and where Francis Bacon and his artistic compatriots celebrated life. From the opulent ceiling to the linen tablecloths and silver service waiters you'll probably be expecting undiscernable nouvelle cuisine made from strange meats. Kettner's isn't like that. Now owned by the same man who runs the Pizza Express chain, it's about normal world food in a posh setting fit for a queen. Make sure you order a bottle of champers – it's a Kettner's must.

Café Emm

17 Frith Street, W1
Tel: 020 7437 0723
Tube: Tottenham Court Road

If you don't get here before 7 p.m., you're going to have to queue in London's unpredictable weather. But it will certainly be worth the wait. It looks a bit dodgy from the front, but come inside and you'll see loads of little tables with local media kids merrily enjoying a beer and a bit of food. The portions are all obese-American-tourist huge, and are the cheapest meals in Soho (mains £5.50). Emm is a culinary find as surprising and interesting as discovering a dead bee in your bellybutton.

Pulcinella

37 Old Compton Street, W1
Tel: 020 7287 3920
Tube: Piccadilly Circus

Sit al fresco and gnaw on one of the restaurant's massive pizzas. Watch the urban tuk tuk drivers dodge gawping tourists, trying not to turn them into cobble grout.

Café Boheme

13 Old Compton Street, W1
Tel: 020 7734 0623
Tube: Leicester Square

Excellent brasserie food is served all day long in this cozy and intimate restaurant. Sit at the outdoor tables, or opt to eat indoors, which is the place to be to eye the fit staff and listen to live jazz from Tuesday to Thursday.

Also in the area

Busaba Eathai, 106–110 Wardour Street, W1. Tel: 020 7255 8686. Tube: Tottenham Court Road. Great modern Thai food; so popular that there's often a queue. At least it moves quickly though.

Satsuma, 56 Wardour Street, W1. Tel: 020 7437 8338. Tube: Piccadilly Circus. Japanese food in a flash. Quick turnover of tables and rapid service.

Spiga, 84–86 Wardour Street, W1. Tel: 020 7734 3444. Tube: Tottenham Court Road. Classic Italian pizza and pasta.

Entertainment

Soho Theatre and Writer's Centre

21 Dean Street, W1
Tel: 020 7478 0100
Tube: Tottenham Court Road.
www.sohotheatre.com

Whether you take a writing workshop, see a play or a comedy sketch, or just relax over coffee or a beer, you'll find something of interest at this modern arts complex.

Cinemas

Curzon Soho, 93–107 Shaftesbury Ave, W1. Tel: 020 7439 4805 or www.curzon.net. Tube: Leicester Square
Odeon Wardour Street, 10 Wardour Street, W1. Tel: 0870 505 0007. Tube: Leicester Square
Metro, 11 Rupert Street, W1. Info: 020 7437 0757 or booking: 020 7734 1506. Tube: Piccadilly Circus
Odeon Panton Street, Panton Street, SW1. Tel: 0870 505 0007. Tube: Piccadilly Circus

Taxis

Soho Cars, 2 Lexington Street, W1. Tel: 020 7734 2002

Freedom Cars, 52 Wardour Street, W1. Tel: 020 7734 1313

A–Z Piccadilly Car Services, W1. Tel: 020 7287 5355

Covent Garden

Covent Garden holds all the mystical allure of an opulent jewelry box, a gilded mobile puppet show and a circus tent stuffed with oddities and amazement. The streets are filled with gawping tourists, but if you follow their gaze you'll see all manner of weird and peculiar sights. A man sprayed silver with rotten apples glued to his clothes standing like a statue waiting for a rogue pigeon to release its bowels. How about a musician hauntingly playing the somber theme tune from *The Deer Hunter* on his clarinet, or a man on a ten-foot unicycle juggling flaming torches with a William Tell-style apple precariously balancing on his head.

But if staring open-mouthed amongst a group of tourists waiting to be targeted by the Artful Dodger as you watch a Punch and Judy marionette show isn't your idea of a rockin' good time, then luckily there are other things to keep you amused. Head down to the shops along Long Acre Road and around the market where you can pick up all sorts of gifts, fashions and necessities. If bohemian is what you're after, then try Neal Street. It is outstanding for shoes, with plenty of boutiques, salons, and veggie cafés.

You may have to search high and low in order to find a place to live around Covent Garden as it is so central, but you'll be right in the thick of things without having to deal with the seedy side of life like in Soho. Your only problem will be the visitors. Whether it's from Covent Garden's mention in *My Fair Lady*, or a lot of guidebook poppycock, tourists love this part of London. The true market moved out decades ago, leaving prime tourist territory. The area is so full of sightseers that you can barely move, and you'll be nearly blinded in the evenings with the flashbulbs igniting. OK, so I exaggerate. But if you have to get from one end of Covent Garden to another in a hurry, you can forget about it unless you have a Go-Go-Gadget Copter.

> Entertainers (buskers) have to audition in order to perform in Covent Garden to ensure that they are of a high standard.

Pubs and bars

Gordon's Wine Bar

47 Villiers Street, WC2
Tel: 020 7930 1408
Tube: Embankment or Charing Cross

This is one of my favorite bars in all of London and, believe me, I've seen a lot. On the cold winter nights, curl up with a nice glass of red in the womb-like rock caves lit only by candlelight. This used to be a wine cellar, and sure enough you can only get wines here. But it is a far cry from your normal City wine bar. Dust looms in every corner, casting an atmospheric haze that glimmers in the candlelight. On the hot summer nights, grab a nice bottle of Sauvingnon Blanc and make your way outside to the little lane that is filled with loungers enjoying the sunshine, the company, and a nice bottle or two.

Freud
198 Shaftesbury Avenue, WC2
Tel: 020 7240 9933
Tube: Covent Garden or Tottenham Court Road
A tiny subterranean drinking cupboard for trendy young things. The twisty wrought-iron staircase should not be navigated by the tipsy, so go easy on the cocktails.

12 Bar Club
22 Denmark Place, WC2
Tel: 020 7916 6989
Tube: Tottenham Court Road
Your first time at this tiny club is as unforgettable as those awkward deflowering fumbles, unless of course you were blackout pie-eyed. It is a great place for listening to live music, quite often chilled acoustic sessions. Plenty of music's greats have lurked around these parts, so stop in for a cold drink and some tunes.

The Poetry Society
22 Betterton Street, WC2
Tel: 020 7420 9880
Tube: Covent Garden
www.poetrysoc.com
A truly literary place for everyone with a love of poetry. The café upstairs serves excellent food, but if it's verses and vino that you're after, head down to the basement. It's intimate, cozy, and a wonderful place to spend a night out drinking without letting your brain completely atrophy. The promoters really know their stuff and the readers are always top-notch. If you don't think you can face a night of constant contemplative stanzas, then pop along for one of their Poetry and Jazz, or Words and Beats nights, which perfectly merge music and poetry.

Also in the area
The Coach and Horses, 42 Wellington Street, WC1. Tel: 020 7240 0553. Tube: Covent Garden. Traditional pub full of smoke and smiles. **Bar des Amis**, 11–14 Hanover Place, WC2. Tel: 020 7379 3444. Tube: Covent Garden. Under the French brasserie, this bar specializes in wines.

Princess Louise, 208–209 High Holborn, WC1. Tel: 020 7405 8816. Tube: Holborn. Very opulent indeed.
Cross Keys, 31 Endell Street, WC2. Tel: 020 7836 5185. Tube: Covent Garden. A lovely little pub stuffed with 60s memorabilia.
Punch and Judy, 40 The Market, WC2. Tel: 020 7836 9931. Tube: Covent Garden. Busy pub with a massive terrace, popular with tourists.
Africa Bar, The Africa Centre, 38 King Street, WC2. Tel: 020 7836 1976. Tube: Covent Garden. A very peculiar bar; see it for yourself.

Late bar

Retox Bar
The Piazza, Covent Garden, WC2.
Tel: 020 7240 5330
Tube: Covent Garden
From the outside this late bar looks like a subterranean dive, but once inside you'll be confronted with loud music, glowing lights and sleek decor. It's a nice place for a late drink in these normally tacky parts.

Also in the area
The Spot, 29–30 Maiden Lane, WC2. Tel: 020 7379 5900. Tube: Covent Garden or Charing Cross. Massive soulless bar, but it's open late.
The Roadhouse, The Piazza, WC2. Tel: 020 7240 6001. Tube: Covent Garden. Hyperactive cheesy party venue.

Clubs

The End
West Central Street, WC1
Tel: 020 7419 9199
Tube: Tottenham Court Road or Holborn
Open 11 p.m.–5 a.m., costs £8–10
www.the-end.co.uk
This purpose-built club, slotted into the converted vault of a nineteenth century post office, is full of the kind of people you want to make friends with. Its relaxed door policy, retro-cool crowd and good sound system make this club one of the best in London. The music sways heavily towards techno, breakbeat, drum 'n' bass and UK garage, so trance-heads will want to steer clear.

Also in the area
Gardening Club, 4 The Piazza, WC2. Tel: 020 7497 3154. Tube: Covent Garden. Back in the 80s, people used to come here all the way from the likes of Birmingham – not anymore.

Browns, 4 Great Queen Street, WC2. Tel: 020 7831 0802. Tube: Covent Garden. About a hundred years ago this was prime paparazzi fodder.

Restaurants

Joe Allen's
13 Exeter Street, WC2
Tel: 020 7836 0651
Tube: Covent Garden

This is the ultimate thespian restaurant. Who needs the paparazzi glare of The Ivy? Joe Allen's is a tiny, dimly lit, hidden gem, which serves classy American food at reasonable prices. As it's right in the heart of Theatreland, this is where performers dine after a show. It's certainly not all too-many-forks and somber conversation. This place is as lively as Burt Bacharach's songbook – and it's a good thing, because that's likely to be what the cute bloke in the corner is playing on the piano.

Manorom Thai Restaurant
16 Maiden Lane, WC2
Tel: 020 7240 4139
Tube: Covent Garden

Having ducked in here for the first time to escape the unexpected sighting of an ex-boyfriend, I was expecting little else than an insalubrious hideaway to sip Thai beer while trouble passed me by. Twenty minutes later, my plate was clean, both waiters knew me by name, and the bill cost less than a ticket to see *Lord of the Rings*. A fantastic find.

PJ's Grill
30 Wellington Street, WC2
Tel: 020 7240 7529
Tube: Covent Garden

PJ's is perfect for pre- or post-theatre dinner as it is located right in the midst of Theatreland. This American restaurant manages to steer clear of the usual Yankee chain restaurant over-the-top tat, and keeps dining intimate. There is a jazz pianist to set the mood at the end of the week.

Also in the area
Hercules Pillars, 18 Great Queen Street, WC2. Tel: 020 7242 2218. Tube: Covent Garden. Bangers and mash for mom, dad, kid sister and grandpa. Take your pick of Cumberland, Thai, Highland, or Vegetarian sausages for as little as £4.25.

Entertainment

Covent Garden Market, WC2

Tube: Covent Garden
Open: Mon–Sun 10 a.m.–7 p.m.
www.coventgardenmarket.co.uk

In 1974, the powers that be moved all the fruit and vegetables out and converted the covered market. They pedestrianized the surrounding area and turned it into a tourist hotspot, selling art and knick-knacks. The shops around the market are basically the normal high street shops, but on no other high street can you shop whilst listening to live music, comedians, or watch a Punch and Judy show.

> The actual Covent Garden Market moved to Vauxhall in 1974. The area was then pedestrianized and turned into the tourist hotspot that it is today.

Jubilee Market

South Piazza, Covent Garden, WC2
Tube: Covent Garden
Open: Mon–Sun 10 a.m.–7 p.m.

The Jubilee Market is just to the south of Covent Garden Market. It's rather more bohemian and is a covered mish-mash of all sorts of stalls selling anything from souvenir hats to handmade crafts and novelty toys.

National Gallery

Trafalgar Square, WC2
Tel: 020 7747 2423
Tube: Leicester Square or Charing Cross
www.nationalgallery.org.uk
Admission: free

This gallery houses over 2,000 Western European paintings dating from the thirteenth century to 1900. See such eminent works as the gallery's prized possessions, *The Virgin and Child with St Anne and St John the Baptist* by Leonardo da Vinci, Michelangelo's *The Manchester Madonna*, Botticelli's *Mystic Nativity*, *The Rokeby Venus* by Velázquez, and works by Van Gogh, Degas, Goya, Turner, Hogarth, and Caravaggio.

National Portrait Gallery

St Martin's Place, WC2
Tel: 020 7306 0055
Tube: Leicester Square or Charing Cross
www.npg.org.uk
Admission: free

The National Portrait Gallery is just behind the National Gallery. It hosts the fantastic BP Portrait Awards each year, which is always a must-see. See portraits by Van Dyck, Thomas Gainsborough, Hogarth, Joshua Reynolds and photographs by Helmut Newton. There are portraits of all sorts of figures that have shaped British history: from kings and duchesses, to Shakespeare and Maggie Thatcher.

> Thinking back to the days of Mary Poppins, pigeons flew freely and birdseed sellers used to sell their wares around Trafalgar Square crying, "Feed the birds, tuppence a bag." But those days are no longer. In a bid to rid the area of these vermin-with-wings, all licences for birdseed sellers have been revoked. There has even been hugely controversial talk about shooting the pigeons to cull their growing numbers.

Trafalgar Square

The area was named in 1835 to celebrate the Battle of Trafalgar in which Horatio Nelson defended British naval supremacy against Napoleon's navy. Now it is a tourist photo opportunity and the scene of revelry every New Year. It used to be that waltzing into the area eating a sandwich would have you swarming in pigeons in a scene reminiscent of Alfred Hitchcock's *The Birds,* but now, due to the Mayor's loathing of winged vermin, pigeons are about as rare as a conversation between strangers on the Tube.

> The lions in Trafalgar Square were sculpted by Sir Edwin Landseer and were finished in 1867. They caused him countless difficulties to create, as the ageing lion that was posing for him died. Landseer was forced to complete the sculpture using the decomposing corpse as a model.

Royal Opera House

Covent Garden, WC2
Tel: 020 7304 4000
Tube: Covent Garden
www.roh.org.uk

This gorgeous building recently reopened after a multimillion pound refit, amidst controversy and nasty allegations of tax money being squandered on elitist entertainment. Sure, tickets to major performances can change hands for hundreds of pounds, but if you go to the box office on the day of the performance you can get tickets for £3. So why not break up the day with some Aida or Turandot? You never know what might be playing.

London Transport Museum

Covent Garden Piazza, WC2
Tel: 020 7565 7299
Tube: Covent Garden
www.ltmuseum.co.uk
Entrance £5.95

If the story of the Tube fascinates you, this exhibition will teach you all you need to know about London's transportation system. This is the place to go if you'd like to pick up a 'Mind the Gap' T-shirt or pencil case for your little sister back home (no entry fee for gift shop only).

Royal Courts of Justice

460 The Strand, WC2
Tel: 020 7936 6000

Yes, it's the very same Gothic building you have seen on the news at least a dozen times when those major civil cases and criminal trials head to the courts. Visitors are welcome to watch cases in progress and admission is free, but make sure you turn up between 9 a.m.–4.30 p.m. Monday to Friday.

Cinema

Odeon Covent Garden, 135 Shaftesbury Avenue, WC2.
Tel: 0870 505 0007. Tube: Leicester Square

Taxis

V&A Cars, 16 Leigh Street, WC1. Tel: 020 7387 8855

Urgent Minicab Service, 27 Tottenham Street, W1. Tel: 020 7580 3607

Freedom Cars, 52 Wardour Street, W1. Tel: 020 7734 1313

Trafalgar Square is night-bus central. Almost all of them stop here eventually, so if you can't afford the skyrocketing price of a cab late at night, then head here. The cost is £1 or you can use your valid Travelcard. Just make sure you don't fall asleep in a drunken stupor, as the driver certainly won't wake you up and you'll end up at the end of the line at the bus depot. Not that I'm, erm, speaking from experience.

Camden

If the four horsemen of the apocalypse all left from the furthest compass points on the Tube network travelling at distinctly varying speeds, they would collide in a mass of wonderous pandemonium at Camden Town. Rebellion, Mayhem, Individuality and Excess would be lovingly stitched into the labels of their underpants by their mothers before their journey. But once they cast their eyes on the outstanding pubs, the DJ bars, the gritty streets, and the anarchic market they would never again return to their maternal bosom. Camden is the place where the abnormal is ordinary, where the bizarre is mundane, and the outlandish is positively dreary. Nothing is shocking in Camden. They've seen it all a million times, but far worse. Nobody would bat an exceptionally long bejewelled eyelash at you if you were to walk down the streets completely naked with a full body tattoo of the Queen Mother, twenty-nine piercings in the left side of your genitals, and stinky four-foot-long neon orange dreadlocks. If you never quite fit in anywhere in your life, you'll fit in at Camden. This is where skaters, Goths, club kids, rastas, crusties, and eco-warriors all coexist in harmony.

If this sounds like your scene, then you should be able to find somewhere in the area to hang your Birkenstocks/black eyeliner/glowsticks/roach clip. Housing ranges from the relatively cheap to the outlandishly expensive in this area. From the scabbier section of Camden Town to the lovingly restored Victorian houses in Kentish Town, you should be able to find something within your budget.

You may be at the center of it all, but you'll have to deal with a sudden influx of thousands of tourists every weekend as they converge on the market. Don't stress about having to dodge Japanese tourists taking pictures of tables with inexpensive novelty t-shirts, just get in touch with your creative side and set up a stall selling retro-kitsch handbags or whistles mimicking the mating call of the horned owl. Never fight the non-conformity of Camden. Embrace it and you will love the place.

Pubs and bars

Blakes
31 Jamestown Road, NW1
Tel: 020 7482 2959
Tube: Camden Town
This relaxed yet civilized bar somehow manages to keep the riff-raff out and caters for the locals who still cling on to their rebellious youth, yet have moved on to the mortgage stage of life. It's not pretentious, it's just a nice change from the mayhem of the market. Pull up a chair outside in the summertime, or cozy up and cower from the rain in the winter. A wonderful pub with a slightly grown-up yet trendy feel. There isn't any graffiti on the walls in the loo,

and there aren't rows of three-wheeled baby buggies outside. It's perfect for that in-between stage.

Monkey Chews

2 Queen's Crescent, NW5
Tel: 020 7267 6406
Tube: Chalk Farm

The front part of this pub is dimly lit and fashionably grubby. Young, beautifully cool people kick back to relax with a few drinks and lounge outside on the benches in the summertime. The peckish can wander to the back for oysters and other dishes in the brighter back room with a large glass ceiling. So relaxed it's almost comatose, this pub is the perfect place to spend a long lackadaisical Sunday. You won't just come here once, you'll wish that it was your local pub.

The Lord Stanley

51 Camden Park Road, NW1
Tel: 020 7428 9488
Tube: Camden Town

Famous faces of Britpop past and present may have graced this pub on numerous occasions, but celebrity stalking is no reason to come here. It exudes an effortlessly cool atmosphere, so leave the rebellious teenagers with too many piercings down at the market and wander up to this part of town.

The Good Mixer

30 Inverness Street, NW1
Tel: 020 7916 7929
Tube: Camden Town

This was the only place to be during the height of the Britpop heyday. Now it's not very likely that you'll find Blur or a Gallagher wreaking havoc in a corner, but it's still pretty packed with musos and indie kids. There's usually a vintage Vespa or Lambretta parked outside with the proud owner clutching their crash helmet under the arm of their fishtail parka, and a few fashion students huddled in the corner discussing the latest in ironic feet-clothes.

Camden Brewing Co

1 Randolph Street, NW1
Tel: 020 7267 9829
Tube: Camden Town

This popular local pub keeps the relaxed atmosphere of an old man's pub, while the summery decor and quirky features keep the trendy young things happy. The garden out back, complete with Dimmock-inspired water feature, is surrounded by the back windows of the neighbour's houses. Keep an eye out for twitching curtains and the gaze of curious little old ladies, then sit back, read the quotes on the tables, and have a laugh with your mates.

World's End

174 Camden High Street, NW1
Tel: 020 7482 1932
Tube: Camden Town

This is probably one of the strangest pubs in all of London. It's really very disgusting, there is always someone on the verge of a coma lying in a corner, there are piles of hot vomit in the corridors, the loos are atrocious, and none of the punters ever look like they particularly want to be there. But it is big. And for that reason, and that reason only, it seems to be a major place where people meet up when they come to Camden. It's included in this book, not because we think it's good, but because at some time or another you will probably end up here. Brace yourself and wear a trench coat, projectile vomit is hard to get out of denim.

Bar Vinyl

6 Inverness Street, NW1
Tel: 020 7681 7898
Tube: Camden Town

Once upon a time, in a land far, far away there was no such thing as a DJ bar. Then over the hills and through the glens came a white knight carrying decks and a love of music. He thrust his sword down on Inverness Street and thus the DJ Bar was born. This bar is the original and is still one of the best. There's no swanning about affecting an uncomfortable pose to look cool, just people merging their love of music and lager. Watch out for the loos, seeing hundreds of reflections of your own face can make you feel like you've just fallen down a rabbit hole. Not good for the nauseous.

Mac Bar

102 Camden Road, NW1
Tel: 020 7485 4530
Tube: Camden Town

Pub-cum-bar. It's amazing what a lick of paint will do to a grubby pub. Not much actually: it's obviously a pub conversion with sofas bunged in for that lounge feel. Out with the naughty little indie-kid scallywags and in with the chinos and pension plans. They have obviously made the change to attract a more moneyed clientele, but I suppose as long as the punters are happy that's all that counts. And they certainly seem to be. The art on the walls is constantly changing and the cocktails are surprisingly good and reasonably priced. Not a Camden Crusty in sight.

The Lock Tavern

35 Chalk Farm Road, NW1
Tel: 020 7482 7163
Tube: Camden Town

Low lighting, comfy sofas, and an artist's loft atmosphere create the sort of bar that attracts laid back trendies from all over. Owned by DJ Jon Carter, a fantastic lineup provides smooth grooves upstairs in the lounge area on a lazy afternoon, or cutting edge beats as the night progresses. A fashionable crowd convenes here on weekends after rifling through the retro gems on offer at The Stables Market across the road.

Lemonia

89 Regent's Park Road, NW1
Tel: 020 7586 7454
Tube: Chalk Farm

This popular Greek restaurant lies right in the heart of the plucked, preened and feather dusted streets of Primrose Hill. Sadie Frost, Kate Moss, Meg Matthews and Jude Law – who all live in the surrounding celeb-ville – have been known to pop in for a tasty feast, and yet prices are not astronomically high.

Also in the area

The Enterprise, 2 Haverstock Hill, NW3. Tel: 020 7485 2659. Tube: Chalk Farm. If you can get past the glare of the gaudy exterior, you'll actually find a pretty good pub.

Spread Eagle, 141 Albert Street, NW1. Tel: 020 7267 1410. Tube: Camden Town. Not much to set it apart from most other pubs, except of course that it's the one from *Withnail and I*. So there you go then.

Lounge-jing, 88–89 Chalk Farm Road, NW1. Tel: 020 7485 8222. Tube: Chalk Farm. A mish-mash of all sorts of mental decor-tastic gimmicks make this place busy on the weekends.

Belgo Noord, 72 Chalk Farm Road, NW1. Tel: 020 7267 0718. Tube: Chalk Farm. A wide variety of Belgian beers and mussels keep this place popular.

Late bars

Bartok

78–79 Chalk Farm Road, NW1
Tel: 020 7916 0595
Tube: Chalk Farm

In a part of London so noted for its diversity and love of music, it is not entirely surprising to see that a relaxed bar that only plays classical music and opera works so well. Sometimes you need to broaden your horizons and bone up on your culture. So leave the breakbeats behind and try Berlioz, forget about techno for a minute and listen to Tchaikovsky, and save the hard house for the weekend and chill to some Handel. You'll be surprised at how much of it you already know from telly ads.

Dublin Castle

94 Parkway, NW1
Tel: 020 7485 1773
Tube: Camden Town
www.dublincastle.co.uk

The Dublin Castle has always been around. Always. Surely even back when Romans ruled the roost, they stopped into this pub to watch a band and have a pint. And when the nukes are fired this way, at least the cockroaches will be able to hang out at the Dub as the world turns to dust. An institution unlike any other, almost every band you could imagine has played here. Go on, head down and see what you can hear.

Bar Gansa

2 Inverness Street, NW1
Tel: 020 7267 8909
Tube: Camden Town

This noisy tapas bar is busy due to good food, a nice atmosphere and that coveted late licence. If you're lucky enough to get a table, you certainly won't want to leave until closing time – even if that means missing the last tube. Eat, drink, and be merry. If you've bagged a table, just smile smugly at those jealous punters with sore feet, and settle in for a long night's session.

The Monarch

49 Chalk Farm Road, NW1
Tel: 020 7916 1049
Tube: Camden Town or Chalk Farm

For Damon Albarn lookalikes, Liam Gallagher try-hards, Issey Miyake stylists and BBC DJs, look no further than this rock 'n' roll posey late bar. Don't miss Casino Royale on Friday nights, playing a mixture of retro tunes from the 60s to modern floorshakers. Or head upstairs to check out some live gigs by up and coming bands. Soon enough, you'll be chucking those Paul Oakenfold CDs out of the window.

Also in the area

Quinns, 65 Kentish Town Road, NW1. Tel: 020 7267 8240. Tube: Camden Town. This traditional old boozer is open until 12 Mon–Thurs, and till 1 on the weekends.

WKD, 18 Kentish Town Road, NW1. Tel: 020 7267 1869. Tube: Camden Town. Café, music, club.

Clubs

Camden Palace

1a Camden High Street, NW1
Tel: 020 7387 0428
Tube: Mornington Crescent

Pumping the hard house and club anthems, this no-fuss venue retains a bit of its old-skool glamour, and it can seriously crank the tunes. Popular with students, antipodeans and Essex girls, plus a few too many hard house victims with hairy backs for my liking. Don't forget your glow sticks.

Electric Ballroom

184 Camden High Street, NW1
Tel: 020 7485 9006
Tube: Camden Town

Tip Camden's streets into this club and what do you get? A mixture of Goths, rebellious teens, angst-ridden students and the odd lost-looking wide-eyed tourist. Even so, this club's Saturday night disco-fests are a cheesy laugh.

Jazz Café

5 Parkway, NW1
Tel: 020 7916 6060
Tube: Camden Town

Smoky, dark and sophisticated, this popular venue attracts a blend of 20 and 30-somethings who've got a few pounds to spend watching some of the biggest jazz and soul acts from around the world. Entrance is £10–15.

Also in the area

HQ's, West Yard, Camden Lock, NW1. Tel: 020 7485 6044. Tube: Chalk Farm. A bit mad. More than a bit.

Restaurants

Café Delancey

3 Delancey Street, Camden, NW1
Tel: 020 7387 1985
Tube: Camden Town

Minimalist decor and a classical style harking back to the 50s give this candlelit restaurant a romantic film set feel. Enter lead character, shaking an umbrella at the entrance and catching the eye of his glamorous date who is sitting at a corner table daintily smoking a cigarette. Composing himself, he takes off his rain-soaked overcoat before reaching behind him and handing the woman a single red rose. Straight out of a French flick.

Andy's Taverna

81 Bayham Street, NW1
Tel: 020 7485 9718
Tube: Camden Town

While tourists foolishly tear away at their rubbery fly-trodden flanks of pizza less than 500 meters away, you are revelling in a sightseer-free environment, satisfying your palette in what is sure to be the best-kept secret in Camden. Tucked away on a quiet street off the main drag, this family-run Greek restaurant serves well prepared dishes including an irresistible spinach pastry for £7.95, salmon steak for £8.50 or baked lamb on the bone served with potatoes and salad for £9.50. You'll have to stop yourself from licking the plate clean.

Marine Ices

8 Haverstock Hill, NW1
Tel: 020 7482 9003
Tube: Chalk Farm

Take refuge from the drizzle and cower inside with a little piece of summer. This is the most famous ice-cream shop in all of London. Rows of brightly colored icy sweetness await you. If you're lucky enough to catch one of the few hot sunny days, then grab a cone of your favorite flavor and head down to the market. Just make sure that a stray dreadlock doesn't encounter your creamy treat. Did you know that there are more germs in human hair than in human poo?

Mario's Café

6 Kelly Street, NW1
Tel: 020 7284 2066
Tube: Kentish Town

Made famous by the St Etienne song, this café deserves all the attention that it gets. A few pictures on the wall, some tables, and the best service of any café in London. Top fry-ups, great chips and always a reason to go back. A few tips though: they don't take credit cards, and are closed on Sundays.

Camden Lock Market

With dozens of food stalls to choose from, this is the place to be for some sweet and sour chicken balls with rice, bagels with cream cheese, strawberry crêpes, or even a curry. Most dishes cost £2–4 and there is an outdoor sitting area to rest your legs after trying on fifty pairs of vintage Levi's.

Food delivery

Domino's Pizza, 157 Regent's Park Road, NW1. Tel: 020 722 0070

Broadway Pizza, 9 Camden High Street, NW1. Tel: 020 7383 5010

The Raj Bhelpoori House, 19 Camden High Street, NW1. Tel: 020 7388 6663

Sizzling China, 273 Eversholt Street, NW1. Tel: 020 7388 2368

Also in the area

The Mango Room, 10 Kentish Town Road, NW1. Tel: 020 7482 5065. Tube: Camden Town. Modern Caribbean food with great retro ska and reggae pleasantly pumping from speakers.
Lemonia, 89 Regent's Park Road, NW1. Tel: 020 7586 7454. Tube: Chalk Farm. Impressive Greek cuisine.

Entertainment

Camden Market
Camden Lock Place, NW1
Tube: Camden Town
Sat and Sun 10 a.m.–6 p.m. (some stalls open weekdays)
The market is awash with everything you could ever dream of. If you want veggies, then veer off to the left on Camden High Street, to the right if you are after inexpensive jewelry and Doc Martins. For retro furniture, Atari's, kitsch E.T. telephones and other childhood memorabilia then head up to the Stables Market on the left after the overhead train bridge and into the Stables area. Just behind there are the arches where you'll find vintage denim and tons of retro clothing. The market is enormous and it will take many trips before you know where you're going. If you get tired, then just stop in at the nearest pub to refuel.

Regent's Park
Just moments away from the mania of Camden is the tranquil beauty of Regent's Park. As one of London's royal parks, it is well maintained and is lovingly stuffed full of flowers. Head up towards the north end to Primrose Hill for some of the best views in London.

London Zoo
Regent's Park, NW1
Tel: 020 7722 3333
Tube: Camden Town
Admission: £11 (£9.30 students)

If staring at caged animals is your idea of entertainment, then head to Regent's Park and have a gander. They have all sorts of critters, creatures and carnivores, so pick a sunny Sunday and spend the day gawping at them. Just the thought of the cockroach exhibit that I saw years ago still sends shivers down my spine and lunch up my throat.

Jongleurs Camden Lock

Middle Yard, Camden Lock, Chalk Farm Road, NW1
Tel: 020 7564 2500 or www.jongleurs.com
Tube: Camden Town or Chalk Farm
More rubber chickens, floppy willies and hairy muff jokes than Uncle Luc's sixtieth birthday party.

Cinema

Odeon Camden Town, Parkway, NW1. Tel: 0870 505 0007 or www.odeon.co.uk. Tube: Camden Town

Theatres

The Roundhouse, Chalk Farm Road, NW1. Tel: 0870 609 1110.
Tube: Chalk Farm
Etcetera Theatre, Camden High Street, NW1. Tel: 020 7482 4857.
Tube: Camden Town

Waterbus

Tel: 020 7482 2550
The Regent's Canal, linking Camden with Little Venice, was first opened in 1820. The London Waterbus Company runs a scheduled service along the canal from Camden Lock to the London Zoo. From March 28-October 27 services are daily. Between October 28-March 31 they operate on weekends.

Taxis

London Radio Cars, 1a Delancey Street, NW1. Tel: 020 7916 2121

A1 Cars, 125 Castlehaven Road, NW1. Tel: 020 7272 9999

New Euston Cars, 184 Eversholt Street, NW1. Tel: 020 7388 9494

Chalk Farm Radio Cars, Chalk Farm Parade, Adelaide Road, NW3. Tel: 020 7722 2111

Hampstead and Finchley

Few places in sprawling, gritty London can stake claim to the name 'village' without any trace of irony, but Hampstead truly is the epitome of an urban village. The quaint, steep high street surrounded by large terraced houses may be filled with the usual chain bars, restaurants and shops, but the tables outside cafés, the well-heeled locals, and the spotlessness of the area all go to show that Hampstead Village is rightly named.

But that isn't to say that it is only suitable for country ramblers and tweed-wearing pooch walkers. Hampstead has long been home to a number of new-money celebrities. Television presenters, pop stars, and a few bad boys of rock have all brought a cutting-edge trendiness to an area that could easily have been lost to the haughty upper-crust gentility. Great bars, pubs, restaurants, cafés and clothing shops line the streets and back lanes to bring a modern feel to the area, while the fabulous Hampstead Heath is the only place to loll in the summertime.

If you haven't caught a summer's evening of free jazz on the Heath, sunbathed by the ponds, or had a drink in the beer garden of the Spaniards Inn then you have certainly missed out on something special. Time to make amends. And don't fret that you'll have to be doused liberally in Prada and Gucci before you head up north, because the locals are too busy enjoying life to the full to wear uncomfortable stilettos.

It sounds marvelous doesn't it? Now for the hard facts. You can't afford to live in Hampstead. You can't even afford an old bedsit in the kitchen cupboard of someone's scullery maid. In this area, flats are rare and even if one comes up, the price will be extortionate. So the next best thing is to live nearby.

Welcome to Finchley. Sure, it doesn't have the same charm as Hampstead Village, but at least you'll be able to find a place to hang your hat. The area is still quite upmarket, and you'll stand a much better chance of finding affordable housing. Finchley has some good restaurants and bars itself, and Hampstead is only an, admittedly slightly lengthy, stroll away. The houses are still big and lovely – up to seven storys in some parts – and the area is shockingly void of council estates. So happy house hunting, because after one lazy Sunday spent in the area, you'll be calling real estate agents.

Pubs and bars

The Holly Bush
22 Holly Mount, NW3
Tel: 020 7435 2892
Tube: Hampstead

Tucked away on a small cobbled lane, this unpretentious cozy pub is the antithesis of what you'd expect in well-to-do Hampstead. There are no overzealous carrot-hued St Tropez tans, no Manolo

Blahnik stiletto holes punched in the wooden floor, and there's never a Cosmopolitan cocktail in sight. In these parts pashminas are used for cleaning out the loo.

Spaniards Inn
Spaniards Road, NW3
Tel: 020 8731 6571
Tube: Hampstead

This pub is as popular now as it has been for generations. The Spaniards was a haunt of Byron, Keats and Goldsmith back in the days, and is even mentioned in *Dracula* and *The Pickwick Papers*. Secluded on the long lane leading up towards Kenwood House at the top of the Heath, it is a great place to stop on your way for a picnic in the park. The only problem is that once you settle into the beer garden and relax to the sounds of their little aviary, you'll probably forget about the Heath altogether. You haven't spent a real summer in London if you haven't spent a Sunday outdoors at the Spaniards.

Bar Room Bar
48 Rosslyn Hill, NW3
Tel: 020 7435 0808
Tube: Hampstead

This is a chain, but you wouldn't know it from the atmosphere. It's got a lot more character than most chains, and the drinkers certainly all look happy. The walls are adorned with brightly colored artwork, and the circular bar in the middle of the main room is well stocked. DJs liven up the bar on the weekends, and midweek it is a nice place for a long evening of drinking. Food is served all day, every day and the speciality is wood-fired pizza. The friendly barman even offered around pieces of a pizza made in error – a kind gesture that wouldn't happen in the crab-infested loins of King's Cross.

Also in the area
Jack Straw's Castle, North End Way, NW3. Tel: 020 7435 8885. Tube: Hampstead. A quiet drinking hole in the winter with warm fires, this pub comes into its own in the summer when you can sit outside with a cold drink and bask in the Hampstead sunshine.

Magdala, 2a South Hill Park, NW3. Tel: 020 7435 2503. Tube: Hampstead. This old pub has now been turned into a wannabe trendy boozer. It misses the mark a bit but look outside for the bullet holes. Ruth Ellis shot her lover on the doorstep. She was the last woman executed in Britain.

Wells Tavern, 30 Wells Walk, NW3. Tel: 020 7794 2806. Tube: Hampstead. A pleasant local boozer filled with ramblers who keep local tweed merchants in business, and non-hooliganistic sports enthusiasts.

Flask, 14 Flask Walk, NW3. Tel: 020 7435 4580. Tube: Hampstead. A lovely yellow-bricked pub with a conservatory at the back and occasional live jazz.

Late bar

Toast
Hampstead High Street, NW3
Tel: 020 7431 2244
Tube: Hampstead

If your wardrobe consists of a varied selection of Burberry garments, you will feel right at home here. Not only will your dress sense fit right into this young professional crowd, but you will also be perfectly camouflaged into Toast's chocolate and taupe color-schemed environment. Although this swanky late bar has an exclusive member's club feel to it, the venue attracts a surprisingly unpretentious and chilled crowd.

Restaurants

Just Around the Corner
446 Finchley Road, NW3
Tel: 020 7431 3300
Tube: Golders Green

There are no prices on the menu at Just Around the Corner; you simply pay what you think the meal was worth. But don't think you'll get away with slapping down a penny and running for it. The food is an absolute dream and of a very high standard, and the charming staff ensure that you never stop smiling. This refurbished church chapel makes for a romantic restaurant, with dark wood walls meeting in a dome at the top, stained glass, and fresh flowers and candles on every table. The profiteroles stuffed with crab, and the chicken in tarragon and juniper sauce come highly recommended. Heavenly.

Al Casbah
Hampstead High Street, NW3
Tel: 020 7431 6356
Tube: Hampstead

You haven't had couscous until you've eaten at Al Casbah. Sit back on your brightly adorned cushions and let the traditional Moroccan music soak into your pores faster than the spices can clear them. Lay back and imagine hazy days in Marrakesh ambling past markets selling bowls of bright spices, and weather-beaten old men supping on hookah pipes. Traditional dishes with a twist, this is North African cooking at its best.

Café Imperial

76 Golders Green Road, NW11
Tel: 020 8455 8186
Tube: Golders Green

This restaurant has been drawing in the crowds since 1928, so it must be doing something right. Perhaps it's the 20s Charleston flapper girl feel of the stylish restaurant, or the classy black piano tucked into the corner. Whatever the reason for its popularity, any member of the roaring 20s jazz scene would have loved this secret gem on Golders Green and you'll certainly love it too. Café Imperial has an eclectic menu with mains ranging from £5.95 for pasta dishes to £12.45 for the steak. A real find.

Food delivery

Passage to India, 279 Finchley Road, NW3. Tel: 020 7794 1097

Perfect Pizza, 177 West End Lane, NW6. Tel: 020 7624 0197

Dominoes Pizza, 262 West End Lane, NW6. Tel: 020 7431 0045

Dominoes Pizza, 166 Finchley Road, NW3. Tel: 020 7794 1086

Basilico Pizza, 515 Finchley Road, NW3. Tel: 0800 316 2656

Also in the area

The Gaucho Grill, 64 Heath Street, NW3. Tel: 020 7431 8222. Tube: Hampstead. This Argentinean steak house serves quality food in a stylish setting.

Pizza Express, 70 Heath Street, NW3. Tel: 020 7433 1600. Tube: Hampstead. Another restaurant in this stylish and dependable pizza chain.

Brew House, Kenwood, Hampstead Lane, NW3. Tel: 020 8341 5384. Tube: Hampstead. Sit out in the sun right on the Heath and enjoy brunch in the sun. A local institution.

Zamoyski Restaurant and Vodka Bar, 85 Fleet Road, NW3. Tel: 020 7794 4792. Tube: Hampstead. A very romantic rustic Polish restaurant.

Sam's Fish 'n' Chips, 68–70 Golders Green Road, NW11. Tel: 020 8455 7171. Tube: Golders Green. You will never be without a seat in this banquet hall-style restaurant. A big place with huge portions.

Entertainment

Hampstead Heath

This 790-acre plot of woodland, hills and meadows is home to a surprising abundance of wildlife, including more than 100 bird species. Some sections of the heath are laid out as sports fields, while acres of roaming forest remain untouched. The park also has several bathing ponds for swimming, and an excellent lookout point on Parliament Hill, where you can see all the way to Canary Wharf on a clear day.

Finchley Road O2 Centre

Finchley Road, NW3
Tube: Finchley Road

This massive shopping center houses a Sainsbury's, Homebase, Warner Village Cinema, an art gallery, a gym, and some American-style restaurants like Ed's Easy Diner, and Smollensky's.

Keats House

Keats Grove, Hampstead, NW3
Tel: 020 7435 2062
Tube: Hampstead or Belsize Park
Admission: £3

Built between 1814 and 1816, poet John Keats (1795–1821) stayed here with friend Charles Armitage Brown from 1818 to 1820. Keats wrote some of his best-known poems here, including *Ode to a Nightingale*. The house is now an international tourist destination with its gallery of exhibitions and displays.

Freud Musuem

20 Maresfield Gardens, NW3
Tel: 020 7435 2002
Tube: Finchley Road
Admission: £4 (£2 students)

The museum is in the house where Sigmund Freud and his family stayed in 1938 when they escaped Nazi annexation of Austria. You can see books and antiques, and even the psychoanalysis couch where it all began.

Golders Green Crematorium

62 Hoop Lane, NW11
Tel: 020 8455 2374
Tube: Golders Green

On a macabre note, you can pop down to the crematorium and pay your respects to numerous greats such as Bram Stoker, author of *Dracula*; Keith Moon, drummer for The Who; actor Peter Sellers; Sigmund Freud; Vivien Liegh, actress in *Gone with the Wind*; and poet T. S. Eliot.

Highgate Cemetery

Off Highgate High Street
Tube: Archway
Opened in 1839 when London was facing a shortage of church burial grounds, this Victorian cemetery is now the resting place to more than 167,000 people, including a number of well-known names like Charles Dickens, Michael Faraday and Karl Marx.

Camden Arts Centre

Arkwright Road, NW3
Tel: 020 7435 2643
Tube: Finchley Road
www.camdenartscentre.org
Exhibitions, events, evening and weekend courses, and a bookshop.

Cinemas

Finchley Warner Village, The O2 Centre, Finchley Road, NW3. 24-hour program info: 08702 406020, or general enquiries: 020 7604 3066. Tube: Finchley Road. www.warnervillage.co.uk
Everyman Hampstead, 5 Hollybush Vale, NW3. Tel: 020 7431 1818 or www.everymancinema.com. Tube: Hampstead
Phoenix, 52 High Road, Finchley, N2. Info line: 020 8883 2233, or bookings: 020 8444 6789. Tube: East Finchley
Screen on the Hill, Haverstock Hill, NW3. Tel: 020 7435 3366. Tube: Belsize Park
North Finchley Lido Warner Village, Great North Leisure Park, Chaplin Square, N12. Tel: 0870 2406020. Tube: East Finchley

Theatres

Hampstead Theatre, Avenue Road, NW3. Tel: 020 7722 9301. Tube: Swiss Cottage
New End Theatre, New End, Heath Street, NW3. Tel: 020 7794 0022. Tube: Hampstead
Pentameters Theatre, Heath Street, NW3. Tel: 020 7435 3648. Tube: Hampstead

---

Taxis

Swiss Cottage Car Services, 311 Finchley Road, NW3. Tel: 020 7433 1000

North West London Radio Cars, 5 Rosemont Road, NW3. Tel: 020 7794 5284

Belsize Radio Cars, 311 Finchley Road, NW3. Tel: 020 7435 8088

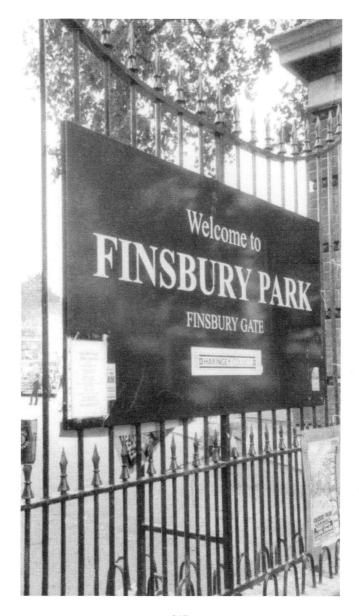

Grimy, seedy, and stuck in an identity crisis, this area has little else going for it other than the fact that it is within the Zone 2 boundaries. Being fairly central, located near a large common, and home to five-bedroom family houses, you'd think that the neighborhood would be more exclusive than it is. Finsbury Park is just south of yuppie Crouch End, where Victorian houses change hands between young executive families for millions, and it's also a short saunter to posh Hampstead and the gorgeous Highgate Village. Holloway is just around the corner from Highbury and Islington where there are rows of trendy bars, but none of that has rubbed off just a few streets away.

Holloway and Finsbury need to inject some life into their streets. Even a dodgy market would be welcome in the area, if only to give it some sort of character. And character is certainly what's missing. An elegant boutique, lovingly restored Victorian theatre, or even a cozy second-hand bookshop run by a devoted owner would provide the neighborhood with at least an ounce of charm. People live here in body but not in spirit.

There are plenty of flat conversions at reasonable prices, because hell, you're not exactly paying for a buzzing atmosphere now are ya? You will find that an abundance of properties in this area are above shopfronts. May I suggest that no matter how desperate you are, you don't choose one above a butcher's shop. Perhaps a nice discount clothing outlet, or maybe a cut-price plastic fantastic supersaver. I once looked at a flat above Raseem's Halal Meats; I was lured all the way to the seediest part of Finsbury on a dark winter's night, only to be met with a sea of goat's blood outside the front door, and I swear I could hear rats mating.

Prices are still vaguely reasonable, but they are rising rapidly, and you'll still have to deal with the homeless picking stamped-out cigarette butts off the ground and the filthy streets covered in random piles of fast food packaging and rotten vegetables. While Finsbury Park has the advantage of having the common nearby and the odd jewel of a street just waiting to be discovered, the bars, pubs and restaurants aren't exactly abundant.

Holloway Road is not much better, judging by the leering eyes and wolf whistles a simple walk through the area attracts. On the upside, things are improving, and if you can score a big house to pile tons of your mates into, you're blessed with having just a short Tube ride into the heart of London.

Pubs and bars

The Old Dairy

1–3 Crouch Hill, N4
Tel: 020 7263 3337
Tube: Finsbury Park

"Trespassers will be shot" a wooden sign reads as you enter this old brick barn. Once a dairy farm, the pub has milked its unique history by hanging buckets and ladders to the walls, pinning up weathered Dairy Supply Co Ltd signs, and retaining the number signs above the various cattle feeding rooms. So honky-tonk that you half expect Dolly Parton to be blasting from the speakers, but thankfully, she's not.

Chapter One

143 Stroud Green Road, N4
Tel: Not listed
Tube: Finsbury Park

A trendy bar in this otherwise rather grotty area. With a stone floor, a matt grey exterior and a young crowd, you'd be forgiven for thinking that you are in Soho.

The Rocket Complex

166–220 Holloway Road, N7
Tel: 020 7753 3200
Tube: Holloway Road

This is the student union bar of the University of North London, so you'll surely find a lot of greasy students in this venue. But it also holds the biggest Mod and Northern Soul all-nighters since the days of the Wigan Casino. That's why you should go. Keep an eye on www.modculture.co.uk for the nights.

Also in the area

The World's End, 21–23 Stoud Green Road, N4. Tel: 020 7281 8679. Tube: Finsbury Park. Attracting a faithful antipodean following, this pub has also got a big screen for cheering on the footballer in life-sized action.

The Bailey, 81 Holloway Road, N7. Tel: not listed. Tube: Highbury & Islington. Large corner pub filled with young locals and students.

Tank Urban Bar, 54 Holloway Road, N7. Tel: 020 7609 9574. Tube: Holloway Road. Live music bar with colorful leather chairs and sofas.

The Coronet, 338–346 Holloway Road, N7. Tel: 020 7609 5014. Tube: Holloway Road. It had so much potential... somehow the bland Weatherspoons pub chain has managed to convert this gorgeous old 1930s cinema into a dull boozer.

Hobgoblin, 274 Holloway Road, N7. Tel: 020 7607 3743. Tube: Holloway Road. Large and rowdy antipodean pub.

Restaurants

Café des Artistes

79 Stroud Green Road, N4
Tel: 020 7281 5557
Tube: Finsbury Park

Wander in past the electric tuk tuk and rest your weary rump on a thick wooden seat. Never mind the French name, this place is a celebration of Thai. Try the Volcano Chicken, £9.50, which is extra hot and served flaming. Not for the faint of heart or the delicate of mouth.

Los Guaduales

53 Stroud Green Road, N4
Tel: 020 7561 1929
Tube: Finsbury Park

Fabric pinned to the ceiling, a technicolored room with open doors facing the high street, and frilly-skirted women wriggling in their seats to salsa music. Follow this up with a fat slab of steak and a shot of tequila, and you've witnessed the South American dining experience. The shot glasses await.

Tbilisi

91 Holloway Road, N7
Tel: 020 7607 2536
Tube: Highbury Islington

In an attempt to modernize this Georgian restaurant's old-world theme featuring dainty wall lamps, china, oil paintings and brown wallpaper, the owners of this peculiar diner have chucked in a couple of blue and yellow Ikea lighting fixtures. Vegetarians will love the Tolma, a dish of stuffed peppers with rice and mushrooms for £6.25, while meat lovers will be in their element with a range of interesting dishes involving steak and lamb.

Food delivery

Garden House Chinese, 42 Stroud Green Road, N4. Tel: 020 7272 8699

Pizza Bella, 30 Crouch Hill, N4. Tel: 020 8348 7050

Pizza Bella, 171 Holloway Road, N7. Tel: 020 7700 0088

Also in the area

Aromi and Gusti, 196 Stroud Green Road, N4. Tel: 020 7263 8900. Tube: Finsbury Park. Artichoke and tuna mayonnaise sandwich, anyone? Eat at this Italian delicatessen and you won't touch a Benjy's cheese sandwich ever again.

La Porchetta, 147 Stroud Green Road, N4. Tel: 020 7281 2892 Tube: Finsbury Park. This is a popular pizza restaurant with a lively atmosphere.

Entertainment

Finsbury Park

When there aren't live concerts, this park isn't a half-bad place for kicking around a football or lazing about in the sun on a summer's evening. Keep an eye out for the mayhem of Mardi Gras and Party in the Park, then join in.

Taxis

Five Star Minicabs, 93 Stroud Green Road (rear), N4. Tel: 020 7272 7200

Lords Minicabs, 198 Seven Sisters Road, N4. Tel: 020 7561 1122

Islington Cars, 197 Holloway Road, N7. Tel: 020 7609 1909

Kwik Minicabs, 85 Holloway Road, N7. Tel: 020 7609 9959

Holloway Cars, 197 Holloway Road, N7. Tel: 020 7700 1249

Islington and Clerkenwell

Clerkenwell is gritty without squalor. Inner city without decay and rot. Graffiti and litter are kept to a minimum, and the area is considered to be near the height of urban cool. Or at least it was once. As interest swells in any area, so do the rents, pushing those in search of trendy nirvana further and further away. Suddenly, instead of being a stomping ground for bohos and style-conscious eccentrics, the area is priced out of creative pockets and into the realms of try-hard executives.

What was once a grimy part of London where no self-respecting Kensington inhabitant would tread the cobbles has now become an area of prime real estate. Fetid factories and derelict warehouses have been hosed off, shined up, and turned into luxury loft dwellings. Clerkenwell attracts well-heeled young trendies with a few pounds in their bank accounts, and due to its close proximity to the City, it also draws bankers with a yearning to cling on to urbane hipness before the liver spots and grey pubic hair start beckoning the Grim Reaper.

Way back before factories and exposed ceiling ducts were cool, the area was known for its Victorian slums and brothels, and the streets were rife with prostitution, murders, muggings, hangings and highwaymen.

Now the area shows almost no signs of its seedy past. Instead inhabitants have to deal with the May Day anarchist's nightmare that is Upper Street. Commercialism strikes with furor in this end of Islington, as major conglomerates, corporations, and multinationals serve tall skinny lattes in cardboard cups, pre-packaged sandwiches filled with coronation chicken, and novelty birthday cards festooned with retro knitting patterns of 70s Y-fronts.

The boom time of Clerkenwell, back when flats were cheap and plentiful, is now fizzling out. It is still a pretty great place to live – it's central and has plenty of good boozers – yet the true setters of trends have moved much further east. But the problem with moving into an area before it undergoes its renaissance, is that these grim areas are usually lacking in safety and amenities.

Areas like Islington and Clerkenwell are just teetering on the verge of their downward plateau, but they do have all you could need, plus plenty of great bars, pubs and restaurants. Living in this area comes with a built-in lifestyle without ever having to dodge the vomit in Soho. Unfortunately your paycheck will have to be fairly hefty if you want to afford a brick and chrome filled, high ceilinged, wood floored conversion in an old custard factory. Otherwise, it would be worth looking through the inky pages of *Loot* until you find a room in a terraced house. You'll be in walking distance of some of London's best clubs and bars.

Pubs and bars

Bar and Dining House

2 Essex Road, N1
Tel: 020 7704 8789

Modern retro? Yes, actually. With kitsch posters on the walls, flickering candles in brash holders on the tables and lounge music playing you'd be forgiven for thinking you had been transported back to the seventies. But this certainly isn't a swinging fondue party for balding council workers and porn-loving housewives. Look past your sea breeze to the exposed brick walls, brown leather sofas, DJ decks and chrome fixtures and you'll know that this is the height of modern stylish decor.

The Duke of Cambridge

30 St Peter's Street, N1
Tel: 020 7359 3066
Tube: Angel

All food and drink is organic in this delightfully large and wooden gastropub. Not only is the food absolutely outstanding, but the organic beer tastes great, has fewer chemicals in it than a Friday night at Fabric, and is said to give you less of a hangover. Say no more.

The Social

Arlington Square, N1
Tel: 020 7354 5809
Tube: Angel

A fantastic pub that's as well known for its great food as it is for its impressive jukebox. In the middle of urban pseudo-suburbia, this pub is the perfect place to spend a long evening. Battered leather sofas, thick wooden tables and chairs, and some wood panelling envelope local attractive young things as a eclectic mixture of tunes belt out from the jukebox or from the DJs. A good time will definitely be had by all. Unless, of course, you're a boring old muppet who would rather be stitching suede elbow patches onto the jumpers your nan knitted you last Christmas.

The Queen's Head

44 Essex Road, N1
Tel: 020 7354 9273
Tube: Angel

Everyone needs a local pub that is free of stuffy suits and rambling old men who have a favorite barstool molded to their flattened arse cheeks. This is the one if you live in Islington. Take my advice and head down for a pint. If you gave this place a miss, you'd be about as sharp as a wet bag of hair.

25 Canonbury Lane
25 Canonbury Lane, N1
Tel: 020 7226 0955
Tube: Highbury & Islington

Lurking behind the frosted ex shop windows just off Upper Street is a welcoming plush yet tranquil lounge bar with chandeliers, velvet seats, and retro leather sofas. The extensive cocktail list will make your head feel like porridge by the morning, but I dare you to try to restrain yourself.

Clerkenwell House
23–27 Hatton Wall, EC1
Tel: 020 7404 1113
Tube: Farringdon

Should you fancy playing with your balls, pool tables are just down the spiral stairs, but the loos are down there too, so make sure you get your footing before descending or else gravity could embarrassingly take hold. The bogs are marked by life-sized retro-kitsch cut-outs of guys and dolls, so make sure you watch where you're going or else you could get a pool cue up your arse. Upstairs, battered sofas are perched on by carefully dishevelled and nonchalant t-shirt and jean wearers.

Also in the area
Cicada, 132–136 St John Street, EC1. Tel: 020 7608 1550. Tube: Farringdon. Lounge bar stuffed full of media types.
19:20, 19–20 Great Sutton Street, EC1. Tel: 020 7253 1920. Tube: Farringdon. Media bar in the basement of an old watchmaker's studio.
Ye Olde Mitre Tavern, 1 Ely Court, Ely Place, EC1. Tel: 020 7405 4751. Tube: Farringdon. Stand in the alley on a warm night for a drink outside this traditional boozer.

Late bars

Dust
27 Clerkenwell Road, EC1
Tel: 020 7490 5120
Tube: Farringdon

Small but perfectly formed, like Kylie Minogue but without the annoying pop tunes. The service may leave a bit to be desired, but they put on some great DJ nights and get in some top spinners from the likes of Paper Records. The crowd is usually a bit older than your average bar punters (they seem to be pushing and passing thirty), but they are still ranting, raving and rocking hard enough to take on the wee kiddies.

The Embassy

119 Essex Road, N1
Tel: 020 7359 7882
Tube: Angel

This is a fantastic, dark, smoky bar with flocked wallpaper and velvet banquettes. Local urbanites come here for the modern and retro DJs and bands. The recently opened downstairs bar is even darker and loungier than the ground floor, so now you have a choice of how much wonderfully eccentric gloom you want of a night.

Fluid

40 Charterhouse Street, EC1
Tel: 020 7253 3444
Tube: Barbican or Farringon

Retro Japanese kitsch. It's a bar with sushi and a Japanese theme but it certainly isn't zen-like and minimalist. A Kirin vending machine looms in the corner, whilst giant Manga pictures adorn the walls. Over the top, but in a good way. All references to Pokemon and Hello Kitty are banned, and you're not likely to see a bunch of little Japanese girls in the corner with large footwear and novelty plastic hair accoutrements. Thank God.

Also in the area

The Garage, 20–22 Highbury Corner, N5. Tel: 020 7607 1818. Tube: Highbury & Islington. A great bar/club where you can see some top bands.

Al's Café Bar, 11–13 Exmouth Market, EC1. Tel: 020 7837 4821. Tube: Farringdon. Open early for breakfast and open late for drinks and bands into the wee hours.

Match EC1, 45–47 Clerkenwell Road, EC1. Tel: 020 7250 4002. Tube: Farringdon. Outstanding cocktail list in this lounge bar.

Restaurants

Le Mercury

140a Upper Street, N1
Tel: 020 7354 4088

This lively, busy restaurant is an absolute treasure nestled in the restaurant-lovers jewelry box that is Upper Street. The food is exquisite with mains such as salmon en croute with julienned vegetables in lobster sauce. The buzzing atmosphere and friendly service are what make this relaxed candlelit restaurant perfect for a night out with mates, a romantic dinner, or a pre or post-theatre meal. But don't expect to pay extortionate prices for this gallic cuisine. Mains are a paltry £5.95 – with such a high standard of meals, this must be the best value food in all of London.

Iznik

19 Highbury Park, N5
Tel: 020 7354 5697

Discover the smells, sights, and tastes of the Ottoman Empire at Iznik. Deservedly, this has been widely known as one of the finest Turkish restaurants in London. Colorful lamps vie for space suspended from the ceiling and painted glass bottles and tea lights are abundantly scattered about. The lively atmosphere is enhanced by the traditional Turkish music that seems to belly dance in the ears of diners. You'll be as keen on this restaurant as a hookah-smoking ageing carpet merchant is to his "special herbs."

La Porchetta

141 Upper Street, N1
Tel: 020 7288 2488
Tube: Angel

This is a great pizza place. It's noisy, bustling, and a favorite of many Islington natives. The food is good, with massive portions, it's reasonably priced, and is merrily laid-back. If you need a bit of eye candy with your meal, then brace yourself, the Italian waiters all wear exceptionally tight jeans. If that's your thing ...

Smiths of Smithfields

67–77 Charterhouse Street, EC1
Tel: 020 7236 6666
Tube: Farringdon

Taking the traditional British class system to new heights, this is a pancake-stack of restaurants with price and quality of cuisine increasing at each level. You minions can stick to the lower floors for a cocktail or a nice meal out with mates, but if the boss or someone who is trying to impress you is paying, then I suggest you go right to the top. And don't forget to order champers.

Food delivery

Mario's Pizza, 159 Essex Road, N1. Tel: 020 7354 0088

Domino's Pizza, 11 Islington High Street, N1. Tel: 020 7713 0707

The Phoenix Chinese Takeaway, 5 Lever Street, EC1. Tel: 020 7251 5386

Also in the area

Casale Franco, Rear of 134-137 Upper Street, N1. Tel: 7226 8994. This romantic restaurant is perfect for impressing a date. Candlelight, wine, and exciting fare such wild boar or mushroom pasta and juniper berry sauce. Italian gusto at its best.

Potemkin, 144 Clerkenwell Road, EC1. Tel: 020 7278 6661. Tube: Farringdon. Posh Russian food in minimalist but chic surroundings.

Stream Bubble and Shell, 50–52 Long Lane, EC1. Tel: 020 7796 0070. Tube: Barbican or Farringdon. Seafood and champagne in modern surroundings.

Clubs

Turnmills

121 Clerkenwell Road, EC1
Tel: 020 7250 3409
Tube: Farringdon
Open 11 p.m.–5 a.m., costs £5–12
www.turnmills.co.uk

Stepping down the stairs into this underground abyss is like stumbling upon Batman's hideaway lair. Beneath the shaking cobblestones, you become part of a secret world, dissected by rainbow stabs of lasers and hugging packs of strangers. Head to Gallery on Friday nights for some serious house, or to Headstart on Saturday for experimental breaks and beats. For those of you who can stick it out, Turnmill's famous gay club night, Trade, kicks off at 5 a.m. on Sunday morning. Five stars.

Fabric

Charterhouse Street, EC1
Tel: 020 7336 8898
Tube: Farringdon
Open 10 p.m.–6 a.m., costs £12–15
www.fabric-london.com

Although its heydey may have dipped somewhat in the past two years, this subterranean drinking cave (which was once a nineteenth-century meat cellar) continues to enlist podium-cracking line-ups, including The Chemical Brothers, Adam Freeland and Sasha. Fabric opened in 1999 and immediately became the place to be, judging by the four-hour queues of impatient ravers tottering in high heels and skimpy clothing. Today, Fabric continues to recruit world-class acts that never fail to please the masses.

Union Chapel

Compton Terrace, N1
Tel: 020 7226 1686
Tube: Highbury & Islington
www.unionchapel.org.uk

Set in a Grade II listed Victorian building, this working chapel still holds church services, but also hires out rooms for concerts and events. Major artists are now playing at this gorgeous venue, and you can hire out a room for parties, exhibits and shows. Stunning. Keep an eye on their website, they've got some great musicians scheduled.

Entertainment

Cinema

Screen on the Green, Upper Street, N1. Tel: 020 7226 3520. Tube: Angel

Warner Village Cinema, N1 Centre, Liverpool Road, N1. Tel: 08702 40 60 20. Tube: Angel

Theatres

Almeida, Omega Place, Caledonian Road, N1. Tel: 020 7359 4404. Tube: King's Cross

Almeida Rehearsal Room, Upper Street, N1. Tel: 020 7359 4404. Tube: Angel

Sadler's Wells Theatre, Roseberry Avenue, EC1. Tel: 020 7863 8000. Tube: Angel

The King's Head Theatre, Upper Street, N1. Tel: 020 7226 1916. Tube: Highbury & Islington

Old Red Lion Theatre, St John Street, EC1. Tel: 020 7837 7816. Tube: Angel

Hen and Chickens Theatre, St Paul's Road, N1. Tel: 020 7704 2001. Tube: Highbury & Islington

Smithfield Market

Smithfield, EC1
Tube: Farringdon
Mon–Fri, 4 a.m.–10 a.m.

This market is all about meat. Housed in a nineteenth-century building, this is where the main meat trade in London occurs. While you're off your face in Turnmills dancing and gurning to the latest breaks track, truckloads of fresh carcasses are changing hands just down the road. I just thought you should know so that you don't get worried in your paranoid stupor when you see all those men in bloodstained white coats wandering around in the morning.

Camden Passage, N1

Tube: Angel
Wed 7 a.m.–2 p.m., Thurs 7 a.m.–4 p.m., Sat 8 a.m.–4 p.m.

Just up towards the Essex Road from Angel station is a fantastic antiques and bric-a-brac market. On Saturdays, the covered section next to the petrol station turns into a farmers' market, but Wednesday is the big day for antiques. The market runs along the back streets of Camden Walk and sells all sorts of interesting jewelry and household items. Take a long wander, you'll be amazed at how big the market actually is.

Chapel Market, N1

Tues–Sun 9 a.m.–6 p.m.
Tube: Angel

The market is just off Liverpool Road, across from Angel station. You'll find fruit and vegetables, and lots of plastic tat like mobile phone covers, novelty lighters and batteries. Not the classiest of markets, but it's endearing and charming, as is the closest thing to Olde Islington that this area has since the influx of chain stores.

Taxis

A&A Cars, 49b Upper Street, N1. Tel: 020 7354 8989

Express 2000 Minicabs, 249 Caledonian Road, N1. Tel: 020 7278 3333

Cabline, 98 Old Street, EC1. Tel: 020 7488 1111

Islington Cars, 197 Holloway Road, N7. Tel: 020 7609 1909

Willesden and Kilburn

It used to be that you would have to follow the trail of blood to get to your mate's party in Willesden, but now it's more likely that you'll be forced to dodge sticky piles of snakebite vomit. The riff-raff are slowly retreating to the mucky bowels of White City and the Aussies are laying down their backpacks and marking their territory in north-west London.

In the past few years, a slowly increasing number of graffiti-sprayed, fly-postered derelict buildings have been cleaned up and transformed into classy Soho-style restaurants and bars, adding some trendier venues to the area's already abundant supply of sullied drinking dens.

Although still slightly seedy – you may want to reconsider blabbing on your shiny new expensive mobile phone at night unless you want it nicked – the area is easily accessible by Tube and bus and is tucked just within the Zone 2 boundaries, promising cheap rent and large properties. This is a good area for antipodeans and greasy students looking for spacious and reasonably priced accommodation.

While the main streets aren't as polished as they could be – you will certainly find yourself dodging crushed cans of Tennants here and there – the main streets are improving rapidly year by year, just going to show that this hood is on the up. In no time, this suburb is sure to steal the "Kangaroo Valley" title away from Earl's Court for being the antipodean hub of the capital.

Kilburn is a rather more upmarket area than Willesden, offering leafy streets and better kept properties, the widely-loved Tricycle Theatre and Cinema, and a couple of top-grade restaurants that you'll return to time and again. If major corporations' market research people are to be trusted, then the sight of a Shelley's Shoes and other major high-street chain stores is probably a good sign of a continually prospering area. Traditionally an Irish neighborhood, the family-run Irish pubs in Kilburn are always good for a rousing night with a few pints of Guinness and great craic.

Although Willesden continues to have its fair share of Bermuda Triangle you'll-never-surface-again streets, it also has some beautifully constructed old buildings that you would never be able to afford if you lived practically anywhere else in London. And with the opening of flash designer restaurants such as Shish, just outside the Willesden Green Tube station, things are only set to get better. From the leafy leprechaun streets and cafés of Kilburn to the grubbier yet upcoming streets of Willesden, this is an area to keep your eye on.

Pubs and bars

The Salusbury

50–52 Salusbury Road, NW6
Tel: 020 7328 3286
Tube: Queen's Park

Free of pretension, posing, and airs of self-importance, the Salusbury is a pleasantly scruffy arty bar stuffed full of local young drinkers sipping on their icy pints. This is a place to drink with a group of mates, have a laugh and get the most out of life before your bum sags like two moldy satsumas in a Christmas stocking dangling over the hearth.

Powers

332 Kilburn High Road, NW6
Tel: 020 7624 6026
Tube: Kilburn

This packed local pub is a popular favorite, especially on a balmy evening, when the outdoor tables catch the late sun. The dim interior provides a nice refuge from the summer heat, and the fireplaces keep you cozy in the wintertime. With the hymnal holder chairs and long church pews, there are plenty of seats for you to park your carcass on, whilst the strange student mural on the wall gives you something to talk about if your drinking partner is duller than a convention of librarians.

Paradise by Way of Kensal Green

19 Kilburn Lane, NW10
Tel: 020 8969 0098
Tube: Kensal Green

With its green color scheme, large windowed doors, and cozy back room with old gold-leafed lounge sofas, shelves of books and palm plants, you'd be forgiven for mistaking this pub for a southern plantation house. Replace the relaxed young chilled out drinkers with Scarlet O'Hara – hey presto, plantation. I don't know about the karma though, as they appear to have nicked some angel statues from a cemetery as decoration – though maybe those southern belles were into grave desecration ...

The upstairs is a lot livelier with a DJ and a darker color scheme, so whether you want a laid-back tipple or a boisterous bop you'll be pleasantly surprised at Paradise.

Also in the area

Astons, 2 Regent Street, NW10. Tel: 020 8969 2184. Tube: Kensal Green. Quiet, nicely decorated bar.

Koz, 87 High Road, NW10. Tel: 020 8451 5277. Tube: Willesden Green. Antipodean DJ bar with a good cocktail list.

ZD Bar, 289 Kilburn High Road, NW6. Tel: 020 7372 2544. Tube: Kilburn. Lively bar with DJs and dancing most nights.
Black Lion, 274 Kilburn High Road, NW6. Tel: 020 7624 1520. Tube: Kilburn. Ornate Victorian boozer with free live bands at weekends.

Late bars

Brondes Age Café and Restaurant

328 Kilburn High Road
Tel: 020 7604 3887
Tube: Kilburn

Attracting a mix of punters ranging from Aussie chicks with bum-length plait extensions to trendy Dieselites and knackered ladder-climbers, this artsy high-ceilinged café is a good alternative to traipsing all the way into central London for a spot of late night frolicking. Plastered with colorful artwork along its exposed brick walls and filled with dark antiquey furniture, you can while away the day sipping lager at one of the outdoor tables, or pop in after closing time for some late-night boogying.

William IV

786 Harrow Road
Tel: 020 8969 5944
Tube: Kensal Green

Hidden away on a shrubby street it is easy to forget how close to dodgy Willesden you really are. Willy's is a large pub with a pleasant restaurant and large outdoor seating area. It stays open late and on the weekend they put a couple of bouncers at the door and set up a DJ to get all the local trendies in the mood for a groove and some serious imbibing.

Restaurants

Small and Beautiful

351–353 Kilburn High Road, NW6
Tel: 020 7328 2637
Tube: Kilburn

Decked out with the same rustic ornaments that you might find at a mate's back garden BBQ party in rural Tuscany, this romantic diner evokes the same feelings that you would get by kicking back to a slap-up feast on a warm summer's evening. In addition to its original exposed brickwork and collection of farm animal wooden carvings, white fairy-lights and dim lighting further set the scene for an intimate evening. Lunchtime specials include a two-course meal for £5.75, or try the delectable main course dishes for less than £6 in the evenings. You will be returning time and again.

Shish

2–6 Station Parade, NW2
Tel: 020 8208 9292
Tube: Willesden Green

The humble kebab has never conjured up the idea of a fine dining experience, but cast all thoughts of greasy meat on a fly-larvae ridden rotating stick from your mind immediately. Shish is no normal kebab shop. It's a massive glass-fronted bar and restaurant that is much more Soho than Willesden. Start with a selection of salad starters and pita, then move onto the large skewers of meat or veggies served in a wrap or on a bed of couscous or rice. Healthy kebabs in a stylish restaurant, and service with a smile and a chuckle – who'd have guessed it?

Cookies and Cream

321–323 Kilburn High Road
Tel: 020 7328 9262
Tube: Kilburn

This lovely little tea shop has the most decadent and drool-inducing selections of fancy cakes, pies, and sweet nothings. This is the perfect place for a post-breakup girly chat and a piece of chocolate cake, or to read the paper on a Sunday morning with caffeine and calories.

Food delivery

Hippo Pizza, 3a Walm Lane, NW2. Tel: 020 8451 7557

US Pizza, 159 High Street, NW10. Tel: 020 8963 1400

Domino's Pizza, 262 West End Lane, NW6. Tel: 020 7431 0045

Perfect Pizza, 177 West End Lane, NW6. Tel: 020 7624 0197

Chasing Dragon, 7 Cricklewood Broadway, NW2. Tel: 020 8208 0805

Top Wok, 74 Cricklewood Broadway, NW2. Tel: 020 8452 9988

Also in the area

Vijay, 49 Willesden Lane, NW6. Tel: 020 7328 1087. Tube: Kilburn. Cheap yet surprisingly good quality Indian food.

Doña Olga, Latin American House, Kingsgate Place, NW6. Tel: 020 7624 3831. Tube: Kilburn Park. Eccentric, busy Colombian restaurant with a great set meal: £12 for three courses. Closed on Mondays.

Sushi-Say, 33b Walm Lane, NW2. Tel: 020 8459 2971. Tube: Willesden Green. Very high quality sushi – pricier than a conveyor belt chain restaurant, and a million times tastier.

Entertainment

Cinema

Tricycle Cinema, 269 Kilburn High Road, Kilburn, NW6. Info line: 020 7328 1900 or bookings: 020 7328 1000. Tube: Kilburn. www.tricycle.co.uk

Theatre

Tricycle Theatre, 269 Kilburn High Road, Kilburn, NW6. Info line: 020 7328 1900 or bookings: 020 7328 1000. Tube: Kilburn. www.tricycle.co.uk

---

Taxis

Mini Cab Express, 204 Kilburn High Road, NW6. Tel: 020 7372 1000

Carlton Mini Cabs, 209 Kilburn High Road, NW6. Tel: 020 7328 3737

Reliable Cars, 75 Willesden Lane, NW6. Tel: 020 7372 5558

Five Stars Express Cars, 62 All Soul's Avenue, NW10. Tel: 020 8933 7706

Entercity, 1 Station Parade, NW2. Tel: 020 8452 4477

South Bank and London Bridge

Once a neglected and rundown area, there used to be little else to do along the South Bank than to visit the National Theatre or the Royal Festival Hall – and then high-tail it out of there again. These days, the walk along the Thames-side footpath is one of the top must-do's when visiting London, leading pedestrians past Shakespeare's Globe Theatre, the Tate Modern gallery, and onwards to the futuristic Millennium Bridge.

In medieval times, the Thames served as a central location for festivities and entertainment. Men stood in boats and did jousting matches over the water, and markets would be set up along the frozen river during winter. Ice-skating was also popular, and Londoners would strap animal bones to their boots with true Blue Peter ingenuity to make ice skates.

But in the heat of summer, a festering stench would come off the water. Not only was the river a major waterway for shipping goods to and from Europe, but it was also the city's main open sewer system until the nineteenth century. The river was highly polluted, and yet Londoners were forced to drink it.

The suburbs of South Bank and London Bridge were historically industrial areas up until the past fifty years, when government-owned council housing estates moved in, creating new pools of communities. Since this time, developers have been wising up by refurbishing old factories into modern open-plan apartments and selling them to City workers at a tidy profit.

Even so, accommodation is relatively sparse and difficult to find around both Waterloo and South Bank, unless you are planning to buy. The posh new Conran restaurants and bars that have moved in along the Thames are just another sign that this area is on the up. It's exclusive if you want a river view.

If you're not on a platinum salary, then look around Borough and London Bridge. You should be able to find some reasonably priced housing in these areas. Whereas Waterloo and the South Bank are home to yuppies in glass-fronted, modern, luxury apartments, just a stroll south-east leads you to the grubby cobbles where highwaymen, murderers, merchants and prostitutes ran rampant hundreds of years ago. Housing is generally more run-down, but if you luck out you'll find a gem of a loft hidden in an old marmalade factory.

> London is one of the most ethnically diverse cities in the world. Twenty-five per cent of workers in London were born overseas, and over three hundred different languages are spoken there.

Pubs and bars

Ruby Lounge

34 Lower Marsh, SE1
Tel: 020 7837 9558
Tube: Waterloo

Pure sex. There's just something about those bright red walls, nipple-shaped lights and pubic hair lampshades. Good-looking bar staff, soft leather pouffe seats and groovy tunes further add to its seductive lounge atmosphere. I half expected to see a sex goddess licking bonbons from the fingers of male punters from a chaise longue in the corner of the room.

Studio Six

Gabriel's Wharf, 56 Upper Ground, SE1
Tel: 020 7928 6243
Tube: Waterloo

You don't find too many bars in London that can get away with flashing disco lights on a Tuesday night, but this funky bar does it well. Studio Six is in its element on a sunny afternoon, when every man and his spaniel heads down to the outdoor tables to drink pints, chat about the latest Tate Modern exhibition, and watch the world pass by. It's a seaside pub without the sea. But if you ask nicely the barmaid might grind some sand in your eye.

The George Inn

77 Borough High Street, SE1
Tel: 020 7407 2056
Tube: London Bridge

Easily one of the most impressive historic pubs in London, this perfectly restored boozer dates back to 1677 and was a popular resting place for the likes of Dickens and Shakespeare. Sit in the outdoor courtyard during the summer, or head into the cozy confines of the low-ceilinged rooms for a quiet drink with the regular old boys and their whippets.

The Anchor Bankside

34 Park Street, SE1
Tel: 020 7407 1577
Tube: London Bridge

Summer wouldn't be the same without your trustworthy riverside boozer to piss those precious sunny hours away. This pub has one of the largest outdoor terraces you'll find in London, and with a postcard-quality view of St Paul's and the City, you can't really go wrong.

Also in the area

Royal Oak, 44 Tabard Street, SE1. Tel: 020 7357 7173. Tube: Borough. Books lining the shelves, black and white photographs, and a big homey fireplace make this eighteenth century pub one of the finest in the area. Closed on weekends, unfortunately.

The King's Arms, 35 Roupell Street, SE1. Tel: 020 7207 0784. Tube: Waterloo. Traditional pub with a nice Thai restaurant in the back conservatory.

Founder's Arms, 52 Hopton Street, SE1. Tel: 020 7928 1899. Tube: Waterloo. This is a good place to stop for a drink after a long day of art-gazing at the Tate Modern.

Market Porter, 9 Stoney Street, SE1. Tel: 020 7407 1577. Tube: Borough or London Bridge. Cozy traditional pub with a warm yellow glow. It attracts locals and market traders and has more beer mats strapped to the walls than a beer mat factory.

> Today, the Thames provides two-thirds of the capital's drinking water. It has been said that every glass of tap water has been gulped down eight times before. However, it should reassure you somewhat to hear that the river has replenished itself since the industrial revolution, and is now actually home to 115 species of fish. Keep an eye out for the odd lost dolphin.

Late bars

Mint

Montague Close, 8–10 Borough High Street, SE1
Tel: 020 7089 5710
Tube: London Bridge

Swanky, charming and reserved, this stylish bar does it right with a candlelit room, an open dancefloor, and simply elegant furnishings. It's located just below Borough High Street next to Southwark Cathedral, but can be tricky to find. Look for the unmarked door to the left of Mint's canopied outdoor-ish area.

Also in the area

Dover, 6a Great Dover Street, SE1. Tel: 020 7403 7773. Tube: Borough. This happily shabby pub caters for students and backpackers from the hostel next door. They offer free pool and they'll even run across the road and get you a takeaway pizza. Look out for cheap drinks on student nights.

Restaurants

Livebait

41-45 The Cut, SE1
Tel: 020 7928 7211

Livebait provides superb food without the conceit of pretension – so there's no need to don the crown jewels and steal your flatmate's Gucci dress just to go for a meal. The hum of pleasure reverberates off the wipe-clean tiles as the high-spirited punters down their seafaring fodder. It's not as cheap as the dress code would fool you into believing, but then if it's economical fish you're after you could just scrape off the frozen fish fingers that are crusted inside your microwave. If you want expertly cooked fish, you'll have to be prepared to shell out for the pleasure. Boom boom, I'll get my coat.

Tas

33 The Cut, SE1
Tel: 020 7928 1444

Turkish without the bazaar accouterments. This modern restaurant doesn't depend on any ethnic gimmickry to entice diners; it just allows the food to belch and speak for itself. Robust aromas ride magic carpets across air from the open kitchen as guests struggle to choose between mousakka or the barbecued mixed grill with yogurt and tomato sauce. A couscous burlesque show with live music and a livelier atmosphere.

Inshoku

23–24 Lower Marsh, SE1
Tel: 020 7928 2311
Tube: Waterloo

This busy minimalist Japanese restaurant pulls in the crowds with a huge variety of reasonably priced sushi, sashimi, and noodle dishes. Try the grilled salmon teriyaki on a bed of oriental vegetables for £6.20, or one of the many bowls of soup noodles.

Honest Cabbage

99 Bermondsey Street, SE1
Tel: 020 7234 0080
Tube: London Bridge

It may feel slightly out of the way, but this green-tiled gastropub is worth venturing off the main drag for some no-nonsense, hearty English food. Jars of pasta, lemons and grain line the window, and the daily menu is neatly inscribed on a blackboard. Simple cooking and decor make this place good value.

Food deliveries

Pizza2Go, 14 Tabbard Street, SE1. Tel: 020 7403 0014

Rickshaw Catering Chinese Food, 11 Tabbard Street, SE1. Tel: 020 7357 6092

Simply Indian, 25 Tabbard Street, SE1. Tel: 020 7407 5005

Britannia Pizza and Pasta, 115 Long Lane, SE1. Tel: 020 7378 0800

Also in the area

House of Crêpes, Gabriel's Wharf, Upper Ground, SE1. Tel: not listed. Tube: Waterloo. Sweet or savory, a fresh crêpe hits the spot on the lovely Gabriel's Wharf.

Konditor and Cook Café, 66 The Cut, SE1, Tel: 020 7620 2700. Tube: Waterloo. Feeling like an alien is hatching in your belly after a night on the vino? We've been there. Flush it out with a Saturday morning breakfast at this great local café.

Kwan Thai, The Riverfront, Hay's Galleria, Tooley Street, SE1. Tel: 020 7403 7373. Tube: London Bridge or Borough. Posh Thai food with a fantastic view.

R. Cook, 84 The Cut, SE1. Tel: 020 7928 5931. Tube: Waterloo. Jellied eels? Pie and mash? Pop in for some traditional East End food.

Entertainment

Tate Modern

25 Sumner Street, SE1
Tel: 020 7887 8000
Tube: London Bridge or Waterloo
www.tate.org.uk
Admission: free, some exhibitions £3–10

Here you will be treated to some of the best Dali, Picasso, Matisse and Warhol originals spanning from 1900 to the present day. Housed in the former Bankside Power Station, the immense brick building is in itself a breathtaking sight.

The Museum of ...

The Barge House, Oxo Tower Wharf, Barge House Street, SE1
Tel: 020 7401 2255
www.themuseumof.org
Tube: Southwark or Waterloo
Admission: free

The Museum of ... is an ever-changing exhibit. It could be the Museum of Me, where the subject matter is about humans and what makes them tick. Or the Museum of the River Thames could teach you everything you ever wanted to know about the history of the river. Or there's the Museum of the Unknown... Take a look and see what exhibit is currently on.

British Airways London Eye

Jubilee Gardens, York Road, SE1
Tel: 0870 500 0600
Admission: £10.50 / £8.50 disabled
www.ba-londoneye.com
Tube: Waterloo

Take a half-hour ride on one of the Eye's 32 hi-tech silver pods for unrivalled views over London. Soaring 135 meters in the air, you will be flying high in slo-mo in the world's largest Ferris wheel. Be sure to book ahead online or over the telephone to avoid the queues.

London Dungeon

28–34 Tooley Street, SE1
Tel: 020 7403 7221
Tube: London Bridge
www.thedungeons.com
Admission: £10.95

Tacky tourist trap. Listen to Henry VIII's wife Anne Boleyn scream as her head is axed off, relive Thomas Becket's murder, and brace yourself for the scary man in dark robes to jump out of the corner and scream in your face. Prepare to endure long queues in July and August.

Southwark Information Centre

London Bridge
6 Tooley Street, SE1
Tel: 020 7403 8299
www.sic.southwark.org.uk
Tube: London Bridge

Get all the tourist info you need on Bankside and Borough.

Millennium Bridge

Open 24 hours and free
Links the South Bank to the City of London

It will forever be known to Londoners as "The wobbly bridge", thanks to those humorous first days when the swaying metallic platform was revealed to the world. But since its latest multimillion-pound renovation, not even the fattest troublemakers have been able to force much movement. Nevertheless, this futuristic pedestrian walkway is worth a photo in the album.

Cinemas

BFI London IMAX Cinema, Charlie Chaplin Walk, SE1. Tel: 020 7902 1234. Tube: Waterloo

National Film Theatre, South Bank, SE1. Tel: 020 7633 0274. Tube: Waterloo

Theatres

National Theatre, South Bank, London, SE1. Tickets: 020 7452 3000 or www.nationaltheatre.org.uk. Tube: Waterloo

Young Vic, Belvedere Road, The Cut, SE1. Tel: 020 7928 6363 or www.sbc.org.uk. Tube: Waterloo

Shakespeare's Globe, New Global Walk, SE1. Tel: 020 7902 1500 or www.shakespeares-globe.org. Tube: Waterloo

South Bank Centre, Royal Festival Hall, Queen Elizabeth Hall and Purcell Room, South Bank, SE1. Tel: 020 7960 4242 or www.rfh.org.uk. Tube: Waterloo

Southwark Playhouse, Southwark Bridge Road, SE1. Tel: 020 7620 3494. Tube: Borough

The Union Theatre, Union Street, SE1. Tel: 020 7261 9876. Tube: Southwark

---

Taxis

Licensed Cars, 296 Old Kent Road, SE1. Tel: 020 7237 4000

Capital Taxis, 28 Great Suffolk Street, SE1. Tel: 020 7633 9733

London Bridge Cars, 28 Southwark Street, SE1. Tel: 020 7357 9999

The Bermondsey Car Company, 14 Tower Bridge Road, SE1. Tel: 020 7252 1400

Brixton and Camberwell

Brixton and Camberwell. In past years, these words were more likely to grace a police radio call, but as gentrification runs riot they have taken on a new downbeat-but-cool image. As with Clapham, new money has added a range of upmarket bars, restaurants and bistros to complement the cheap and cheerful old faithfuls. Camberwell itself is surprisingly green and leafy when you're off the main roads and away from the Green itself, which still plays host to an exciting variety of skag nutters, while Brixton has back roads unlike anywhere else in London. Don't be surprised when someone whispers "hashish" in your ear as they pass you on the street.

After the Second World War, a large number of immigrants from the West Indies settled in the Brixton area, giving it a distinct Caribbean flavor. But gradual hostility between police and blacks led to the riots of the 1980s, when shops were looted and battles raged. Since this time, more relaxed police measures and a continued thriving arts culture have made Brixton a popular place to live amongst the gay community, actors and artists. It is also the center for black media and culture, home to Choice FM radio and the *Voice* newspaper, several galleries, and art and design projects.

In terms of housing developments, Camberwell has remained pretty much the same for the past millennia, though unlike Brixton, it is most likely due to its total lack of Tube transportation. Trains and buses are the only way to travel, and give occasional glimpses of the locals at their best – market day afternoons see hundreds of Jamaican housewives haggling and cussing – colorful and hilarious at the worst.

The Green may be the center of Camberwell, but the best venues are to be found lurking up its main tributaries: further south-east towards Peckham, up to Denmark Hill, and west to Brixton.

Pubs and bars

Sun and Doves
61–63 Coldharbour Lane, SW9
Tel: 020 7733 1525
Tube: Brixton

A brightly-colored pub, but if you aren't put off by the color scheme, a cocktail bar is revealed. Arty bohemian types hang and chill on the sofas, and new media things discuss matters of importance over hot laptops. Bar food is pricey considering the content (microwave fantastic), and enthusiastically punted cocktails tend to represent more willingness than skill. In summer months the Spanish-inspired garden lit by fairy-lights is a pleasure with a splash of wine from the reasonable list.

Late bars

Redstar

319 Camberwell Road, SE5
Tel: 020 7703 7779
Tube: Oval
www.redstarbar.co.uk

It's not starry, but it is red and it's definitely a bar. Unfortunately given to 80s retro cheese nights, this venue does occasionally have passable house and techno nights, depending on how the DJ feels. Two rooms allow some flexibility in music choice, but they're usually pretty similar. Comfy armchairs provide somewhere to park your dancing gear, and if you can see the bar, buy a drink – it's usually four or five deep at least. Open until 4 a.m. weekends.

Living Room

443 Coldharbour Lane, SW9
Tel: 020 7326 4040
Tube: Brixton
www.livingbar.co.uk

Flyer says: "Records you know + music you like + lots of fun + sweets ..." This used to be vaguely accurate, with a crowd of pretentious pre-Fridge prunes in residence. They were soon scared off by the uncompromising attitude of Coldharbour denizens, and the place took a nosedive when serious security was introduced. There aren't enough seats to call it a bar, and not enough space to dance, thus falling between the stools of sense (although a new section upstairs may aid this somewhat). Free before 10 p.m., £5 after.

Bug Bar

The Crypt, St Matthew's Church, SW2
Tel: 020 7738 3184
Tube: Brixton
www.bugbar.co.uk

Situated in the crypt below St Matthew's Church, the Bug Bar is a great starting point for a night on the town. Intimate, dark and friendly, there's good nights with drum 'n' bass, reggae and house on the decks along with the occasional live band and comedy night. Beer's a bit expensive but entrance is usually free on weekdays and stays open till 1 a.m., or 2 a.m. weekends. Clientele includes hip out-of-towners, locals and those too screwed to make it anywhere else. The fact that the venue is huge, on a roundabout and floodlit tends to draw in all sorts.

Brixtonian Havana Club

11 Beehive Place, SW9
Tel: 020 7924 9262
Tube: Brixton

Rum connoisseurs and piss artists can't get enough of this place, which stocks more than 300 varieties of rum, and stays open till 2 a.m. The relaxed vibe matches the Caribbean flavors; evening entertainment ranges from DJ sets to open-mic gigs.

Snug

65 Camberwell Church Street, SE5
Tel: 020 7277 2601
Tube: Oval

Snug by name, snug by nature. This outpost of the Bubushka empire is one of the areas best – leather sofas, bar and chandeliers conspire to create the impression of an old boys' club, but the tunes are anything but. Dub, acid jazz and reggae ooze from the double doors most nights of the week, and the Jamaican 'cat in the hat' DJ knows his stuff. The cocktails are strong but tepidly priced, and the fresh flowers on the bar add a further touch of class. Recent late licence till 1 or 2 a.m. makes this a definite winner.

Restaurants

Café Tadim

Camberwell Church Street, SE5
Tel: 020 7708 838
Tube: Oval

It may look like a Turkish bakery, but this is one of the best coffee cafés in London. Out the back, a narrow conservatory and garden seat around 40 enlightened souls. The genuine Turkish coffee certainly has a kick, and the stuffed breads are cheap, filling and damn tasty – highly recommended.

Hey Babe

22 Camberwell Church Street, SE5
Tel: 020 7252 4800
Tube: Oval

Tricky. Is it a curry house, comedy nonsense, or a restaurant? I'm still not sure. The logo is a large golden kangaroo with a woman rising from its pouch and the menu continues the madness. The Pepper Lamb is billed as: "Sounds boring but is exciting"; the Calamari: "This outrageous calamari will funk up your day and is definitely worth waiting for"; the Dom Dom Mushroom: "Unknown, but guaranteed it will be popular like yourself." Not to forget the Cumin Potato: "Oh yes, you have to take my word, it's the best potato you can think of in this world." You see the problem. This said, there's always a meal deal on: recently a dinner for two would get you, variously, a calculator, calendar and free bottle of wine. The food's good too ...

Jungle Grill

Camberwell Church Street, SE5
Tel: Not listed.
Tube: Oval

A proper sarf-east café – melamine tables, plastic chairs, mountains of chips with everything, beans as standard, and no price over a fiver – this is the perfect place for nursing the Sunday morning hangover. Portions are generous though, so if you're still feeling queasy don't attempt this one. The inmates really show the area's diversity. Old Italians meet and greet in the corner, bike couriers scoff the full English, and young 20-somethings wave burgers about.

Willows Wine Bar

81 Denmark Hill, SE5
Tel: 020 7701 0188
Tube: Oval

Candlelight spills onto the pavements of Denmark Hill; not the first place you'd go looking for it, but once uncovered, this café's never forgotten. A small, intimate café whose prices surely don't pay the staff wages, never mind the rent. Service tends to be slow, but very apologetic, and the food is good, although unadventurous. Upcoming renovations include the conversion of the downstairs into a restaurant and the upstairs into a bistro bar – one to keep an eye on.

Food delivery

Chicago Pizza, 129 South Lambeth Road, SW8. Tel: 020 7735 4444

Pizza Go Go, 703 Wandsworth Road, SW8. Tel: 020 7978 1238

Dragon Wok, 40 Peckham Road, SE5. Tel: 020 7708 3898

Also in the area

Phoenix Café, 441 Coldharbour Lane, SW9. Tel: 020 7733 4430
Tube: Brixton. Old-skool, no nonsense café serving up bacon sarnies, fry-ups and beverages in a friendly atmosphere. Residents generally pack the place, so be willing to battle for a table at peak times.

The Lounge, 88 Atlantic Road, SW9. Tel: 020 7733 5229. Tube: Brixton. Small and laid back and pleasingly stocked up with the day's newspapers, this is a top place to pass away a few chilled-out hours. There's a couple of computers available for net access, the breakfast options are good, plus the coffee and shakes are great. **Noodle House**, 426 Coldharbour Lane, SW9. Tel: 0207 274 1492. Tube: Brixton. Strangely pretentious, considering this is a Vietnamese noodle bar of the most stolid sort. Dishes are cheap and bear little resemblance to the original recipes. Open late, which is where its niche lies. No matter, it's better than a kebab.

Clubs

Club 414

414 Coldharbour Lane, SW9
Tel: 020 7924 9322
Tube: Brixton

Remember free squat parties? No? Well, this looks like one. The manager will hit the roof if such a thing is suggested, 'always 'ad a license 'ere mate', but the collection of road furniture and old fans upstairs has that unmistakeable air to it. On the other side of the coin, this is one of South London's oldest techno/trance venues, and everyone who's anyone has played a few sets here. The Liberators night, Nuclear Free, guarantees steaming acid tunes and a dirty come-down the next day. Entry is cheap, lager tends to come in cans, and drugs are rife – nothing particularly surprising then. The hoi-polloi of the scene tend to head to Fridge just around the corner ...

Dogstar

389 Coldharbour Lane, SW9
Tel: 020 7733 7515
Tube: Brixton

The Dogstar is one of Brixton's most popular bar/clubs. During the week it's free to get in, with the reasonably priced beer and excellent DJs pulling a lively Brixton crowd. Come the weekend, however, and it's a very different story as the place is transformed into cheesy stiletto disco hell. Hordes of Tamara's and Tarquin's descend en masse, having been ejected from Essex Road, leaping straight out of their taxis and into the drunken chat-up inferno inside. It is truly ghastly. Avoid at all costs.

Funky Monky

25 Camberwell Church Street, SE5
Tel: 020 7277 1803
Tube: Oval

At first sight this small bar seems to be a café, until you wind your way upstairs to find a similar sized club. Weekly tango classes and weekend parties use the space well, and the regular DJs on the ground floor provide a solid warm-up every time. Cocktails tend to be bucket-sized bargains and are best avoided. Weekend nights are frequently overrun with locals who have overindulged in their respective poisons too early to make it to Brixton – usually entertaining with a hint of danger ...

Fridge
1 Town Hall Parade, SW9
Tel: 020 7326 5100
Tube: Brixton

Another trance club, which garnered a strong following a few years ago by hosting underground techno and hard trance "Escape from Samsara" and Pendragon nights. However, continued heavy-handed security, trickling water taps and overcrowding have reduced the appeal of late. Still, if leaping around a sweaty mass of fluorescent trance heads is your bag, go along. Admission varies but is generally around £8–12. The Fridge also hosts several popular gay nights.

Fridge Bar
1 Town Hall Parade, SW9
Tel: 020 7326 5100
Tube: Brixton

Right next door to the Fridge, this is a small and friendly joint with a busy street level bar and a delightfully sleazy dark dance floor downstairs. It attracts a busy mixed gay/straight crowd on weekends, but the bouncing can get a bit energetic at times – maybe the crack dealers in the park opposite spark paranoia? Best for chilling on Sundays after the mob has passed through. Admission is free weekdays (open till 2 a.m., weekends till 4 a.m.).

Entertainment

Brixton Market
East of Brixton Road area, SW9
Tube: Brixton
Mon–Sat, 10 a.m.–sunset

This market has around 300 market stalls specializing in African and Caribbean foodstuff, fabrics, and even gospel music. It has always been a central trading point of Brixton, and, for you pub quizmasters out there, Electric Avenue was one of the first shopping streets in London to be lit by electricity.

Brockwell Park's Evian Lido

Brockwell Park, Dulwich Road, SE24
Tel: 020 7274 3088
www.thelido.co.uk
Admission: £2–£5

It's hard to believe that this outdoor oasis is just in the outskirts of one of London's grimiest suburbs. Surrounded with lush greenery, this refurbished pool is the cheapest ticket out of London one could get on a sunny afternoon. Open from May to September, weekdays 6.45–10 a.m., and 12–6 p.m. Weekends 12–6 p.m.

Cinemas

Ritzy, Brixton Oval, Coldharbour Lane, Brixton, SW9. Tel: 020 7731 2121 or bookings: 020 7733 2229. Tube: Brixton
Peckham Premier, Rye Lane, SE15. Tel: 020 7732 1010. Rail: Peckham Rye

Taxis

Brixton Mini Cabs, 270 Brixton Road, SW9. Tel: 020 7733 2165

Bluebell Mini Cabs, 63 Stockwell Road, SW9. Tel: 020 7326 1616

South Lambeth Mini Cabs, 12a Victoria Mansions, South Lambeth Road, SW8. Tel: 020 7582 7755

Camberwell Cars, 27 Denmark Hill, SE5. Tel: 020 7703 4461

Clapham and Battersea

The young professional crowd has taken over Clapham. There was a time when this well-groomed bunch wouldn't have even dreamed of setting foot anywhere near the Lambeth council borderline. But as a result of an overspill from the nearby affluent region of Fulham, plus some sugar-coated city jobs under their belts, Cambridge grads are snapping up properties with more glee than four-year-old children leaping through water sprinklers.

In the area of Clapham Junction and Clapham South, where properties would have sold for just £40k in the 50s, you would be lucky to find a two-bedroom flat for less than £300,000. Along the yuppy-esque boundaries of Northcoate Road, prepare to see bouncy packs of loud and proud public schoolboys strutting in khaki chinos, tucked-in collared shirts, and deck shoes. As for the women, your typical well-fed city girl comes suited and booted with well-groomed hair, polished fingernails, and last season's designer handbags.

Actually, it's no real surprise why Clapham has become an appealing area to live during the past two decades. With its vast common, and the nearby wild greenery of Battersea Park, the area has plenty of foliage and open space for going for a walk, playing "badders", or for chucking the rugby ball around.

In the summertime, Clapham Common becomes home to a range of outdoor events, skateboard shows, and open-air concerts. The park also has a reputation for being a gay pick-up joint, and come nightfall, the fields come alive with the sounds of erogenous groaning.

Just a 20-minute walk from Clapham Junction across the common lies the village of Clapham Common, which boasts enormous houses which have proved to be popular amongst budgeting students, first-jobbers, travellers, and artsy types. Its large properties, lush back gardens, and the nearby common makes this area a pleasant place to live.

> Built in 1851, Wandsworth Prison housed a number of famous people including Oscar Wilde, incarcerated in 1895, and Ronnie Biggs, the great train robber, who famously escaped in 1965.

Pubs and bars

Arch 635

15–16 Lendal Terrace, SW4
Tel: 020 7720 7343 or www.arch635.co.uk
Tube: Clapham North
This subterranean cave, built under the railway arches, has all the

components to make it a cool bar. Exposed brickwork, live DJ sets, fairy-lights, and industrial aluminium decor. Definitely one of the coolest bars in Clapham, but somehow feeling a bit out of place, enticing a strange mixture of people – from the ultra-trendy to the I've-just-come-from-the-country-club type.

The Alexandra

14 Clapham Common Southside, SW4
Tel: 020 7627 5102
Tube: Clapham Common

One of the few pubs in Clapham to have retained its brick-and-wood historic pub feel, while throwing in a smattering of enamelled signs and old farming tools to defy the whole aluminium-covered bar sensation that is sweeping through Clapham. Its punters are mainly relaxed 20 and 30-somethings who wouldn't dream of slapping on a pashmina to mix with the nearby All Bar One crowd.

Frog and Forget Me Not

The Pavement, SW4
Tel: 020 7622 5230
Tube: Clapham Common

Something about this pub makes it feel like it is the scummy lounge room of a student house. Perhaps it's the well-worn mismatched second-hand couches scattered throughout the place, or maybe it's the young and slightly scruffier crowd that tends to gather here. So get off your lazy arse, turn off the telly, and get down to the pub. You won't even have to worry about ironing pleats into your trousers.

The Sun

47 Old Town, SW4
Tel: 020 7622 4980
Tube: Clapham Common

For those days when London feels like the sweaty armpit of the world, take a seat at one of the Sun's outdoor tables and you can almost imagine yourself kicking back at a beachside café. This sociable pub is the place to be on a sunny afternoon in Clapham, when all the middle-class 20-somethings in the area gather to check out the local talent. On really busy days, the crowd spills out onto the road, creating a party atmosphere within a 100-meter radius of the pub. If you can't make it down to Brighton for the day, this might be your next best option.

Also in the area

100 Pub, 100 Clapham Park Road, SW4. Tel: 020 7720 8902. Tube: Clapham Common. A friendly vibe and funky music make this pub well worth the walk from the station.

The Bread and Roses, 68 Clapham Manor Street, SW4. Tel: 020 7498 1779. Tube: Clapham Common. Comedy and poetry readings in your own backyard. You now have no excuse to stay in.

B@1, 85 Battersea Rise, SW11. Tel: 020 7978 6595. Rail: Clapham Junction. Don't miss their 2-for-1 cocktails from 6–8 p.m. weeknights. Men will love the talent this venue attracts.

Kazbar, 50 Clapham High Street, SW4. Tel: 020 7622 0070. Tube: Clapham Common. Lycra, men in pink neon, and disco. Say no more.

Windmill on the Common, Clapham Common Southside, SW4. Tel: 020 8673 4578. Tube: Clapham Common. One of the few traditional British pubs left in the area. Sit here in the summer and check out the eye-candy on the Common.

Drawing Room and Sofa Bar, 103 Lavender Hill, SW11. Tel: 020 7350 2564. Tube: Clapham North. Looking for a quiet, sensual place to flirt with a potential lover? This is the perfect place.

The Holy Drinker, 59 Northcoate Road, SW11. Tel: 020 7801 0544. Rail: Clapham Junction. If you're stuck on Northcoate Road looking for a good place to go, this bar may be a bit posey, but it's the best in the area.

Late bars

Tearoom des Artistes

697 Wandsworth Road, SW8
Tel: 020 7652 6526
Tube: Clapham North

Decorated like the inside of a child's jewelry box, this over-the-top artist's haven glitters with red plastic chandeliers, white fairy-lights and visuals illuminating the walls. Originally a sixteenth-century barn, this split-level bar is a groovy watering hole attracting a mixed crowd of Claphamite try-hards and sociable trendsetters. Don't miss Sunday Best, a mellow clubbing session on Sunday afternoons brought to you by DJ Rob Da Bank.

SO.UK

165 Clapham High Street, SW4
Tel: 020 7622 4004
Tube: Clapham Common

One of the classier late night drinking options in Clapham, this darkly lit Moroccan themed bar is popular amongst yuppified city workers and trust fund darlings. Groovy DJ sets and plenty of pouffe seating make for a relaxed lounge atmosphere for wine sipping sophisticos. Not your glow stick waving party venue, then, but those messy wet snogs do tend to emerge long before closing time at midnight.

Sand

156 Clapham Park Road, SW4
Tel: 020 7622 3022
Tube: Clapham Common

With a name like Sand, I half expected to stumble into a rugged beach bar after lazing about in the common in a pair of shorts and flip-flops. Sadly, nothing could be further from the truth. This style bar has nothing to do with sand at all, except for perhaps the creamy color of the walls. Drinks are pretentiously expensive and the bar is packed with your obligatory rugby boys and tarted up investment bankers. On a plus note, it's open late.

Also in the area

Café Sol, 56 Clapham High Street, SW4. Tel: 020 7498 9319. Tube: Clapham Common. Perfect place for a drunken snog. Quality not guaranteed.

Restaurants

Castilla

82 Battersea Rise, SW11
Tel: 020 7738 9597
Rail: Clapham Junction

One night, while dancing in some cheesy club in the West End, one of my mates decided it would be funny to pour an entire pint of lager over my head. My eyes burned from the alcohol, black mascara smeared my eyes, and sodden hair stuck to my face. But this shocking experience was nothing compared to the "I'm not in Kansas anymore" knock I got when stepping into this obscure Spanish restaurant tucked away just off the main drag in Clapham Junction. This surprisingly authentic tapas bar not only serves mouthwatering food, but it has a late license and gets packed on weekends.

The Pepper Tree

19 Clapham Common, SW4
Tel: 020 7622 1759
Tube: Clapham Common

Recreating the hysteria of a school cafeteria, this Thai restaurant packs in its patrons by sitting them side-by-side in long rows of picnic-style benches. You may find yourself sitting next to a Rastafarian, a slicked-up office girl, or a pack of Aussies. Anything goes. As for the food, it can't fail to impress. Try the Thai curries for an assault of spices.

Gastro

67 Venn Street, SW4
Tel: 020 7627 0222
Tube: Clapham Common

At first glance, this dingy diner may look more like your local greasy spoon than a classy French fooderie, with red vinyl bench seating and plastic fish tacked to the wall. But take a seat and you'll soon discover why this place comes so highly recommended. French waitresses, fine wines, and authentic dishes made to perfection are to be expected, and you will surely be returning time and again.

Fish in the Tie

105 Falcon Road, SW11
Tel: 020 7924 1913
Rail: Clapham Junction

Not only is this one of the best restaurants in Clapham, but Fish in a Tie creates some of the finest fish feasts in all of London. A dark candlelit dining area, scribbled menus, and simply prepared dishes make dining here an absolute pleasure. Wash your meal down with some good house wine and you'll walk away with change from a £10 note.

Food deliveries

Basilico, 175 Lavender Hill, SW11. Tel: 020 7924 4070

Bombay Bicycle Club, 28 Queenstown Road, SW8. Tel: 020 7720 0500

Chinese Kitchen, 37 Falcon Road, SW11. Tel: 020 7223 5559

Pizza Tuscona, 127a Lavender Hill, SW11. Tel: 020 7223 6664

Domino's Pizza, 48 Battersea Rise, SW11. Tel: 020 7924 2572

Also in the area

Bento's, 70 Clapham Park Road, SW4. Tel: 020 7622 3456. Tube: Clapham Common. Places like this deserve to be packed out every night. Divine Japanese food in a modern setting for great value.

Thyme, 14 Clapham Park Road, SW4. Tel: 020 7627 2468. Tube: Clapham Common. Voted the best local in the *Time Out* awards, 2002.

Tsunami, 1–7 Voltaire Road, SW4. Tel: 020 7978 1610. Tube: Clapham Common. The best sushi in South London.

Gourmet Burger Kitchen, 44 Northcote Road, SW11. Tel: 020 7228 3309. Rail: Clapham Junction. Gone are the days when golden arches and nuked meat-processed patties ruled the fast food burger world. This posh burger joint has a vast menu of tasty beef beauties or meatless options for vegetarians.

Alba Pizzeria, 3 Bedford Road, SW4. Tel: 020 7733 3636. Tube: Clapham Common. You'll be loosening your belt after this fantastic pizza.

Clubs

Clapham Grand

Grand Theatre, 21–25 St John's Hill, SW11
Tel: 020 7228 1070
Tube: Clapham Junction train station

Cheesy tunes from the 70s and 80s, women in heels and painted on skirts, and spotty-faced city boys with perma-puckered lips. All this for £15. Sounds about as appealing as a kiss on the lips from Aunt Sally who smells of wee. Even so, the club continues to pack 'em in on weekends, and can even be a good laugh – if you're up for a grope or two and a boogy to YMCA.

Also in the area

Wessex House, 1a St John's Hill, SW1. Tel: 020 7228 0501. Rail: Clapham Junction. Cheaper entrance than neighbouring Clapham Grand, and shorter queues, but even further down on the club food chain.

White House, 65 Clapham Park Road, SW4. Tel: 020 7498 3388. Rail: Clapham Junction. Fashion labels, girly drinks and egos are abundant in this tiny club, which is more a place for posing than dancing.

Entertainment

Jongleurs Battersea

The Cornet, 49 Lavender Hill Gardens, SW11
Tel: 0870 7870 707 or www.jongleurs.com
Rail: Clapham Junction

An enormous blacked-out room serves as a perfect destination for eating, drinking and laughing until pee runs down your leg.

Clapham Common, SW4

Clapham comes alive in summer when all the 20- and 30-somethings in the area head to the Common with a picnic basket, a football, and a case of beer. Utterly divine.

> You may remember reading about Clapham Common in Graham Greene's book, *The End of the Affair*, which was later made into a film starring Ralph Fiennes. Filming was largely shot on location on the Common and around London.

Battersea Park, SW11

What? Deer in London? Yes, *and* peacocks *and* a Japanese Buddhist Peace Pagoda. This 200-acre park has got it all – from forests to sports fields and endless trails to explore.

> Familiar from a million Pink Floyd album covers, Battersea Power Station is the large brick building with four white smokestacks near Battersea Park, SW11. Since it was closed in the 80s, the power station has since received approval from the city council to be redeveloped as a leisure complex with a seating capacity of 2,100, a hotel, exhibition space, shopping center and offices. Watch this space.

Clapham Northcote Road Antiques Market

155a Northcote Road, SW11
OPENING TIMES
Tel: 020 7228 6850
Rail: Clapham Junction
Open: Mon–Sat 10 a.m. – 6 p.m., Sun 12 noon – 5 p.m.
One man's junk is another man's treasure, so they say. Whatever you're looking for – china, furniture, glass ornaments or various bric-a-brac – you'll find it here, with 40 dealers under one roof to choose from.

Northcote Road Market

Northcote Road, SW11
Rail: Clapham Junction
For those fresh loaves of bread, vegetables, fruit and fish, there is no better place in Clapham for purchasing your weekly groceries than this street-long market. Takes place every Saturday.

Battersea Dogs' Home

4 Battersea Park Road, SW8
Tel: 020 7622 3626
Rail: Battersea Park or Queenstown Road
www.dogshome.org

Looking for a new pet? Help by giving these rescued stray cats and dogs a new home. The home is open every day except Thursday and costs £1 admission.

Cinema

Clapham Picture House, 76 Venn Street, SW4. Tel: 020 7498 3323. Tube: Clapham Common. Converted from the site of a former snooker hall, this intimate four-screen cinema also has a licensed café and bar, so give yourself some extra time for a pint before the flick.

Theatre

Battersea Arts Centre, Lavender Hill, SW11. Tel: 020 7223 2223 or see www.bac.org.uk. Tube: Clapham North

Landor Theatre, Landor Street, SW9. Tel: 020 7737 7276. Tube: Clapham North

Taxis

All Area Cars, 1 Lothair Street, SW11. Tel: 020 7978 7979

Keen's Quality Car Service, 87a Falcon Road, SW11. Tel: 020 7223 1111

Street Wise Cars, 4a Lavender Hill, SW11. Tel: 020 7350 1111

Mr Cabbie, 175 Battersea Park Road, SW8. Tel: 020 7220 6003

Wimbledon and Richmond

Groups of affluent young professionals have been led to the edge of the river by the Pied Piper of Richmond. But instead of drowning in the murky water, they must have all used their ample investment portfolios as flotation devices and clambered out to stake claim to the area's big old mansions. Wimbledon and Richmond are little nests of suburbia along the river. Think sports utility vehicles and three-wheeled prams. Sprawling but carefully manicured lawns wander down to the river, capped by massive old properties kept in as good condition as Grandmother's favorite pearls. This is where the rich live their idyllic lives in blissful Pimms and lemonade hazes.

Come summertime, tennis fans converge on the otherwise peaceful Wimbledon. The world's finest tennis tournament takes over the area for two weeks every year as men in little white shorts battle with their balls. Two – Love. Mixed doubles. Women's singles final. That's when the boys dip their strawberries in cream and watch Anna Kournikova jiggle out of her sports bra, smiling and posing her way to the bottom of the league in a flurry of cash.

But the fittest athletes in racket sports aren't the only stars down south. In contrast to his normal rock 'n' roll antics, Mick Jagger has moved his stairmaster and Grecian 2000 stockpile down to tranquil Wimbledon when he's not picking sand out of his wrinkles in Mauritius.

If you want to live in Wimbledon or Richmond, you will probably be able to find a place to string your racket in some of the area's less respectable outer regions: just don't get your heart set on a river view. Plenty of property is available in the slightly more ramshackle streets; the lawns won't be quite so manicured, but at least you'll get to share the great local pubs and restaurants with the local moneyed aristos.

> The first Wimbledon Tennis Championship was held in 1877, when 200 spectators turned up to watch the sets. Now the tournament is broadcast to millions around the world.

Pubs and bars

The Old Ship
3 King Street, TW9
Tel: 020 8940 3461
Tube: Richmond

In keeping with the seafaring theme of the riverside area, the landlord has strapped some nautical memorabilia to the walls. The pub is nice and snug in the winter, but as there isn't any outdoor seating, the punters head elsewhere for an al fresco pint in the summertime. Still, that just leaves the place peaceful if a quiet drink is what you're after. Ah well, those pasty Brits sipping drinks on the river will probably just get sunburnt anyway.

The Alexandra
33 Wimbledon Hill Road, SW19
Tel: 020 8947 7691
Tube: Wimbledon
Escape Wimbledon's pinball-like pedestrian traffic flows during the height of summer to discuss the latest tennis scores, gossip about Andre Agassi's ball smashing techniques, or wind down with a Pimms and lemonade at this pub's leafy rooftop terrace. Drink the time away until your mouth tastes like the bottom of a birdcage.

The White Cross
Water Lane, TW9
Tel: 020 8940 6844
Tube: Richmond
Whatever happened to those childhood summertime hobbies of building go-carts, chasing ice cream vans, and recreating James Bond films? Five stubbed toes, a diploma, and a string of ex-boyfriends later, the adult equivalent of summertime bliss is sitting out in the sunshine with a pint of lager. This pub is the perfect lazy drinking place.

Restaurants

Tide Tables
2 The Arches, Riverside
Tel: 020 8948 8285
Tube: Richmond
This is a fantastic veggie café set under the arches along the river. Order a pumpkin pancake or veggie lasagne with a fresh fruit smoothie and head into the massive courtyard overlooking the river. This leafy area is a wonderful place to sit and read a good book over a cappuccino; luckily, if you've forgotten to bring a tome of your own, you can read one of the used books from their library.

Le Piaf
40 Wimbledon Hill Road, SW19
Tel: 020 8946 3823
Tube: Wimbledon
Le Piaf is a French café/restaurant in the heart of Wimbledon. The pavement tables are gold dust on a weekend evening as the locals pile in for outstanding cuisine such as grilled tuna steak and salad niçoise. The prices are very reasonable for such high-quality provisions and the staff are friendly and knowledgeable.

Kozachok Restaurant

10 Red Lion Street, TW9
Tel: 020 8948 2366
Tube: Richmond

When it came to painting the walls of this fabulous Russian/Ukranian restaurant, the owners seemed to have taken inspiration from the pages of their children's coloring book. With cartoon-like figures drawn on the walls, carved Matryoshka dolls perched on the shelves, and an extensive list of vodka flavors to enhance the senses, this flamboyant diner is one deliciously vibrant and lively eating place. Oh, and the food's good too.

Food delivery

Perfect Pizza, 164 The Broadway, SW19. Tel: 020 8542 6634

RK Indian Takeaway, 286 Haydons Road, SW19. Tel: 020 8543 4008

Papillon Pizza, 224 Merton High Street, SW19. Tel: 020 8543 3470

Bengal Village, 72 Sheen Road, TW9. Tel: 020 8940 0792

Entertainment

Boat trip

From the bank of the Thames
Tube: Richmond

Boat trips leave from the Thames in Richmond and go to Teddington Locks, taking tourists on a 45-minute expedition for £4 a head.

Richmond Park

Richmond, Surrey
Tube: Richmond

Hide out in the grass and watch the deer go at it during mating season, but make sure you don't get too close. This massive park is one of the wildest and most impressive parks in London, with deer roaming the forests and walking trails winding about the fields.

Royal Botanic Gardens of Kew

Richmond, Surrey
Tel: 020 8332 5000
Tube: Kew Gardens
Admission: £5

Spend a civilized afternoon perusing the gardens of this 300-acre plot with over 40,000 varieties of plants. The Palm House is world famous and has a delightful collection of tropical, alpine and temperate plants. This is a great place to take your mom when she's in town.

Recipe for Pimms No. 1

50 ml Pimms gin-based liqueur
1 slice orange
1 slice lime
1 slice cucumber
1 sliced strawberry
1 sprig of mint
ice
lemonade to fill
Fill a tall glass with ice and fruit, add Pimms and top with lemonade.

Cinemas

Richmond Odeon, Hill Street, TW9. Tel: 0870 505 0007.
Tube: Richmond
Richmond Odeon Studio, Red Lion Street, TW9. Tel: 0870 505 0007.
Tube: Richmond
Wimbledon Odeon, The Broadway, SW19. Tel: 0870 505 0007.
Tube: Wimbledon
Richmond Filmhouse, Water Lane, TW9. Tel: 020 8332 0030.
Tube: Richmond
Watermans Arts Centre, High Street, TW8. Tel: 020 8232 1010.
Rail: Kew Bridge
Putney Odeon, Putney High Street, SW15. Tel: 0870 505 007.
Tube: Putney Bridge

Theatre

Wimbledon Theatre, The Broadway, SW19. Tel: 020 8540 0362.
Tube: Wimbledon

Taxis

A&H Mini Cabs, 282 Haydons Road, SW19. Tel: 020 8296 8484

Central Cars, 279 The Broadway, SW19. Tel: 020 8543 5555

Kensington and Chelsea

The words Kensington and Chelsea are synonymous with wealth, class and grandeur. Renowned for its Georgian houses, private gardens and designer boutiques, it is home to London's poshest postcodes, where dukes, foreign investors, and old money families rub shoulders at exclusive restaurants, bars and clubs.

Trust funds, ageing celebrities and friends to the Queen choose South Kensington as the ideal neighborhood in which to settle. This new generation of 30-something well-heeled A-listers are dubbed "Sloanies" by Londoners because of their nose-in-the-air nature and the simple fact that they live near Sloane Square Tube station.

But Chelsea's history is very different from the modern world of Botox injections and Manolo Blahnik kitten heels. In the early 60s, the King's Road was the height of "swinging London" cool. Think Austin Powers, the Beatles, and Steve McQueen "blowing the bloody doors off" a Mini Cooper.

Merseybeat ruled the airwaves and dedicated followers of fashion in Mary Quant miniskirts strutted up and down the streets of Chelsea, occasionally venturing out east to Carnaby Street. London swung, and it was never groovier to be British.

A mere decade later, the area was again fundamental to the creation of a new movement. Vivienne Westwood's radical clothing company Sex, a rubber and fetish emporium, opened on the King's Road. Soon after, Westwood's lover, Malcolm McLaren, became the Svengali of a new band of musical misfits, The Sex Pistols. Westwood dressed the boys in strapped trousers and ripped shirts as they made their way to stages around London, shouting and cursing. The mods moved out and the punks lay down their safety pins and hair dye. The age of punk had now dawned – leaving parents grimacing in fear all across the land. But over the years, punk soon fizzled out, and these days the closest thing you'll see to anarchy along the streets is someone wearing last season's Pringle pullover.

Kensington is one of the most elite shopping areas within the capital. On the outskirts of Hyde Park lies the exclusive area of Knightsbridge, where you'll find London's poshest department store, Harrods, and a string of designer shops like Harvey Nichols and trendy Urban Outfitters. Need a new pair of designer lightbulbs? A new tea cozy from this season's collection? An Alexander McQueen handkerchief? Leave the minions and peasants to scrap it out during the sales down at Oxford Street: the refined shopping is done in Kensington.

All in all, Kensington is an area with a great deal of history – and money – floating around. For most of us, however, even the thought of finding a scummy one-bedroom flat on the outskirts is unlikely, unless Daddy's left you a nice free-range macrobiotic nest egg to sort out your life. Even so, the area is densely populated, and most apartments do not have a garden, sufficient parking, or even a balcony. And, frankly, once you have been to one posh bar, you've seen them all. So there.

Head to the Cadogan Hotel at 75 Sloane Street if you want to see the very spot where Oscar Wilde was arrested in 1895 after it was discovered that he had a "special relationship" with young chum Lord Alfred Douglas.

Pubs and bars

Janet's Bar

30 Old Brompton Road, SW3
Tel: 020 7581 3160
Tube: South Kensington

Resurrecting a slice of retro Americana, this delightfully kitsch bar is a time warp for those of us itching to play dress-up in mom's old bobby socks and poodle skirts. Photographs of cheerful punters plaster the walls of this cozy local and childish paintings of a woman with a blonde bob and 50s glasses – Janet, the owner – are pinned to the colorful walls. Music from the beloved era further sets the tone of this friendly watering hole, which attracts a mixture of Sloanies and casual media types.

Anglesea Arms

15 Selwood Terrace, SW7
Tel: 020 7373 7960
Tube: South Kensington

Setting the tone with its floral wallpaper and nude oil paintings, this old-world pub is chilled, sophisticated and friendly. A large outdoor seating area overlooks a quiet street in one of Kensington's most exclusive neighborhoods, ideal for spending a civilized afternoon over a bottle of white wine.

The Collection

264 Old Brompton Road, SW3
Tel: 020 7225 1212
Tube: South Kensington

A long corridor with illuminated glass floor panels guides the way into this refurbished African-themed style bar, which has been built into a converted brick factory. Upmarket and stylish, be sure to slap on the warpaint if you plan to impress.

The Blenheim

27 Cale Street, SW3
Tel: 020 7349 0056

Tube: South Kensington or Sloane Square

Don't make the mistake of wandering into this place while the football is on unless you are prepared to go full-on with the red and white facepaint, snare drums and foghorns. Having black and white Chelsea football photographs pinned to the wall, and matches playing from the TV screen, this is a football fan's heaven. Arrive on any other day, and the pub is transformed into a quiet local pub with your obligatory grey-haired regulars and a smattering of softly spoken pint huggers.

Food deliveries

Alpha Pizza, 351 Edgware Road, W2. Tel: 020 7402 4002

Domino's Pizza, 129 Westbourne Park Road, W2. Tel: 020 7229 7770

Home Delivery Pizza Co, 116 Holland Park Ave, W11. Tel: 020 7221 3380

Also in the area

The Builder's Arms, 13 Britten Street, SW3. Tel: 020 7349 9040. Tube: Sloane Square. Slip off those shoes, sink into a good novel, and lounge away your afternoon in this serene pub just off the King's Road.

Cross Keys, 1 Lawrence Street, SW3. Tel: 020 7349 9111. Tube: Sloane Square. That modern Goth decor gets me every time.

Admiral Codington, 17 Mossop Street, SW3. Tel: 020 7581 0005. Tube: South Kensington. Its swanky location means that its clientele is made up of a mixture of city chaps in chinos and old boys trying to keep a stronghold on their refurbished local pub.

Late bars

Cactus Blue

86 Fulham Road, SW3
Tel: 020 7823 7858
Tube: South Kensington

If modern Mexican theme bars appeal to you, then this is as good as it gets. Slightly cheesy, yes, but that's to be expected. As a bonus, this place stays open until midnight, offering just enough time to humiliate yourself by dancing on the table, snogging your prepubescent intern, and projectile vomiting tequila into your boss's face. May God be with you.

Jimmie's Bar, 18 Kensington Church Street, W8. Tel: 020 7937 9988. Step back in time to New York in the 70s. It's young, sexy, and has pouffe seats that light up when you sit on them.
Isola, 145 Knightsbridge, SW1. Tel: 020 7838 1044. Tube: Knightsbridge. Pricey but fashionable cocktail bar.

Restaurants

Chelsea Kitchen
98 Kings Road, SW3
Tel: 020 7589 1330
Tube: Sloane Square
Looking like the 70s diner in *Pulp Fiction*, this no-frills greasy spoon has put little effort into the decor but serves basic British food at surprisingly low prices. If you can get past the red vinyl benches and tacky wildflower paintings, this place is one of your best bets for a cheap feed in Chelsea. Keep your snouts out of the trough ladies, have some decorum.

Phat Phuc Noodle Bar
The Chelsea Courtyard, 151 Sydney Street, SW3
Tel: 0976 276 808
Tube: South Kensington or Sloane Square
With a name like Phat Phuc, the owner's either got a great sense of humor, or he's so out of touch that he thinks that Earl Jeans is the name of an aristocrat in Wessex. As it turns out, the name means "happy buddha" in Vietnamese – now with that out of the way, bring on the noodles.

Chelsea Bun Diner, 9a Limerston Street, SW10. Tel: 020 7352 3635. Tube: South Kensington. Head here for a proper English fry-up breakfast to banish those hangover blues.
GW8, 3 Abingdon Road, W8. Tel: 020 7376 2191. Tube: High Street Kensington. This catering company has opened up shop for the neighbouring public to sell fresh quiches and healthy homemade dishes. It would make mom proud.

Entertainment

Chelsea Physic Garden
66 Royal Hospital Road, SW3
Tel: 020 7352 5646
Tube: Sloane Square
Originally created in 1673 as a garden for studying botany, it is

now home to the Chelsea Flower Show in May and the Chelsea Festival each June.

Carlyle's House

24 Cheyne Row, SW3
Tel: 020 7352 7087
Admission: £3.50
Tube: Sloane Square

The Victorian essayist and historian Thomas Carlyle lived in this three-story house from 1834 until his death in 1881. Head to the attic to see where he wrote his famous history of the French Revolution.

Kensington Palace

Kensington Gardens, W8
Tel: 020 7937 9561
Tube: Queensway

See where Princessess Margaret and Diana rested their pretty little heads. This palace dates back to 1605, when it was home to the second Earl of Nottingham.

Chelsea Farmers Market

Sydney Street, SW3
Tube: South Kensington

An outdoor marketplace with various merchants flogging everything from organic food and fresh meat to plants. If it's all too much, have a rest at one of the outdoor tables and feast upon the delicacies on sale.

Cinemas

Chelsea Cinema, 206 King's Road, SW3. Tel: 020 7351 3742.
Tube: Sloane Square
UGC Chelsea, 279 King's Road, SW3. Tel: 0870 907 0710.
Tube: Sloane Square
Odeon Kensington, Kensington High Street, W8. Tel: 0870 505 0007 or www.odeon.co.uk. Tube: High Street Kensington

---

Taxis

Mercury Radio Cars, 15 All Saints Road, W11. Tel: 020 7727 3535

Local Radio Cars, 3a Harrington Road, SW7. Tel: 020 7584 5566

Elite Chauffeur Services, 34 Porchester Square, W2. Tel: 020 7262 9962

Earls Court and Fulham

When your manicure bill equals the weekly salary of your average Londoner, it's time to move to Fulham. Mix in with grinning Hugh Grant lookalikes, women flashing suntanned flesh year-round and babies getting the grand tours around the parks in bejewelled four-horsepower deluxe Chanel prams. This is the breeding place of the quintessentially English, with posh accents, restored Georgian houses and antique furniture. Old money, trust funds and bottomless gold card accounts. Tea and crumpets.

Actually, it is a lovely place to live if you can afford it. It is also a rampant breeding ground for young couples eager to rustle up an heir to their fortunes. The local parks are filled with post-coital executives enjoying the sunshine before rushing back home to check the ovulation chart, and happy young families telling Ulsa, the Swedish nanny, to put a muzzle on young Edward Thomas William Windsor-Smythe III. Loud children are soooo passé. Those not yet embracing the fruit of their loins spend long afternoons planning next year's trip to Ascot while sipping Moet in the sunshine.

In contrast, neighbouring Earls Court is largely made up of a mixture of European travellers, Americans, and tireless antipodean backpackers leaving trails of sweat as they struggle beneath their packs with stinky trainers strapped to the side, and Turkish carpets rolled at the top.

Once known as Kangaroo Court due to the large number of Australian nomads who flocked there, it was later reborn as the gay center of London in the 80s. Now offering a mixture of Fulhamites, Aussies and rainbow power, Earls Court isn't the sort of place that you would seek out to take in the nightlife – but not a bad area to live, especially if you are looking for short-term accommodation. Fulham however, is one of the most expensive boroughs in London to find a flat, making it popular amongst City workers and banking professionals.

Pubs and bars

Babushka House

648 King's Road
Tel: 020 7736 4501
Tube: Fulham Broadway

If those codpiece-protruding rapscallions of *A Clockwork Orange* moved into the goody-two-shoes Brady Bunch homestead, the result would be the Babushka House. With its eclectic 70s pic 'n' mix of kitsch trinkets, naked mannequins and retro flowered wallpaper, this is certainly one of the most unique bars you'll find in Fulham. Granny's house on LSD.

Lunasa

575 Kings Road
Tel: 020 7371 7664
Tube: Parson's Green

Thin slats of angled mirrors positioned strategically behind the bar make this slinky establishment a Peeping Tom's ideal hangout. Take a seat at one of the barstools and spy away – nobody will ever be the wiser. With big windows, tall ceilings and modern decor, this classy joint is one of the finest on the strip, attracting a trendier crowd than most of its bland try-hard neighbours.

The White Horse

1–3 Parson's Green, SW6
Tel: 020 7736 2115
Tube: Parson's Green

When the sun is out, this is the place to see – and be seen. Those who live in the area simply walk across the manicured common in their shined leather brogues to take a seat at an outdoor table and sip Merlot. Others pull up in their latest-edition Mini Coopers to park just out front. A favorite with well-heeled emaciated Barbie dolls and tanned public school boys, the 'Sloany Pony' is a popular meeting place among the moneyed crowd. Saying that, don't get glammed up for the occasion. The dress code here is casual. But I'm not talking ratty Levi's – casual here doesn't dip below this season's Marc Jacobs or Paul Smith active wear.

The Atlas

16 Seagrave Road, SW6
Tel: 020 7385 9129
Tube: West Brompton

Tucked away in the far corner of a nearly deserted street, it is hard to believe that this lovingly restored gastropub manages to fill up nearly every night. Secluded from the hubbub of Earls Court, word of mouth attracts punters to this chilled pub where jazz, New Orleans swing music and Mediterranean food set the mood.

Also in the area

Novelos, 47 Parsons Green Lane, SW6. Tel: 020 7736 2713. Tube: Parsons Green. Get all shook up with this bar's Elvis impersonation shows every Thursday and Saturday night.

Deco, 294 Fulham Road, SW10. Tel: 020 7351 0044. Tube: Fulham Broadway. Step downstairs into a stylish Art Deco world with an equally trendy clientele.

The King's Head, 17 Hogarth Place, SW5. Tel: 020 7244 5931. Tube: Earls Court. Proof that there are still Aussies living in Earls Court. It may not be as busy as the good ol' days, but Friday night is always a lively one, especially when the *TNT* magazine staff head down to cheer on the weekend.

Bootsy Brogans, 1 Fulham Broadway, SW6. Tel: 020 7385 2003. Tube: Fulham Broadway. Come here on a weekend and you will hardly be able to move. A hotspot with the local backpacker crowd.

The Hansom Cab, 86 Earls Court Road, SW5. Tel: 020 7795 4821. Tube: Earls Court. One of the best pubs in the area with an outdoor seating area. Glorious in summertime.

Late bars

Crazy Larry's

222–224 Fulham Road, SW10
Tel: 020 7352 5978
Tube: Fulham Broadway

If you spend a lot of time going out in Fulham, it is pretty much guaranteed that you will stumble into this tacky joint at some point in your unfortunate post-work drunk history. We're not recommending that you go out of your way to check out this place, but it actually isn't too bad if you're up for a cheesy laugh. Don't attempt it unless you are already absolutely pie-eyed.

Also in the area

Embargo, 553b Kings Road, SW8. Tel: 020 7351 5038. With its Bedouin-style draped curtains and candlelit chillout room, this is one sophisticated joint, popular with the well-off bland chino-wearing crowd.

Po Na Na Fez Club, 222–224 Fulham Road, SW10. Tel: 020 7352 5978. Tube: Fulham Broadway. Possibly one of the best late night watering holes, popular with posers, fashion models and sexy (or so they believe) men.

Restaurants

Troubadour

265 Old Brompton Road, SW5
Tel: 020 7370 1434
Tube: Earls Court or West Brompton

A brightly painted wooden door marks the entrance to this enchanting dining place where creative folk gather to sip red wine, discuss the latest photography exhibitions and indulge in ambrosial dishes. The café could almost be confused for an old man's workshop, with farming tools, musical instruments and a motley collection of pots dangling from the walls. Bob Dylan, Jimi Hendrix, and Paul Simon all played in the club downstairs in the 60s and today this eccentric gathering place is a favorite among bohemian types who drop in for live gigs, poetry readings and comedy nights.

Mona Lisa
417 Kings Road, SW10
Tel: 020 7376 5447
Tube: Fulham Broadway
Don't let your eyes deceive you. While the minimalist decor in this family-run restaurant is nothing to speak of, the service and quality of food ranks Mona Lisa as one of the best eateries in London. After sitting down at a table, a waiter presents you with a silver platter of uncooked meats and seafood for your perusal. Though they skimp on interior decorating, they fuss on the food. And the prices are definitely retro.

The Blue Elephant
4–6 Fulham Broadway, SW6
Tel: 020 7385 6595
Tube: Fulham Broadway
If Disneyland invented a ride for Bangkok's Golden Palace, it would look something like the Blue Elephant. After passing through its entrance (marked by bamboo spears and Thai straw hats), the dining room is a lush rainforest of vegetation with a fountain and gaudy ornaments.

Jim Thompson's
617 Kings Road, SW6
Tel: 020 7731 0999
Tube: Fulham Broadway
It could nearly be mistaken for a trinket shop, given the clutter of ethnic paraphernalia hanging from the ceiling, perched against the walls, and even under your bum. The idea is that while you are slurping back a plate of Thai food, or simply mulling over a pint in the bar, you can also feast your eyes on the imported goods on sale. If anything catches your beady little eye, don't be afraid to barter a good price.

Food delivery

Eastern Star, 14 Hogarth Place, SW5. Tel: 020 7373 2407

Pronto, 162, Brompton Road, SW3. Tel: 020 7581 1333

La Cuisine Deliveries, 89 Lillie Road, SW6. Tel: 020 7381 4060

Queuejumper.com, 159 Dawes Road, SW6. Tel: 020 7385 8999

Domino's Pizza, 613 Fulham Road, SW6. Tel: 020 7381 9898

Basilico, 690 Fulham Road, SW6. Tel: 0800 028 3531

Also in the area

Saffron, 306b Fulham Road, SW10. Tel: 020 7351 1282. Tube: Fulham Broadway. It may feel like you're going for a dinner at a mate's flat when you walk up to this split-level diner, but this modern Indian restaurant serves a mean curry.

Nikita's, 65 Ilfield Road, SW5. Tel: 020 7352 6326. Tube: Earls Court. Although on the pricier side, this restaurant is rumored to create the best Russian food in London.

Café Blue, 451 Fulham Road, SW10. Tel: 020 7352 8636. Tube: South Kensington. Your classic Italian café with reasonable prices.

Entertainment

Earls Court Exhibition Centre

Warwick Road, Earls Court, SW5
Tel: 020 7385 1200.
Tube: Earls Court

This massive auditorium can pack in 40,000 people, making it a popular venue for corporate exhibition extravaganzas and large-scale concerts by the biggest musical acts from around the world.

Taxis

Minicabs, 204 Earls Court Road, SW5. Tel: 020 7244 8380

Fulham Minicabs, 183a Dawes Road, SW6. Tel: 020 7381 8181

Airport Taxis and Beaufort Cars, 28 Old Brompton Road, SW7. Tel: 020 7349 8765

Notting Hill

New York has Greenwich Village. London has Notting Hill. Eclectic bohemia is painted over every inch of this community without ever staining it with the grubby hues of the eco-hippy. This is where the young rich creatives call home, away from daddy's estate in Buckinghamshire. Locals are too hip for the old money world of Kensington, but too frightened of grit to move to Hoxton. The area is constantly buzzing as it remains a creative oasis in West London.

Adding to the eclectic vibe of the neighborhood, every August the Notting Hill Carnival takes over the streets in an extravaganza of Jamaican music, food, drink, and a colorful parade of outstanding costumes. Thousands of people converge on the area over this weekend, which is one of the largest Mardi Gras outside of Rio.

Notting Hill is where artists, designers, songwriters and thespians cultivate their passions safe in the knowledge that if they don't get their lucky break, at least their trust funds will pay the rent. Jealous, moi? Of course. This is where dreams are pursued with fervent passion, uninhibited by the daily worries of your average working-class art student.

The houses in the area are massive white rows of ancestral pearls running along tree-lined streets, interspersed with the odd candy-colored Art Deco dwelling. But the crowning gem of the area is Portobello Road Market. Flowers, antiques, vintage gowns, and music ... everything a young boho needs. Never mind about locally set romantic comedies with Hugh Grant finding true love at the market, the area is truly worth a wander on a sunny Sunday.

Unless you are reading this book whilst lounging on an antique chair in the parlor of the west wing of your ageing rocker father's palatial pied-à-terre in Manhattan, then you probably won't be able to live right in Notting Hill. Keep trawling the *Loot* newspaper as there is a remote chance that you may be able to find a crumbling flat in the area for a vaguely reasonable price, but you'll probably have to search a bit further out towards Westbourne Park or Ladbroke Grove.

Pubs and bars

The Westbourne

101 Westbourne Park Villas, W2
Tel: 020 7221 1332
Tube: Westbourne Park

This busy, trendy pub with a massive forecourt sets it apart from similar boozers in the area. Snuggle inside away from the elements in the cozy back room on the cold winter evenings, or sit on an outdoor bench until your anaemic complexion resembles a portly chap after a cherry pie eating contest. See, be seen, be seen to not be seeing. Too cool to care and too busy having a good time anyway.

Bed

310 Portobello Road, W10
Tel: 020 8969 4500
Tube: Ladbroke Grove

Childish innuendoes aside, Bed is actually a pretty good bar in the rougher end of Portobello Road. In keeping with the ethnic vibe of the neighborhood, the owners of Bed have brought the North African feel inside and made it trendy. You won't see the place littered with randy couples cavorting on four-posters. The beds are comfy foam-covered platforms all around the bar and the only lusting going on is over their selection of cocktails. The bar is thankfully laid-back and bohemian.

The Cow

89 Wesbourne Park Road, W2
Tel: 020 7221 0021
Tube: Ladbroke Grove

It's pubs like this that turn casual drinkers into social-holics. Casual, homey, and attracting an uninhibited, trendy crowd, The Cow is the local pub you wish you had. A sign above the bar reads "oysters on ice" for those seductive after work snacks. Suck and sip your night away.

Beach Blanket Babylon

45 Ledbury Road, W11
Tel: 020 7229 2907
Tube: Notting Hill Gate

Enough of all those Zen-like, bland, flat-packed pubs. I want a feast for the eyes when I go out, and Beach Blanket Babylon is more than a feast; it's a Henry VIII banquet. Step through the looking glass, open the back of your wardrobe and lose yourself around the labyrinth. This bar is a secret garden in the middle of fantasia, and surely is the result of designers sitting in the poppy fields for too long before setting off for the Emerald City.

Grand Union

45 Woodfield Road, W9
Tel: 020 7286 1886
Tube: Ladbroke Grove

With the sound of water lapping along the canal, and the sight of kayakers sedately paddling past, this is the closest London gets to recreating the Venetian café ambience. But this isn't about mustachioed men singing about ice cream. This is Britain, baby, and this pub is famed for its gastronomic cuisine.

Market Bar

240a Portobello Road, W11
Tel: 020 7229 6427
Tube: Notting Hill Gate

Candlestick holders bearing the wax of a thousand melted candles and the whispers of long-forgotten conversations, its simple Gothic-glam decor is a favorite amongst locals and market traders.

Also in the area

Golborne House, 36 Golborne Road, W10. Tel: 020 8960 6260. Tube: Westbourne Park. The carefully chosen classy fixtures and the bouncer on the door belie the fact that this is actually a gastropub, and a good one at that.

Canvas, 177 Portobello Road, W11. Tel: 020 7727 2700. Tube: Notting Hill Gate. Neutral colors and minimalist design create the feeling that the people are the art against a blank canvas. Profound.

Mau Mau, 265 Portobello Road, W10. Tel: 020 7229 8528. Tube: Notting Hill Gate. A small artsy venue that has gained great respect. Home of comedy nights each Thursday and film screenings during the international film festivals.

Pharmacy, 150 Notting Hill Gate, W11. Tel: 020 7221 2442. Tube: Notting Hill Gate. Attention to detail as only an artist's bar could be. Yes, this is Damien Hirst's creation. Theme bar extraordinaire, complete with tablet seats and staff in scrubs.

The Elbow Rooms, 103 Westbourne Grove, W2. Tel: 020 7221 5211. Tube: Notting Hill Gate. A popular and classy snooker hall.

Late bars

Notting Hill Arts Club

21 Notting Hill Gate, W11
Tel: 020 7460 4459
Tube: Notting Hill Gate

Rumored to be a hotspot with nonchalant celebs, its live gigs, groovy DJ sets and legendary Wednesday night events attract a varied mixture of people. Anything goes.

Gate

67 Notting Hill Gate, W11
Tel: 020 7727 9007
Tube: Notting Hill Gate

Deep below the Gate Cinema, this DJ bar concocts cocktails for well-heeled locals. The bar is decorated with the normal chocolate brown leather pouffes and dim lighting, and there is a cozy dining area just off to the right of the DJ booth. Note the strange sign in the loos that discourages tandem toilet visits. Naughty children.

Restaurants

Lucky Seven
127 Westbourne Park Rd, W2
Tel: 020 7727 6771
Tube: Westbourne Park

Veiled behind a bright red exterior and a few neon signs lies the kitsch-tastic Lucky Seven. Polythene, formica, and retro Americana swathe this golden nugget of a pseudo fifties diner. Shimmy into one of the wipe-clean booths, order a thick burger and a thicker milkshake and pretend you're on your way to the sock-hop. It's a time warp not seen since McFly hopped into the Delorian.

Portobello Gold
95–97 Portobello Road, W11
Tel: 020 7460 4900
Tube: Notting Hill Gate

Before you immerse yourself in the dusty antiques and crumbling musty ballgowns of the market, wander into Portobello Gold for a delicious meal. In keeping with the boho nature of the area, they do loads of fantastic veggie dishes. The restaurant/bar is decorated like a cheesy 70s garden party, with plenty of vegetation and the sounds of singing birds. Yes, birds.

Food delivery

The Home Delivery Pizza Co, 116 Holland Park Avenue, W11. Tel: 020 7221 3380

Hippo Pizza, 167 Ladbroke Grove, W10. Tel: 020 7221 2040

Domino's Pizza, 129 Westbourne Park Road, W2. Tel: 020 7229 7770

Also in the area

Assaggi, 39 Chepstow Place, W2. Tel: 020 7792 5501. Tube: Notting Hill Gate. Apparently this chic French restaurant is one of Jamie Oliver's old favorites. Book well in advance or you'll be disappointed.

Sausage and Mash Café, 268 Portobello Road, W10. Tel: 020 8968 8898. Tube: Notting Hill Gate. Bringing this traditional English comfort food up to date. Check out the phallic photos on the walls and tuck into some meaty or veggie sausages.

Entertainment

Notting Hill Carnival

www.carnivalnet.org.uk

Over the August Bank Holiday, this upmarket and sedate neighborhood turns upside down and inside out. Jamaican jerk chicken is cooked on open barbecues in the streets, ear-piercing whistles abound as scantily-clad bejewelled people parade on floats through the streets. The carnival is all about eating, drinking, and being merry whilst listening to stands booming out all sorts of tunes.

Portobello Road Market

Portobello Road, W11

Tube: Notting Hill Gate or Ladbroke Grove

Saturdays 8 a.m. – 6 p.m.

www.portobelloroad.co.uk

Antiques and collectibles from over 1500 dealers, as well as stalls of vintage clothing, records, flowers, and just about anything you could want. The market makes a wonderful afternoon out.

Cinemas

Electric Cinema, 191 Portobello Road, W11. Tel: 020 7229 8688. Tube: Notting Hill Gate

The Coronet Cinema, 103 Notting Hill Gate, W11. Tel: 020 7727 6705. Tube: Notting Hill Gate

The Gate Cinema, 87 Notting Hill Gate, W11. Tel: 020 7727 4043. Tube: Notting Hill Gate

UCI Cinemas, Whitely's Shopping Centre, Queensway, W2. Tel: 0870 010 2030. Tube: Queensway

Theatres

Gate Theatre, 11 Pembridge Road, W11. Tel: 020 7229 0706. Tube: Notting Hill Gate

Canal Café Theatre, Bridge House, Delamere Terrace, W2. Tel: 020 7289 6056 or www.newsrevue.fsnet.com. Tube: Warwick Avenue

---

Taxis

Lancaster Cars, 112 Ladbroke Grove, W10. Tel: 020 7727 3113

Mercury Minicabs, 15 All Saints Road, W11. Tel: 020 7727 1434

Chepstow Cars, 23a Chepstow Corner, Chepstow Place, W2. Tel: 020 7229 1166

Drive 24 Passenger Service, 94 Golborne Road, W10. Tel: 020 8968 0100

Shepherd's Bush and Hammersmith

Shepherd's Bush is a rather dirty place. Sorry, but it is. As you come out of the Tube station, you're faced with a derelict park full of empty cans of Tennents Super, sleeping homeless people and massive grey al fresco urinals. Not a pretty sight.

The cheap rents in the area have brought the onslaught of backpackers, and thus plenty of the bars in the area are soulless, dingy, antipodean pubs. But the area seems to be undergoing a change lately. As the rents in Soho and the West End soar, many media companies are now following the BBC's lead and are moving to the area. Slowly, more and more fashionable bars have started to spring up, and locals don't necessarily have to head to nearby Notting Hill for a drink.

In fact, the area's close proximity to Notting Hill is precisely why it is so puzzling that no bohemian coolness has rubbed off a bit further out west. Maybe it will soon. Shepherd's Bush does have some nice areas, such as the wonderfully pretty village of Brackenbury, it's just a shame that the nice bits are surrounded by ramshackle crumbling houses.

Hammersmith is much the same, with sharp contrasts between nice areas and rundown squalor. Hammersmith does have a tad more beauty and less grime than the Bush, but then it's right on the Thames, so it's no wonder that it has been faster to take off as a smart residential area. Adding to the peculiarities of the area, the Shepherd's Bush Tube is split into two stations (Central and Hammersmith & City lines) that are down the street from each other. Confusing and unnecessary.

With a few exceptions, the whole area of Shepherd's Bush and Hammersmith leaves a bit to be desired, but then maybe the affluent people that live there are just onto a good thing ahead of its time. Give it a few years, and maybe Shepherd's Bush and Hammersmith will be the new Notting Hill. Then again, maybe not. It's a gamble. But at least you'll be able to find affordable rental accommodation in the meantime.

Pubs and bars

Havelock Tavern
57 Masbro Road, W14
Tel: 020 7603 5374
Tube: Shepherd's Bush or Hammersmith

This outstanding gastropub has such good food that it's nearly impossible to get a table at lunchtime during the week. I know: I've tried often enough. But it's certainly worth leaving for lunch a bit early or going on the weekend, because the food really does live up to all the impressive reviews. The pub is full of stripped chunky wooden tables and chairs and is deservedly buzzing. One of the best.

The Dove

19 Upper Mall, W6
Tel: 020 8748 5405
Tube: Hammersmith

This great little pub overlooking the Thames has cozy rooms and a nice conservatory out the back leading to an open balcony. It has been around for over 300 years, and in that time has poured drinks for the likes of Ernest Hemingway, Graham Greene and William Morris. The public bar made its way into *The Guinness Book of Records* for having the smallest bar in the UK, and indeed, it is only big enough for three people. Or two people, a pair of chess-playing dwarves and a sack of sprouts. Not that I've tried.

The Queen's Head

13 Brook Green, W6
Tel: 020 7603 3174
Tube: Hammersmith

You'll walk into this pub and be pleasantly surprised when you see the quaint and cozy atmosphere, the candlelight, and hear the sounds of swing and jazz. Sounds brilliant doesn't it? Well wait until you see the garden. It's huge, full of tables, and is lush with foliage. It's Eden, but with alcohol. And no snakes. And people are wearing clothes.

The Old Ship

25 Upper Mall, W6
Tel: 020 8748 2593
Tube: Hammersmith

Oh captain my captain. Ship, ship ahoy. Well you can't have a pub on the river without strapping a few oars to the wall, can you? This large pub is an excellent vantage point to watch rowers practicing on the river as it is located right on the Thames Path. Perfect for long summer days of drinking al fresco, or great for snuggling up with a mulled wine next to a crackling fire in the winter.

Vesbar

15–19 Goldhawk Road, W12
Tel: 020 8762 0215
Tube: Goldhawk Road or Shepherd's Bush

This has got to be the best bar in the area and is the perfect spot for a drink before catching a concert at the Shepherd's Bush Empire. A few sofas linger in the large front windows, with plenty of tables scattered about the main room. Reminisce about those eighties heydays and try to get the seats at the old table computer game – gold dust with a pac man on top.

Also in the area
Brook Green Hotel, 170 Shepherd's Bush Road, W6. Tel: 020 7603 2516. Tube: Hammersmith. Massive bar with comedy nights.
Stonemason's Arms, 54 Cambridge Grove, W6. Tel: 020 8748 1397. Tube: Hammersmith. Large range of beers and vegetarian food.

Late bar

West 12
74 Askew Road, W12
Tel: 020 8762 0215
Tube: Goldhawk Road or Shepherd's Bush
Cocktails, nice food and a late licence. All that, and in Shepherd's Bush. They have a good selection of surprisingly well-made cocktails so you can drink until you turn into a pumpkin at midnight. Then you're out on your arse to drink with the winos on the green.

Restaurants

Patio
5 Goldhawk Road, W12
Tel: 020 8743 5194
Tube: Goldhawk Road or Shepherd's Bush
OK, so it looks like a dodgy café from the outside, but that's only because you can barely see it for all the review clippings. This is a fantastic Polish restaurant and a great place for some traditional home cooking. Go on, drink too much vodka, eat too much beetroot and blinis, and have a great time. This place is all about enjoying food, drink and company. Two thumbs-down to stuffy, overpriced, minimalist restaurants.

Bush Bar and Grill
45a Goldhawk Road, W12
Tel: 020 8746 2111
Tube: Goldhawk Road
It's as if the posh eateries in Notting Hill became as tight as a mouth full of wisdom teeth and the Bush Bar and Grill popped out from the pressure and landed in Shepherd's Bush. It doesn't really fit in with the area's graffiti and dilapidated corner shops, but it does provide a refuge for the local richies. A bit gritty urban warehouse, a bit Habitat showroom, this trendy bar and restaurant attracts a clientele that probably wouldn't normally come to this dingy end of Shepherd's Bush. The modern European food is well made and the ingredients are always fresh. If you can afford a nice night out in the area, then this is the place to be.

Food delivery

Domino's Pizza, 224 Uxbridge Road, W12. Tel: 020 8743 8900

Pizza Go Go, 2 Western Avenue, W3. Tel: 020 8742 9701

Akash Tandoori, 177 King Street, W6. Tel: 020 8748 4567

Also in the area
Blythe Road, 71 Blythe Road, W14. Tel: 020 7371 3635. Tube: Kensington Olympia. Modern European food at reasonable prices.
Blah Blah Blah, 78 Goldhawk Road, W12. Tel: 020 8746 1337. Tube: Goldhawk Road. Lovely vegetarian cuisine.
Paulo's, 30 Greyhound Road, W6. Tel: 020 7385 9264. Tube: Hammersmith. Traditional Brazilian grub.

Entertainment

Shepherd's Bush Empire
Shepherd's Bush Green, W12
Tel: 020 8354 3300
Tube: Shepherd's Bush
www.shepherds-bush-empire.co.uk
This is a fabulous old venue that hosts some of the best bands around.

Shepherd's Bush Market
Between Uxbridge Road and Goldhawk Road, W12
Tues, Wed, Fri, Sat 8.30 a.m. – 6 p.m. Sun 8.30 a.m. – 3 p.m.
Tube: Shepherd's Bush or Goldhawk Road
Not the best market in London by any means, but if you're in the area and need a new novelty lighter or some batteries for your Rampant Rabbit then visit this daily street market across from the tube.

Theatres
Riverside Studios, Crisp Road, W6. Tel: 020 8237 1111.
Tube: Hammersmith
Lyric Theatre, King Street, W6. Tel: 020 8741 2311.
Tube: Hammersmith

Cinemas
Hammersmith UCG Cinemas, King Street, W6. Tel: 0870 907 0718.
Tube: Hammersmith
Warner Village Cinemas, Shepherd's Bush Green, W12.
Tel: 0870 240 6020. Tube: Shepherd's Bush

Taxis

Oaklands Minicabs, 1a Oaklands Grove, W12. Tel: 020 8743 3871

Astoria Minicabs, 111 Uxbrdige Road, W12. Tel: 020 8742 9944

GLT Minicabs, 54 Shepherd's Bush Green, W12. Tel: 020 8749 6000

City

Workers in dapper suits and shiny brogues rush through the streets of the City every weekday like famished ants on a half-sucked boiled sweet. With faces drawn with worry and calculated lists of numbers dancing in their heads they rush from meeting to meeting clad in sober pinstripes and sedate dark hues. Sensible hairstyles cover their highly trained brains, as the widgets and cogs churn constantly under the weight of multimillion-pound stock portfolios.

This is the financial center of London and though these high-powered stockbroker types work hard, they certainly play hard too. Come evening, investment bankers and financial consultants slowly loosen their ties, roll up the sleeves of their Savile Row suits, and drink themselves into wine comas. But then, if you were on expenses, wouldn't you? Your finest champagne, *garçon*.

The area is impeccably clean and geared towards workers who commute. There isn't a launderette, a supermarket or a bookie in sight. But there are wine bars, oh yes, there are. Plenty. However, come the weekend, the area is as dead as shares in a 16-year-old dotcom entrepreneur's website. All the workers scuttle back to Tunbridge Wells, remove their suits and curl up in misshapen cardigans and sheepskin-lined leather slippers, to smoke Montecristos and drink 75-year-old brandy in the conservatory, or so legend says.

You probably won't be able to live in the City, but then I doubt that you'd want to anyway. It really does become a ghost town, but worse than tumbleweed, this is where real ghosts wander the cobbled streets of the bullion district. The pubs may be filled with wanky city boys with their cufflinks screwed on too tight, but they are steeped with history and many are utterly stunning.

If you work in finance, then chances are you'll pass through the City at one time or another, but no matter what your profession, you should definitely see the sights in the City. The area is so sodden with history that if you took it to the drycleaners, they'd give you back nothing but a handful of Roman numerals. What little housing that is available in the City is at the Barbican, a massive monstrosity filled with luxury flats, a theatre, cinema, art gallery and concert hall. Good luck.

Sir Christopher Wren, painter Joshua Reynolds, Admiral Lord Nelson, the Duke of Wellington, sculptor Henry Moore, Florence Nightingale, and scientist Alexander Fleming are among the 200 people buried in the crypt of St Paul's Cathedral.

Pubs and bars

Black Friar

174 Queen Victoria Street, EC4
Tel: 020 7236 5474
Tube: Blackfriars

Only the City can provide so much history on a pub crawl. From 1279 to 1539, the site of this pub was a monastery for the Priory of Dominicans. They wore black habits and thus the pub, and the area, became known as Blackfriars. The pub has an impressive exterior and the inside is filled with marble and brass friars, or merry monks, who watch over the thirsty punters below. The grotto next to the bar is covered in Italian marble, with a Roman-esque ceiling of gold leaf. Be careful, this pub is haunted by a ghost who likes to open and close doors, and levitate ashtrays off the tables. Boo!

Old Bank of England

194 Fleet Street, EC4
Tel: 020 7430 2255
Tube: Chancery Lane or Temple

During the 1780s, Sweeney Todd, the Demon Barber of Fleet Street, went around the neighborhood killing unsuspecting victims, stripping them of their valuables and the skin off their bones, before passing the flesh on to his lover's pie shop on Bell Yard, where she sold her 'meat' pies to locals. When the police finally became aware of what was going on, the remains of 160 people were discovered, and the evil barber was hanged on January 25, 1802. This elegant pub – with its tall ceilings, large chandeliers and opulently draped windows – lies on the spot between the old barbershop and pie shop.

Ye Olde Cheshire Cheese

Wine Office Court, 145 Fleet Street, EC4
Tel: 020 7353 6170
Tube: Blackfriars

The stone threshold at the entrance to this pub is almost entirely worn away from years of use, and the list of historical literary names that has crossed it is immense. Voltaire ordered his drinks in this boozer, as did Yeats, Thackeray, Pope and Conan Doyle. But the Cheese's most famous punters were Dr Samuel Johnson and Charles Dickens. Apparently Dickens favored the seat at the right of the fireplace on the ground floor opposite the bar, so feel free to try to score the chair if you believe in genius by arse osmosis.

Also in the area

Shaw's Bookseller's, 31–34 St Andrew's Hill, EC4. Tel: 020 7489 7999. Tube: Blackfriars. Stylish pub/bar that can be seen in the 1997 film, *The Wings of the Dove.*

Vertigo, Tower 42, 25 Old Broad Street, EC2. Tel: 020 7877 2424. Tube: Bank. Impressive views, but you have to call before you go. Ooh, how clandestine.

Tsunami, 1 St Katherine's Way, EC2. Tel: 020 7481 0972. Tube: Tower Hill. Arty young bar in an otherwise devoid area.

Williamson's Tavern, 1 Groveland Court, off Bow Lane, EC4. Tel: 020 7240 5750. Tube: Mansion House. Apparently this is located at the exact center of the city. Pretty good pub too.

Punch Tavern, 9 Fleet Street, EC4. Tel: 020 7353 6658. Tube: Blackfriars. A fabulous Victorian pub sparkling with gold and rammed with colorful trinkets and marionettes. Perfect place for a quiet drink.

Restaurants

Pizza Express
125 Alban Gate, London Wall, EC2
Tel: 020 7600 8880
Tube: St Paul's
It may be the Starbucks of the pizza world, but in an area saturated with overpriced dining places populated by City boys in pink-checkered shirts, this chain eatery is one of the best options around St Paul's. Big two-story windows and high ceilings make for a bright and airy seating place, but as usual the female-sized pizzas will leave most strapping men feeling ravenous. Better start with the dough balls.

Le Coq d'Argent
1 Poultry, EC2
Tel: 020 7395 5000
Tube: Bank
www.conran.co.uk
Right, it's not cheap. But the City isn't about saving a few quid, it's about being flash and waving about more cash than you have. And this is the best place to do it. If it's on expenses, better go here. Flashy, in an understated and masculine way, with an emphasis on top quality food.

Just the Bridge
1 Paul's Walk, off High Timber Street, EC4
Tel: 020 7236 0000
Tube: Blackfriars

This lovely minimalist brasserie is in a gorgeous location, near the Millennium Bridge on the north bank of the Thames opposite the Tate Modern. It doesn't exactly have panoramic views of the south bank, but its modern British food will keep you staring at your plate, regardless.

Food delivery

Sandwich Supreme Delivery Service, 74 Leather Lane, EC1. Tel: 020 7831 8653

Domino's Pizza, 11 High Street, N1. Tel: 020 7713 0707

The Gourmet Oriental, 132 Curtain Road, EC2. Tel: 020 7729 3132

Entertainment

Museum of London
London Wall, EC2
Tel: 020 7600 3699
Tube: Barbican
www.museumoflondon.org.uk
Admission: free
Walk through the different stages of London, from the Ice Age to modern day. This is one of the best museums for Londoners because you can chart out where you live on the maps and check whether prehistoric people used to bury their meat nearby. Fascinating.

Bank of England Museum
Bartholemew Lane, EC2
Tel: 020 7601 5545
Tube: Bank
Find out the history of the Bank of England from 1694 to today. Riveting entertainment.

The Great Fire of London was started in the wee hours of September 2, 1666 at a bakery on Pudding Lane. The fire spread quickly and blazed for four days and nights, destroying 430 acres of the medieval city. A total of 13,200 houses and 87 churches burned down, along with the old St Paul's Cathedral, but amazingly only nine lives were lost.

Cinema
The Barbican Screen Cinema, Silk Street, EC2. Tel: 020 7382 7000.
Tube: Barbican

Theatre
Bridewell Theatre, Bride Lane, off Fleet Street, EC4. Tel: 020 7936
3456. Tube: Blackfriars

Taxis

London and City Carriage, 18-20 Laystall Street, EC1.
Tel: 020 7250 0099

City Green Cars, 23 Roseberry Avenue, EC1. Tel: 020 7713
7766

City Fleet, 192 Goswell Road, EC1. Tel: 020 7250 0111

Whitechapel and Spitalfields

Whitechapel is notorious for its seedy and violent history. In the 1880s the area was rampant with poverty, homelessness and prostitution. To escape their dismal, fetid and squalid lives, people turned to drink: resorting to crime and violence to pay for it. Gangs ruled the filthy streets, and the East End of London became one of the most unpleasant places to live. Then in the autumn of 1888, a series of gruesome and vile murders took place that shocked and appalled the nation. Five local prostitutes were killed and mutilated around the Whitechapel area; their organs had been removed and their bodies butchered. The killer, Jack the Ripper, was never found.

Many of the streets where the bodies were found have been renamed in recent years to stop perverse sightseeing, but if you have a morbid curiosity for the macabre, you can have a pint in the Ten Bells on Commercial Street, as that's where many of the victims used to drink.

Nowadays, the area is still lingering on the grimy side and is completely devoid of bland high street chain bars and shops. You certainly won't find a Gap or a Slug and Lettuce around this area. The area is most notable for the curry houses and market on Brick Lane, which has turned rather trendy in recent years, bringing with it first-rate bars like 93 Feet East and Vibe. Heading north on Brick Lane you'll find retro clothing shops and the famous Brick Lane Beigel Bake – perfect for cheap 24-hour snacks. Further west of the area is Nicholas Hawksmoor's gorgeous Christ Church Spitalfields, and Spitalfields market, which is great for up and coming designer clothes and jewelry.

The streets are constantly used for filming period dramas, so if you live here, expect to be held up on your way to work occasionally by a horse-drawn carriage in a Dickens film. The area is crammed with converted lofts and warehouses, and plenty of ramshackle old houses. You'll probably be able to find somewhere reasonably priced to rent, but you may have to trawl through a lot of rundown rat-infested piles until you find something good. Bethnal Green is just slightly east of the area, but is quite good for finding big terraced houses with low rent. If you do hit upon somewhere in the area to live, you'll have the markets on your doorstep, grotty history around you, and a short walk to Shoreditch for the best bars in town.

In 1888, Professor Bill Fishman, a noted lecturer and author of East End culture, described Whitechapel as, "a place of sickness, premature death, prostitution, and obscene extremes of poverty."

Pubs and bars

Vibe Bar

Old Truman Brewery
91–95 Brick Lane, E1
Tel: 020 7377 2899
Tube: Aldgate East

Local arty loafers and music aficionados loiter outside the large front beer garden of this student bar on the hot summer evenings. Inside is a bizarre jumble, with a stage area for bands, plenty of leather sofas, graffiti murals on the walls and, bizarrely, computers where you can surf the web and check your e-mails. A hodgepodge reminiscent of those hazy childhood days when Timmy, the boy who ate glue, tried to affix your braid to his collage with sticky tape.

The Golden Heart

110 Commercial Street, E1
Tel: 020 7247 2158
Tube: Liverpool Street

Leave your airs and graces in the umbrella bin when you come in; you can pick them up at closing time. No posing allowed. This traditional pub has anything but conventional customers. Every local artist, musician and thespian knows about the Golden Heart and has probably spent far too much time here. One word of warning though: don't get on the wrong side of the landlady; she's a tough wee nut who never forgets a face, but stay on her good side and you have a pub for life.

Blind Beggar

337 Whitechapel Road, E1
Tel: 020 7247 6195
Tube: Aldgate East

This nondescript pub hides a sinister past. This is where, in 1966, infamous local gangster Ronnie Kray shot rival villain George Cornell after the latter called Kray a 'fat poofter'. The ensuing fracas in the pub caused the needle on the jukebox to stick on the Walker Brothers' *The Sun Ain't Gonna Shine Anymore ... anymore ... anymore ...*

Public Life

82a Commercial Street, E1
Tel: 020 7375 2425
Tube: Liverpool Street

From those people who dispense soap and ration paper towels in seedy bars, to the girl I once knew who somehow went through an entire loo roll every day, some people like to waste considerable amounts of time in the toilet. Instead, spend a penny down in Public Life. This converted Victorian toilet still has some of the original fixtures, but the old porcelain lavatories have been ripped out and replaced by a well-stocked bar with friendly staff. DJs pump out some great tunes as graphics are flashed onto the walls. Oddly enough, the toilets are crap.

Indo

133 Whitechapel Road, E1
Tel: 020 7247 4926
Tube: Whitechapel

Nestled between the dirty half-derelict shops on a street strewn with garbage leftover from the market, lies a little gem called Indo. Credible struggling artists and musicians want panache with a few granules of grit, so they drink at Indo. It's a tiny arty little cupboard of a bar and is a great place for an evening drink.

In Victorian times, a common ploy to attract customers to a shop was to install a sideshow exhibit, perhaps involving a bearded woman, a two-headed chicken, or a midget. In the late 1800s, a merchant named Tom Norman had a number of attractions, mostly made of wax, at his shop on Whitechapel Road. Among these curiosities was Joseph Merrick, the Elephant Man. His head and face were severely disfigured with random growths and his skin hung in folds. He was kept in a dark cage and when curious passers-by paid their money, Merrick had to remove his hood and clothes and stand before them naked. Though he could speak and function almost normally, and was in fact a highly intelligent man, he was ordered around like a dog for maximum shock value. He was later bought by a doctor at the London Hospital and was kept isolated in an attic room of the nurses' quarters. Though initially frightened of him, they eventually found him to be a likeable man underneath his hideous exterior. The doctor continued to run tests on him, and told him that to sleep on his back would be very unsafe due to his severe deformities. Merrick longed to be like normal people and one night, in 1890, he did indeed fall asleep on his back, never to wake again. Suicide or unfortunate accident?

Late bars

Pleasure Unit

359 Bethnal Green Road, E2
Tel: 020 7729 0167
Tube: Bethnal Green

This retro-tastic DJ bar is host to some of London's grooviest Mod and Northern Soul nights. The place is swathed in purple and an old Vespa adorns the window. Think back to the days when the pinnacle of marvelous was the music, *We are the Mods, we are the Mods, we are, we are, we are the Mods*.

93 Feet East

Brick Lane, E1
Tel: 020 7247 3293
Tube: Aldgate East

Half of this venue is an experimental club reminiscent of a school gymnasium, and the other is a brilliant bar with platforms to sit on surrounded by reams of flowing gossamer curtains, and filled with street-cool natives.

Also in the area

The Spitz, 109 Commercial Street, E1. Tel: 020 7392 9032. Tube: Liverpool Street. Music, food, drinks, art, bands. Covers all bases.

Restaurants

Brick Lane Beigel Bake

159 Brick Lane, E1
Tel: 020 7729 0616
Tube: Aldgate East

This 24-hour bagel shop is always packed. There isn't anywhere to sit down, but by the time the pubs shut, the hoards of hungry punters are more than happy to converge on this little shop for cheap and tasty bagels to devour on the streets. It's also a welcome break from trawling through the retro furniture and cheap bin liners on Sunday mornings at the market. If you're lucky enough to live in the area, you can bet you'll be sending down a flatmate for half a dozen bagels on a Saturday morning to ease your hangover.

Curry Houses

Brick Lane
Tube: Aldgate East

If you don't know where Brick Lane is, you'll definitely know when you're getting close. Inspector Clueso wouldn't have needed the Pink Panther's nose as the area is marinated in garam masala. The entire south end of Brick Lane and the neighbouring streets are all packed with curry houses. There are too many great ones to mention here – so you'll just have to try all of them. Almost all let you bring your own alcohol and don't charge corkage, so make sure that you stop at one of the off-licenses before you sit down to your meal. The huge amount of competition between the restaurants keeps the food quality up and the prices down.

Les Trois Garçons

1 Club Row, E1
Tel: 020 7613 1924
Tube: Liverpool Street

This listed pub was recently turned into a fantastic French restaurant, which is frighteningly over the top. Stuffed creatures, from amphibians to fowl, dangle from every corner watching you eat your expertly-made dishes. Think fois gras, asparagus, and tarte tatin. This is not a budget restaurant, mains £15.50–£20.50, but then it's not just about the food, it's about fine dining in an atmosphere that cackles uproariously in the featureless faces of the drab minimalist restaurants of the West End.

Food delivery

Perfect Pizza, 460 Kingsland Road, E8. Tel: 020 7249 6661

Pizza Go Go, 86 Hamlets Way, E3. Tel: 020 8980 4999

Entertainment

Whitechapel Art Gallery

80–82 Whitechapel High Street, E1
Tel: 020 7522 7878
Tube: Whitechapel

This is one of London's best exhibition spaces, which sees art from some of the country's best artists. Check out www.whitechapel.org to see what they have on.

Brick Lane Market

Brick Lane, Cheshire Street and Slater Street, E1
Tube: Aldgate East or Liverpool Street
Sunday 8 a.m.–2 p.m.

A real cockney market selling fresh fruit and veggies, vintage clothing, cheap household basics and various bric-a-brac. You never know what you'll find; I've even seen a stall selling, erm, small animal skins – though I don't know where they came from or what you were supposed to do with them. Another time, a man tried to sell a piece of toast on a pile of rubble, a woman was selling plants uprooted from someone's garden, and my mate spotted his stolen bicycle. A market certainly worth getting up early on a Sunday morning for.

Spitalfields Market

Commercial Street, E1
Tube: Liverpool Street
Mon–Fri 11 a.m.–3.30 p.m., Sun 10 a.m.–3 p.m.
Organic fruit and veggies, clothing and accessories by upcoming designers, retro sportswear, trendy vintage home furnishings, art, and records. A posh market and a great way to spend the morning. Grab a fresh fruit drink and wander about the handicrafts.

Cockney Slang

Cockney rhyming slang originated as a way for traders to secretly communicate when carrying out illegal trade in the mid-nineteenth century. Much of this slang has slipped into everyday usage now for many true Londoners (but don't try and use it yourself – you'll just look like an idiot). Just keep your logic and rhyming skills about you and you might just understand the traders down the market. Then again, maybe not.

Butcher's (hook)	= look
Rosie (Lee)	= tea
Trouble and strife	= wife
Apples and pears	= stairs
Bo-peep	= sleep
Jam jar	= car
Tiddly-wink	= drink
Loaf (of bread)	= head

Cinema

Mile End Genesis Cinema, Mile End Road, E1. Tel: 020 7780 2000.
Tube: Stepney Green

Taxis

White Horse Cars, 118 Mile End Road, E1. Tel: 020 7790 1072

Euro Cars, 361 Commercial Road, E1. Tel: 020 7780 9999

London Capital Cars, 132a Commercial Road, E1. Tel: 020 7481 8283

Hoxton and Shoreditch

Hoxton is the all-absorbing artist's idea of utopia. Pilgrimages are made to the finest galleries, and treks are made from all across the land so that artists can immerse themselves in the best that the London art scene has to offer. These East End galleries began to spring up in the early 90s and the archetypal Hoxton bars soon followed. This is where the often-copied brick, chrome and leather bar design was born – a technique that has now been copied in venues, not only all across London, but further and further afield.

There is a distinct buzz in the area. With such a high concentration of musicians, actors, designers and artists, the air around Shoreditch is permanently electric with creativity. People seem to be fuelled by a form of petrol made from the decomposed bodies of the Victorian prostitutes who died on their doorsteps, long before living in a Marmite factory would ever have signified anything but severe destitution. The area's seedy history is rife with degradation, murders, poverty and hardship.

Oh, how things change. Up until about ten years ago, the area was nothing but a rat-infested derelict dump that didn't even have the grin-and-bear-it tough love of the real East End. Where Pearly Kings were proud of their jellied eel past out beyond Bethnal Green, Shoreditch was more of a no-man's wasteland of boarded up factories and warehouses. Then the young trendy crowd spotted the potential. They didn't see the crumbling buildings as condemned cesspits; they saw vast spaces with untold promise. These enormous urban dwellings are extremely hard to come by, but if you find one you will have the best bars, pubs and restaurants right on your threshold cobbles.

You can spend summer days lounging in Hoxton Park with a few beers, wander down the streets and watch up-and-coming bands, or listen to poetry readings by potential laureates. Shoreditch is the kind of place where a breeze on the back of the neck is like a kick up the arse with a wink and a smile – smug and whiny, but content all the same.

If you want to see Hoxton in all its glory then you'd better hurry up because the trendy bourgeoisie have lit their torches, raised their pitchforks and are rapidly encroaching to take complete control and turn everything with charm and character into another pea in the superfluously budding Starbucks pod. Rents have been escalating for the past few years, and now most property in the near vicinity has been priced right out of the realm of all the starving artists, writers, and actors who gave the area its beguiling allure in the first place.

Pubs and bars

The George & Dragon

1 Hackney Road, E1
Tel: Unlisted
Tube: Old Street

Enough of this minimalism already. The George and Dragon spits up on bland bars and counters their claim to cool by strapping great lots of crap to the walls and pumping out some fab music from top guest DJs. Fairy lights twinkle, trendies pout, and the odd doll is dangling above the bar next to a dented trombone. Pulling in the best of the fashionista set as well as scraggily coiffed music lovers, this popular bar makes a perfect local pub.

The Foundry

84–86 Great Eastern Street, EC2
Tel: 020 7739 6900
Tube: Old Street

Avant-garde eccentrics meet in this grimy former bank for poetry nights, exhibits, and DJs playing quirky tunes. Downstairs the bank notes and bullion have been cleared out and the vaults now serve as a gallery for contemporary art. Don't expect silver service; this is the opposite of the identikit chain bars. It's rough around the edges and thankfully bohemian. As you sit down to your cool pint on an early afternoon, take a moment to observe the sun illuminating the thick layer of dust lingering like a blanket of dead cells. Disturbing.

The Red Lion

41 Hoxton Street, N1
Tel: 020 7739 3736
Tube: Old Street

A happily conventional pub that provides solace for punters who are tired of the new style bars that are sprouting like mold on petri dishes smeared with bio-yogurt. Being on Hoxton Street, it attracts all the usual suspects from the area, and the odd old-timer who remembers what the area was like back before tweed was twee.

The Bricklayer's Arms

63 Charlotte Road, EC2
Tel: 020 7739 5245
Tube: Old Street

If you've been to Shoreditch, you've probably been to the Bricklayer's. It's always completely packed out with more retro T-shirts than a redneck's laundry bin. The crowds tumble out into the street at the slightest rise in temperature, but you'll have to dodge the odd lost pizza deliveryman as he wildly navigates Charlotte Road at 20 miles per hour on his moped. It won't take a pervert with promises of chocolate to invite you in here, just your mates and the sweet smell of fermented hops.

Dragon
5 Leonard Street, EC2
Tel: 020 7490 7110
Tube: Old Street

The fashionable have been coming to Dragon for years, and though it is one of the most popular Shoreditch haunts, the only real pretension is the lack of a door sign. But then if you're already pulling in the punters, you hardly need a day-glo cartoon dragon's head stuck on a flagpole protruding from the roof.

Also in the area
The Reliance, 336 Old Street, EC1. Tel: 020 7729 6888. Tube: Old Street. A laid-back pub with a bizarre seafaring theme.
Cocomo, 323 Old Street, EC1. Tel: 020 7613 0315. Tube: Old Street. It looks like a café upstairs, but the basement is littered with comfy cushions and pouffes. DJs most nights.
New Inn, 1 New Inn Yard, EC2. Tel: 020 7739 7775. Tube: Old Street. Small cozy bar hidden down a little alleyway.

East End Celebrities

Cockney cockles may be a distant memory from their palatial estates, but these celebrities started life among the Pearly Kings and Queens of the East End.

David Bowie, singer – Stepney Green

Damon Albarn, singer with the band Blur – Whitechapel

Lennox Lewis, boxer – West Ham

Alexander McQueen, fashion designer – Stratford

David Beckham, footballer – Leytonstone

Late bars

Smersh
Ravey Street, EC2
Tel: not listed
Tube: Old Street

If it weren't for the front half of an old scooter strapped to the front of this building, you might miss it. And what a shame that would be. Don't try to get here early as the bar is only open after 7 or 8 in the evenings, but it is certainly worth checking out. They host Mod and Northern Soul nights, such as The Hideaway Club Goes South, so keep an eye out in the listings, as it's a great venue for intimate retro R&B. Brighton? Wigan? The Isle of Wight? Nah, Shoreditch.

Mother

333 Old Street, EC1
Tel: 020 7739 5949
Tube: Old Street

Mother Bar has long been the secret drinking den of Shoreditch. If you're growing out your ironic haircut or nouveau mullet, and if you're pondering purchasing that vintage Lambretta, chances are you've already been to Mother. It's a gathering place for locals, and a home away from home for many. The crowd is well up for a laugh and aren't afraid to get up and grind. You will have to queue for ages as it is a member's bar, but they let in non-members if it isn't too crowded.

Bedroom Bar

62 Rivington Street, EC2
Tel: 020 7613 5637
Tube: Old Street

In just a few years Rivington Street has turned from derelict cobbles full of rat-runs and decay into an entertainment destination. Cargo, the Comedy Café and now Bedroom. Yes, it has a bed in it, but immature pick-up lines aren't the reason why you should drink here. It has great DJs at the end of the week and it's even open late. It serves as the private view bar for the outstanding Vilma Gold gallery, so expect lots of promising new art talent to be gyrating to the crescendos whilst their haircuts pay homage to the days when you turned Barbie into Ken with mom's garden shears.

Shoreditch Electricity Showrooms

39a Hoxton Square, N1
Tel: 020 7739 6934
Tube: Old Street

Right on the corner of Hoxton Square, this place is pretty hard to miss, as the old cinema sign hanging precariously over the door is a beacon in the night. The mural behind the bar is always changing, from a pile of steaming sprouts to a Hungry Hungry Hippo, and the Austrian alpine scene at the back reminds you that you're nowhere near any kids in curtains or edelweiss. Can I suggest however, that no matter how pissed you get, don't go downstairs for a dance. It's a petrifying world of dodgy taxi drivers dancing like Willy Wonka after too many snozzcumbers.

Hoxton Bar and Kitchen

2–4 Hoxton Square, N1
Tel: 020 7613 0709
Tube: Old Street

A bit of brick, an exposed duct, and some well-worn leather seating. Sounds like typical decor in the area, and it is, but this bar was one of the first, and is a faithful boozer for local paint-stainers, note-scribblers, and pattern cutters. The bar is sunken and has a large back window at street level for that Bladerunner industrial effect. You'll be thirsting for margaritas before noon.

Also in the area

Catch, 22 Kingsland Road, E2. Tel: 020 7729 6097. Tube: Old Street. Popular wood-filled DJ bar with experimental music.

Home, 100 Leonard Street, EC2. Tel: 020 7684 8618. Tube: Old Street. www.homebar.co.uk. An old favorite in the area with all the typical decor and punters.

Sosho, 2a Tabernacle Street, EC2. Tel: 020 7920 0701. Tube: Old Street.www.matchbar.com. This relatively new addition to the cocktail-tastic Match chain has been widely lauded for its quality drinks and great atmosphere.

Medicine Shoreditch, 89 Great Eastern Street, EC2. Tel: 020 7739 5173. Tube: Old Street. www.medicinebar.net. This is the second Medicine, which follows in the fantastic footsteps of the branch on Upper Street. Mohammed Ali beckons you into this stylish late DJ bar.

Clubs

333

333 Old Street, EC1
Tel: 020 7739 5949
Tube: Old Street
Open 10 p.m.–5 a.m., costs £5–10

Taking an anti-superclubbing stance, this non-commercialized venue caters to an up-for-it crowd just looking to have a good dance. Head to Off Centre for a blend of jazz house and hip-hop or Mènage a Trois for some hedonistic beats and breaks. Unbeatable.

Bridge 'n' Tunnel

4 Calvert Avenue, E2
Tel: 020 7739 5451
Tube: Old Street
Open: 7 p.m.–12 a.m., costs up to £3

This two-floor DJ bar is creating quite a stir since opening its doors in 2002, raking in globally famous DJs including Groove Armada, Fatboy Slim and Andrew Weatherall. Get it while it's hot.

Herbal

12–14 Kingsland Road, E2
Tel: 020 7613 4462
Tube: Old Street
Open 7.30 p.m.–2 a.m., costs £3–5
www.herbaluk.com

Listen to DJs in the upstairs New York-esque relaxed bar, then move downstairs for a dance to anything from house and funky beats to electronica. You'll know you're at Herbal when you see the fake grass strapped to the outside of this otherwise unassuming building.

Cargo

Kingsland Viaduct, 83 Rivington Street, EC2
Tel: 020 7739 3440
Tube: Old Street
Open noon–1 a.m., costs £5–8
www.cargo-london.com

This bar/club/restaurant has everything you could want, mixing up experimental beats, rare grooves and world music with an eclectic assortment of people. One of the newest clubs on the scene and certainly one of the best.

Restaurants

Hoxton Furnace

1 Rufus Street, N1
Tel: 020 7613 0598
Tube: Old Street

If you aren't drunk enough for a greasy stomach lining-dissolving kebab, then a quick stroll around Hoxton will take you to some fantastic food. This busy Italian serves massive pizzas with rizla-thin bases covered in numerous toppings such as spinach, goats cheese and pine nuts. If pizzas aren't what you're after there is a blackboard boasting a variety of other mains, both meaty and veggie. One word of warning though, go easy on the chili oil. It's hotter than Marilyn Monroe sunbathing naked with jalapenos stapled to her nipples.

Viet Hoa

70–72 Kingsland Road, E2
Tel: 020 7729 8293
Tube: Old Street

This Shoreditch institution is always popular and packed with dribbling masses. It's a noisy and buzzing café downstairs and a bit more chilled out on the upper floor. The cheap and high quality Vietnamese food is what entices, and mains are from £2.15–£6.90, so you can afford to sample lots of the weird and wonderful delights.

Great Eastern Dining Room

54–56 Great Eastern Street, EC2
Tel: 020 7613 4545
Tube: Old Street

This is a touch of class in an area so known for its street-cool. The restaurant serves modern Italian food that will definitely impress on a first date, and if it goes well, head to the bar downstairs, which has an exclusive celebrity feel to it. Who knows where things could lead from there, if your debit card allows?

The Real Greek

15 Hoxton Market, N1
Tel: 020 7739 8212
Tube: Old Street
www.therealgreek.co.uk

Dropped into Hoxton Market like a plate at a Greek wedding, addresses don't come much better. But you won't come here time and again because of the location, you'll come for the great food. This isn't slop from a dodgy beachfront restaurant in Santorini, this is proper chic Greek made with high quality fresh ingredients. Oh, and if you recognize the restaurant, it's not a creepy déjà vu feeling, it's because this is where Hugh Grant and Colin Firth battled for their lady's affection during the fight scene in *Bridget Jones's Diary*.

Food delivery

Pizza Go Go, 86 Hamlets Way, E3. Tel: 020 7249 6661

The Gourmet Oriental, 132 Curtain Road, EC2. Tel: 020 7729 3132

Millennium Pizza, 106 Hoxton Street, N1. Tel: 020 7729 2959

Also in the area

Little Georgia, 8 Broadway Market, E8. Tel: 020 7249 9070. Tube: Old Street. Eastern European food in a lovely atmosphere.

Lennie's, 6 Calvert Avenue, E2. Tel: 020 7739 3628. Tube: Old Street. Greasy spoon whips off its egg and bacon-splattered apron and goes Thai at nightfall.

Yelo, 8–9 Hoxton Square, N1. Tel: 020 7729 4626. Tube: Old Street. Thai in 70s retro-kitsch restaurant. Bit of brick and leather makes it Hoxton.

Traditional Cockney Eats

Searching for pie and mash or jellied eels? Head to the East End and try one of these traditional family-run shops.

F. Cooke, 150 Hoxton Street, N1. Tel: 020 7729 7718

G. Kelly, 526 Roman Road, E3. Tel: 020 8980 3156

M. Manze, 87 Tower Bridge Road, SE1. Tel: 020 7407 2985

Entertainment

Geffrye Museum
Kingsland Road, E2
Tel: 020 7739 9893
Tube: Old Street
www.geffrye-museum.org.uk
Admission: free
This stunning Grade I listed, eighteenth-century almshouse houses the UK's only specialist furniture and interior design museum. See the history of English domestic interiors from 1600 to the present.

Arcola Theatre and Gallery
27 Arcola Street, E8
Tel: 020 7503 1646
Rail: Dalston Kingsland, or Tube: Liverpool Street then bus 149
www.arcolatheatre.com
This converted clothing factory houses the largest studio theatres in London. The Arcola is a buzzing new addition to the local artistic and cultural community. See live folk or jazz music in the bar, watch some outstanding plays in the theatres, check out the art exhibits, or get in touch with your creative side at one of their workshops.

Comedy Café
66–68 Rivington Street, EC2
Tel: 020 7739 5706
Tube: Old Street
This Shoreditch venue, located on the same street as the popular Cargo nightclub, attracts some of the most talented comedians on the circuit. Open 7 p.m. until midnight Wednesday to Thursday, 7 p.m.–2 a.m. weekends. Shows 9–11.30 p.m. Wednesday to Saturday. Admission: free on Wednesdays, £3–£12 other nights.

Cinema
Rio, 103–107 Kingsland Road, E8. Tel: 020 7241 9410. Rail: Dalston Kingsland or Tube: Old Street, then bus 8.

Taxis

Atlas Cars, 21–22 Shoreditch High Street, E1. Tel: 020 7480 7000

Hoxton Cars, 56 Hoxton Square, N1. Tel: 020 7729 2929

Dial A Car, 103 Shoreditch High Street, E1. Tel: 020 7613 0222

Crown Cabs, 75 Pitfield Street, N1. Tel: 020 7253 7888

Docklands and Greenwich

You've heard the term "concrete jungle" but until you've been to the Docklands, you've never really seen one. No trees, no greenery: nothing but repetitive reflections of cement slabs. During the daytime, businessmen engrossed in their nefarious dealings and bland City girls twilling about for a scrap of attention scamper about the streets gathering sandwiches and newspapers. But come evening, the area is as dead as a dysentery victim left to rot in Mudchute during the unseasonably hot summer of 1764.

The Isle of Dogs has always been known for its bleak past of murderers, prostitution, and poverty. Once home to panders, petty touts, hookers, perverts, sodomites and general riff-raff, dockside hovels of the past centuries were indeed a fetid and miserable place in which to live.

In recent years, steps have been taken to build up the area again; condemned buildings have been steamrollered, leaving some areas barren while waiting for new luxury apartments to be built in their place. The past ten years have seen a boom in brick and aluminium fronted multi-levelled buildings, providing thousands of modern flats for the City and financial workers who have been trickling in steadily.

Fleet Street newspaper groups and City financial corporations have taken over the northern part of the Isle of Dogs and around Canary Wharf, creating Hong Kong-style glass towers. Any newcomer to the area would find it hard to believe that beneath the reflective skyscrapers lie centuries of decaying bones, lost treasures, and historical artifacts.

However, a walk under the murky depths of the Thames brings you into Greenwich, a lively area with a youthful and arty vibe. Best known for its market, where you can pick up anything from a fishtail parka to second-hand books or retro furniture, the area is far more vibrant than the Docklands, and yet it is only a footpath under the Thames away.

So if you are after a hot local pub, the deserted Docklands may not be the place for you, unless you don't mind popping over to Greenwich or commuting into central London to take in the nightlife. On the upside, you can find a nice flat for reasonable rent here, although if you're considering this area at all, Greenwich is certainly the better option.

Pubs and bars

Time
7a College Approach, SE10
Tel: 020 8305 9767
Tube: Greenwich (DLR)
Built in the oldest ex-music hall in Great Britain, this revamped vast studio space is full of art and fashion students radiating creative

pheromones. Tall ceilings, graffiti art, worn leather couches, and a mirror with the word "Girls" in flashing lights further add to the effortlessly cool vibe this place secretes.

Bar du Musée

17 Nelson Road, SE10
Tel: not listed
Tube: Greenwich (DLR)

A French-style bar, Musée holds back on obvious gimmickry and instead focuses on atmosphere. A fantastic wine list, dim candlelight, and dark crimson walls create the air of Gallic genteel charm. Serge Gainsbourg or Edith Piaf? Beaujolais or Merlot? *Je t'aime*.

The Trafalgar Tavern

Park Row, SE10
Tel: 020 8858 2437
Tube: Greenwich (DLR)

Excellent views across the Thames of the Isle of Dogs, Canary Wharf, and the giant pustulating boil on Tony Blair's arse, The Dome, draw punters to this traditional old pub. Candles in wine bottles and two pianos (must make for a rousing game of duelling organs), add a bit of romance for loved-up couples watching the river rolling on by.

The Cutty Sark Tavern

4–6 Ballast Quay, off Lassell Street, SE10
Tel: 020 8858 3146
Tube: Greenwich (DLR)

A musty, comforting smell resembling a second-hand bookstore is the first thing you notice when stepping into this 1695 Georgian pub, which is decorated like the interior of a ship. Beer barrels used as tables, old pictures of boats on the walls, and worn carpets tick back the decades to those festering days of scurvy as you gaze out at the smashed windows of a nearby factory overlooking the river.

The North Pole

Greenwich High Street
Tube: Greenwich (DLR)

Seek refuge from haggling over an Art Deco pineapple-shaped toastrack at the colossal sprawling market, and duck into The North Pole for a drink. Sink into the comfy brown leather sofas and leave a nice wide bum indent, because before you know it, five hours will have passed and you'll be totally drunk. This is an ideal place to loiter and linger, especially on Wednesday nights when you can listen to live jazz.

Also in the area

The Tollesbury Barge, Millwall Inner Dock, Marsh Wall, E14. Tel: 020 7363 1183. DLR: South Quay. It survived Dunkirk in 1940, the bombing of the London Docks in 1942, and the IRA bombing of 1996. And yet, if the bar staff don't lighten up a little, this place is bound to be doomed. Even so, the novelty of being on a boat won't wear off before your first pint.

Late bar

Via Fossa
West India Quay, E14
Tel: 020 7515 8549
Tube: West India Quay (DLR)

It is a very strange experience walking through masses of erect concrete office blocks before stumbling upon a lit footbridge carrying you to rows of bars and restaurants with huge outdoor seating areas. It's a bit reminiscent of being on vacation with all the young punters drinking far too much on a warm summer night. Via Fossa is a large bar set in an old brick factory in stark juxtaposition to the sleek glass office buildings on the other side of the water. Old mirrors adorn the brightly colored walls around the massive carved wood bar, as local office workers enjoy cocktails and beers late into the night.

Restaurants

Hubbub
269 Westferry Road, E14
Tel: 020 7515 5577
Tube: Mudchute (DLR)
www.space.org.uk

Hubbub is a trendy gastropub that serves excellent food in surroundings filled with local art, fairy-lights, battered leather sofas and stacks of board games. The meals are outstanding, with quality fare such as fillet of seabass, Greek salad, and ciabatta with all manner of stuffings. But as good as this place is as a pub/restaurant, it has the added cachet of the attached arts venue, The Space. Grab a meal from the bar and take it through to the other side of this converted church to watch a band, a cabaret show, or a play.

Noodle Time
10–11 Nelson Road, SE10
Tel: 020 8293 5263
Tube: Greenwich (DLR)

Those radical color schemes so embraced in *Austin Powers* must have rubbed off on the owners of this noodle bar chain, which has eagerly adopted the use of bright orange, green and yellow. Standing on this otherwise bland street like a Rubik's Cube dropped in a bathtub, this oriental noodle bar screams cheap food. And cheap it is, with Homer-sized dishes of noodles and soups for as little as £3.40. Popular with the locals, this fast-food chain eatery alternative packs 'em as tight as David Beckham's rear end.

> ### Food delivery
>
> **Tandoori Nights**, 3 West India Dock Road, E14. Tel: 020 7515 6048
>
> **Domino's Pizza**, 2–8 Beccles Street, E14. Tel: 020 7517 9494
>
> **Millennium Pizza**, 119 Woolwich Road, SE10. Tel: 020 8858 2221

Also in the area

Beachcomber Seafood Café, Greenwich Church Street, SE10. Tel: 020 8853 0055. Tube: Greenwich (DLR). Mermaids, fishermen's nets and stuffed fish aside, don't look any further than this colorful café for fresh seafood.

Spread Eagle, 1–2 Stockwell Street, SE10. Tel: 020 8853 2333. Tube: Greenwich (DLR). Homey French cuisine in a pubby atmosphere.

Royal China, 30 Westferry Circus, E14. Tel: 020 7719 0888. Tube: Canary Wharf. Kick back at this riverside chinoiserie.

Entertainment

Greenwich Market

Church Road, SE10
Tube: Cutty Sark (DLR) or Island Gardens (DLR)
Mon–Sun 9.30 a.m.–5.30 p.m.

Almost anything you could possibly want can be found in Greenwich and it is certainly worth the trek out on the Docklands Light Railway. Pick up some great retro and vintage clothing, vinyl records, or kitsch furniture.

Cutty Sark

Cutty Sark Gardens, SE10
Tel: 020 8858 3445
Admission: £3.50
Tube: Greenwich (DLR)

The Cutty Sark is the sole survivor of the type of clipper ships that used to dominate the seas during the mid-nineteenth century when tea and wool used to be traded across the Pacific and Atlantic oceans. It is free to view the ship from the outside, but if you'd like to take a closer look below the decks, you'll have to pay for the pleasure.

National Maritime Museum

Romney Road, SE10
Tel: 020 8312 6565
Tube: Greenwich (DLR)
Admission: free

It's got all the maps, charts, boats and uniforms you would expect to find in a maritime museum, plus a few modern day extras such as interactive displays and video art teaching the history of Britain's convoluted seafaring history.

Royal Observatory

Greenwich Park, SE19
Tel: 020 8312 6565
Tube: Greenwich (DLR)
www.nmm.ac.uk

The birthplace of Greenwich Mean Time (GMT) and all that scientific mumbo-jumbo about longitudes and latitudes. The observatory is divided between east and west, and you can place one foot on either side of the meridian line to straddle the two hemispheres.

Greenwich Park

After snatching up that vintage leather jacket for £10 at the market, take it for a test run with a stroll through the rose gardens of this rambling, ideal English park.

London Arena

Limeharbour, Isle of Dogs, E14
Tel: 020 7538 1212
Tube: Crossharbour (DLR)
www.londonarena.co.uk

There's always something going on at this massive arena, from London Knights hockey games to Kylie Minogue concerts. It's like being the only kid in the neighborhood with a trampoline in the backyard.

Cinemas

Greenwich Cinema, 180 Greenwich High Road, SE10.
Info line: 01426 919 020 or booking: 020 8293 0101.
Tube: Greenwich (DLR)
Surrey Quays UCI, Redriff Road, SE16. Tel: 0870 010 2030.
Tube: Surrey Quays (DLR)
West India Quay UCG, Hertsmere Road, E14. Tel: 0870 907 0722.
Tube: West India Quay (DLR)

Taxis

Station Cars, East India Dock Road, E14. Tel: 020 7987 7777

Island Cars, The Quarterdeck, E14. Tel: 020 7537 7999

Directory of Useful Numbers

Emergencies	999
UK Operator	100
Directory Enquiries	192
International Operator	155
International Directory Enquiries	153

Health

Aids National Helpline (24 hours)	0800 567 123
Al Anon	020 7403 0888
Alcoholics Anonymous	020 7833 0022
British Pregnancy Advisory Service	08457 30 40 30
Crime Victims Support	020 7735 9166
Domestic Violence Women's Aid Helpline	0845 702 3468
Drugs and Advice Helpline	020 8960 5023
Eating Disorder Association	01603 621 414
Mind National Association For Mental Health	0845 766 0163
Marie Stopes Pregnancy Advisory Line	0845 300 80 90
National Blood Donor Service	08457 711 711
Organ Donor Cards	0845 60 60 400
Quitline (advice on how to quit smoking)	0800 00 22 00
Rape and Sex Abuse Support	020 8683 3300
Samaritans (London number)	020 7734 2800
(National number)	08457 90 90 90

(A friendly ear whether you are depressed, suicidal, lonely or just need someone to talk to)

Shelter (The National Campaign for Homeless People)	0808 800 444

Transportation

London Transport	020 7222 1234
	www.tfl.gov.uk

National Rail Enquiries	0845 48 49 50 www.rail.co.uk
National Express	08705 808 080 www.gobycoach.com
24-hour Radio Taxis	020 7272 0272
Heathrow Airport Enquiries	0870 00 00 123
Gatwick Airport Enquiries	0870 00 02 468
Stanstead Airport Enquiries	0870 00 00 303
Luton Airport Enquiries	0158 24 05 100
City Airport Enquiries	0207 646 0088
GNER Enquiries	08457 225 225 www.gner.co.uk
Eurostar reservations	0870 160 6600 www.eurostar.co.uk
Computer Cabs (Black Cabs)	020 7432 1432 www.computercab.co.uk

Utilities

London Electricity	0845 744 4555
British Gas	0845 600 6113
Powergen	0800 015 20 29
Transco Gas Emergency	0800 111 999
Thames Water	020 7636 8686
British Telecommunications	0800 800 150
Cable and Wireless	0800 092 0636

Embassies

The Home Office (Immigration), 40 Wellesley Road, Croydon, CR9. Tel: 0870 606 7766 or www.homeoffice.gov.uk

Australian High Commission, Australia House, The Strand, WC2. Tel: 020 7379 4334 or www.australia.org.uk

New Zealand High Commission, 80 Haymarket, W1. Tel: 020 7930 8422 or www.nzembassy.com

American Embassy, 24 Grosvenor Square, W1. Tel. 020 7499 9000 or www.usembassy.org.uk

South African High Commission, 15 Whitehall, SW1. Tel: 020 7925 8900 or www.southafricahouse.com

Canadian High Commission, Grosvenor Street, W1. Tel: 020 7258 6600 or www.canada.org.uk

Entertainment

Ticketmaster	020 7344 4444
London events info line	09068 663 344

International Codes

Australia	61	Ireland	353
Austria	43	Israel	972
Belgium	32	Italy	39
Brazil	55	Japan	81
Canada	1	Netherlands	31
Czech Republic	420	New Zealand	64
Denmark	45	Norway	47
France	33	Portugal	351
Germany	49	South Africa	27
Greece	30	Spain	34
Hong Kong	852	Sweden	46
Iceland	354	Switzerland	41
India	91	USA	1